ENERGY-EFFICIENT BUILDINGS

AN ARCHITECTURAL RECORD BOOK

McGraw-Hill Book Company

New York   St. Louis   San Francisco
Auckland   Bogotá   Hamburg
Johannesburg   London   Madrid
Mexico   Montreal   New Delhi
Panama   Paris   São Paulo
Singapore   Sydney   Tokyo   Toronto

ENERGY-EFFICIENT BUILDINGS

EDITED BY
WALTER F. WAGNER, JR., AIA

The editors for this book were Jeremy Robinson and Patricia Markert.
The designer was William Bennett.
The production supervisors were Elizabeth Dineen and Tom Kowalczyk
The book was set in Optima by Publishers' Computype Service, Inc.,
  New York, New York

Printed and bound by Halliday Lithograph Corporation.

1234567890   HDHD   89876543210

Library of Congress Cataloging in Publication Data

Main entry under title:

Energy-efficient buildings.

"An Architectural record book."

Includes index.

1. Buildings—Energy conservation.   I.   Wagner,
Walter F.

TJ163.5.B84T68   696   80-11572

ISBN 0-07-002344-1

Architectural Record Books

Affordable Houses
Apartments, Townhouses and Condominiums, 2/e
The Architectural Record Book of Vacation Houses, 2/e
Architecture 1970-1980: A Decade of Change
Buildings for Commerce and Industry
Buildings for the Arts
Engineering for Architecture
Great Houses for View Sites, Beach Sites, Sites in the Woods, Meadow Sites,
    Small Sites, Sloping Sites, Steep Sites and Flat Sites,
Hospitals and Health Care Facilities, 2/e
Houses Architects Design for Themselves
Houses of the West
Institutional Buildings: Architecture for the Controlled Environment
Interior Spaces Designed by Architects
Office Building Design, 2/e
Places for People: Hotels, Motels, Restaurants, Bars, Clubs, Community
    Recreation Facilities, Camps, Parks, Plazas, Playgrounds
Public, Municipal and Community Buildings
Religious Buildings
Recycling Buildings: Renovations, Remodelings, Restorations and Reuses
Techniques of Successful Practice, 2/e
A Treasury of Contemporary Houses

Architectural Record Series Books

Ayers: Specifications for Architecture, Engineering and Construction
Feldman: Building Design for Maintainability
Heery: Time, Cost and Architecture
Heimsath: Behavioral Architecture
Hopf: Designer's Guide to OSHA
Portman and Barnett: The Architect As Developer

CONTENTS

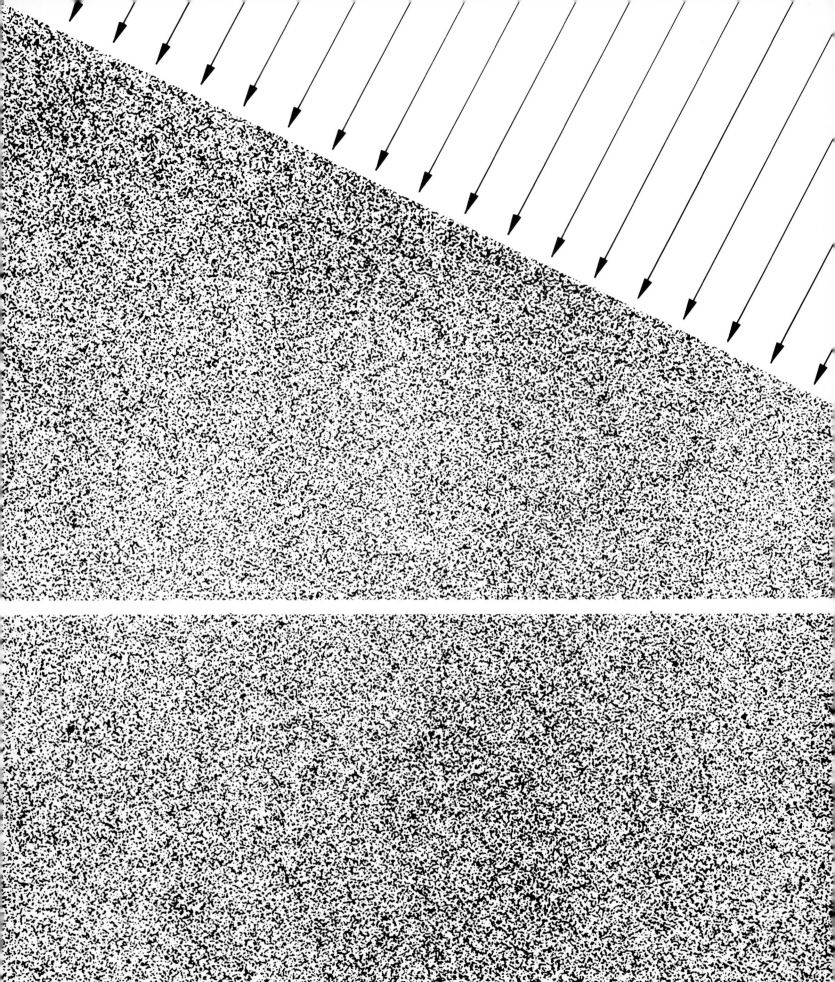

INTRODUCTION

It was not many years ago that the idea of energy conservation was far from people's minds—indeed, almost un-American. This was the land of cheap power, big automobiles—and buildings which used technology (and energy) to simply "outmuscle" the laws of nature. We designed buildings with sealed windows and without reference to solar orientation, with high standards of comfort but without reference to operating costs, with the newest technology but without much sense of what tomorrow might bring.

Well, what the early 1970s brought was a growing awareness that energy was becoming a problem. Shortages of natural gas turned up in some parts of the country; brown-outs in other parts of the country. We experienced—briefly, but ominously—a period of long lines at gas stations. If we were willing and able to ignore those warnings, we did have to react to growing problems of generating new power, increasingly shaky supplies of oil from overseas, and—on every front—growing costs and prices. In a very short time, power wasn't cheap any more.

It was time for re-examination. . . .

In this book (page 7) you'll find a broad analysis of the enormous strides made by architects, engineers, manufacturers, and building owners to reduce energy consumption in buildings. From the first days of energy awareness, it was clear that there were plenty of things that architects and engineers could do to conserve energy, but that there was not much incentive—no reason for most building owners to care. The reasoning was simple: electricity has traditionally been cheap and abundant; and almost anything a designer can do to conserve energy adds something to first cost—even if it does reduce operating costs. . . .

In the last few years under the impact of escalating fuel and energy costs, we have seen the whole equation of first cost vs. operating cost change—and thus the priorities and the engineering and design practice change in response.

This book explains those changing cost equations, the changing priorities, and the growing body of design expertise that has developed to respond to the need for energy conservation and the wish for more energy-efficient buildings.

On the next pages you'll find a thought-provoking bit of perspective—from architect and respected energy expert Donald Watson's *Energy Conservation through Building Design* (McGraw-Hill, 1979)—that reminds us that there is really nothing new (indeed, a lot that is centuries old) about the techniques of energy conservation.

Chapter 1, which begins on page 7, describes the progress of design professionals and the industry in analyzing the problem, reassessing the "rules" and priorities, revising our thinking, and developing voluntary and finally (and alas) mandatory standards.

Chapter 2, which begins on page 29, explores our progress towards making use of our only "free" and endlessly renewable resource, the sun. . . .

Chapter 3, beginning on page 79, takes a look at how inventive architects are exploring building underground (at least partially underground) to conserve energy—and the environment.

And chapter 4, beginning on page 113, offers a score of design case histories—of major buildings of all types in which the architects and engineers have saved energy through the most advanced kinds of mechanical systems, hvac systems, lighting systems, and building controls.

This book, of course, marks only a beginning. In the years ahead, we will see more advances—in our thinking, in our priorities, and in the techniques and tools of more energy-efficient building. But—as *Architectural Record's* editors have seen it—this is the state of the art as we enter the 1980s. . . .

THREE PERSPECTIVES ON ENERGY

This essay argues that it is not nearly enough to concern ourselves with the technology of the energy problem—but that we also need to concern ourselves with its historical, economic, and cultural aspects if we are to solve it.

by Donald Watson

Pueblo Bonito in New Mexico. An analysis of the structure shows irradiation in winter to be constant from 8:00 A.M. to 4:00 P.M. and greater than in summer, during which it decreases during the hot afternoon (from *Contributions to North American Ethnology 1881*).

Energy is limited only because of limits in the way it is viewed, a "crisis" only because its implications have been too long overlooked. Energy efficiency is not a new criterion of design, for the context of building has always been defined by climatic and material limitations. Even when these are severe, they have not prevented building designers from evolving solutions of great craft and elegance.

Indigenous and vernacular building at its best is a direct expression of adaptation to climate and to constraints of resources. Pueblo structures in the American Southwest, for instance, could hardly be improved on for natural control of seasonal climatic impacts, and early American building styles can in some measure be traced to the exigencies imposed by the environment and by building methods. Most recently, a renewed appreciation of the indigenous tradition in architecture has resulted in a literature devoted quite expressly to its analysis—not just from an interest in cultural preservation, but also to find lessons for modern designers working in similar cultures and climates.[1] One elegant example is the vernacular house of Baghdad

Donald Watson is an architect and visiting professor at the Yale School of Architecture, where he serves as chairman of the Environmental Design Program; he is author of numerous publications on energy-efficient building design, including *Designing and Building a Solar House*. This essay is excerpted from the book *Energy Conservation through Building Design*, published in March 1979 by Architectural Record Books, including essays by Francisco Arumi, J. Douglas Balcomb, Robert Bruegmann, Jeffrey Cook, Fred S. Dubin, Eugene Eccli, Baruch Givoni, James C. Hedstrom, Ralph Knowles, Harold E. Marshall, Robert D. McFarland, Murray Milne, Donald Prowler, Rosalie Ruegg, Diane Serber, Lawrence G. Spielvogel, John Philip Steadman, Richard G. Stein, Sim Van der Ryn, and John I. Yellot.

in Iraq. Its adaptive strategies include zoning of the plan: family activities move between lower rooms (of heavy masonry) on summer days and courtyard and roof terraces on summer nights, and to the second floor (of light wood and glass) during the winter, thus taking advantage of distinct building solutions for different seasons.

An example from Roman antiquity, the Forum Baths in Ostia (about 250 AD), combined direct solar heating and "hypocaust," or under-the-floor, warm-air heating. The Forum Baths are a large public building with a series of rooms used in sequence, each with a distinct temperature and humidity requirement. The fireplace-flue heating system used the wall and floor structure—an early and exemplary application of radiant heating.

But after the fall of Rome and the emergence of European countries from the dark ages the lessons of the past had to be relearned. The history of the fireplace characterizes this relearning. First there was the open fire in the center of a room, with smoke exiting as best it could through doors and roof openings. Then, in the multistoried feudal castles, flues were incorporated into the wall—an early example, from about 1090, being in Colchester in England. The stove appeared first in Europe in Alsace in 1490, made of brick and tile. Subsequently wood and coal fires were enclosed in special metal and masonry ovens, often with extended flues built in a labyrinthine pattern within the fireplace wall, so that its mass was heated from the combustion flue and became a radiant heating element. The dimensioning of such a flue—developed from German and

Russian precedents—was the subject of a treatise by Carl John Cronstedt and Fabian Wrede in Sweden in 1775.

Thereafter the fireplace or stove was developed as a piece of equipment engineered not only for heating but also for ventilation. Iron stoves could also be mass-produced, the first manufactured cast-iron stove reputedly dating from 1642, built in Lynn, Massachusetts. The science was, of course, further developed by Benjamin Franklin, who had introduced the "Pennsylvania Stove" in 1744. Franklin's royalist counterpart and contemporary, Benjamin Thompson, Count of Rumford, practiced and wrote about improved fireplace design in London and in the colonies.

The efforts of Franklin and Count Rumford to reduce the smoke in rooms indicate that an effective tradition of designing satisfactory fuel-burning devices had not evolved very far for over 500 years. But the chimney doctors popularized their art too late, for by 1748 James Watt had already heated his office by steam, fulfilling Renaissance proposals to use piped hot water for space heating. Pipes allowed designers to remove the fires to a remote location.

Succeeding generations of architects, and the new profession of mechanical engineering, then began to develop and use central heating and ventilation systems. Coal, the primary fuel for the nineteenth century, determined not only the relationship between heating technology and design within buildings, but patterns of human settlement. Agreeable living conditions could not be found next to coal-burning factories, or even commercial districts. And so decentralization

2

> **"The context of building has always been defined by climatic and material limitations. That has not prevented building designers from evolving solutions of craft and elegance."**

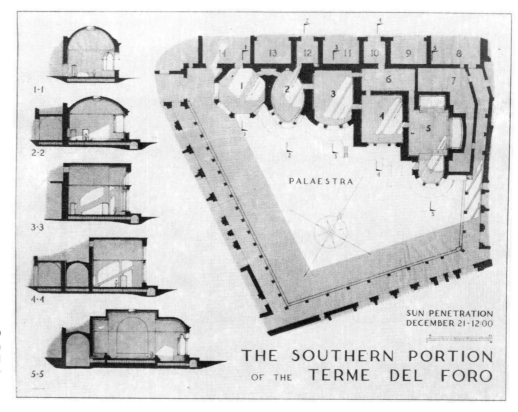

PALAESTRA

SUN PENETRATION
DECEMBER 21-12:00

THE SOUTHERN PORTION OF THE TERME DEL FORO

The Forum Baths in Ostia (about 250 AD) received heat from solar radiation and supplemented it with an early and exemplary application of radiant heating (drawing by permission of Edwin D. Thatcher).

and the separation of work from residence resulted in urban segregation by zone.

Oil and natural gas, cleaner to burn and easier to transport and store, simply cleaned up coal's act. Their uniform quality enabled much finer control of energy conversion and transport, and since heat could be moved more easily from the point of production to the point of use, the energy performance of the building envelope itself could be disregarded. Thus in the end fossil fuels became a substitute for climate-responsive buildings.

But the impact of climate was not altogether ignored by the early-twentieth-century architects who contributed to the development of the Modern Movement. Walter Gropius designed his own house in Lincoln, Massachusetts, as a "sun-tempered" structure. The Keck brothers in Chicago built the Crystal House for the Chicago World's Fair in 1933-1934 as an exploration of the esthetics of glass and steel and discovered it was so well heated by direct solar radiation that they then embarked on a decade-long investigation of solar-oriented dwellings that gave occasion for the first popular use of the term "solar house" in local newspapers at the time. In 1927, Buckminster Fuller proposed the Dymaxion house, based upon concepts of energy efficiency and industrial production. Le Corbusier, of course, was inspired by the industrial esthetic of oceanliners and airplanes, and in *Precisions*, published in 1930, proposed his own vision of the modern house, in which the walls are plenums—or "neutral walls" as he called them—for artificial control of heating and cooling. Sun control was developed into an architectural science by the Olgyay brothers in the early

1950s, and their subsequent publications are classics still in print today.

Much more recently, contemporary architects have begun to use the relative freedom of expression which modern technology offers to pursue design styles of their own invention, and "energy design" has been used as the rationale for esthetic gymnastics like putting buildings up in the air or under the ground. Now some commentators predict that energy conservation will provide the impetus for a total rethinking of architectural style as dramatic as that which followed the industrial revolution.

What, after all, is the energy crisis? And how does it affect building design? The projections of future fossil fuel supplies vary, being based more on assumptions than on substantiated fact. But in an authoritative summary of recent fuel-availability projections, V. E. McKelvey, director of the U.S. Geological Survey, presents the conclusion that known reserves of all recoverable world fuel resources would last 34 years if world consumption continued to grow by 5 per cent a year, the average rate from 1960 to 1973. If the consumption rate were reduced to 2 per cent a year, then the time to exhaustion would be 90 years. The projections are based only on known reserves, and they do not include total world resources thought to exist but still unproven. But counting the number of years to depletion is not a particularly relevant exercise once it has properly alerted us to the social and political implications of fuel scarcity. The important points are simply that supplying additional energy will in the future become increasingly costly no matter what the future source is to be,

and that continuing to increase energy demand involves unprecedented economic risk due to trade imbalances and their domestic repercussions—as well as social and environmental stresses due to the loss of natural resources, pollution, and other related health and safety costs associated with the energy-intensive development required by profligate energy use.

All of these points could be true, but why the connection with building design? The connection exists because of the combination of several facts. First, around 40 per cent of our national energy consumption is used in the building sector to heat, cool, and illuminate our buildings; to manufacture building products; and to construct buildings. Second, as much as one half of this energy could be saved by proper building design, construction, and use. Energy waste in the building sector has obvious economic impact on building owners and, beyond that, aggravates indirect environmental and health costs borne by future generations. The urgent decision is when to invest in energy conservation in the building sector. The longer the decision is delayed, the more difficult that option will be, as a greater portion of available capital is assigned each year to escalating energy expenditures to operate buildings.

These facts build the case for the energy conservation alternatives: an effort, equal to or greater than that now projected for energy development, should be devoted to conserve energy by improved design of buildings, transport, and other energy-intensive consumer products. The argument has been taken up by many authors that, due to energy waste in conversion and transmission,

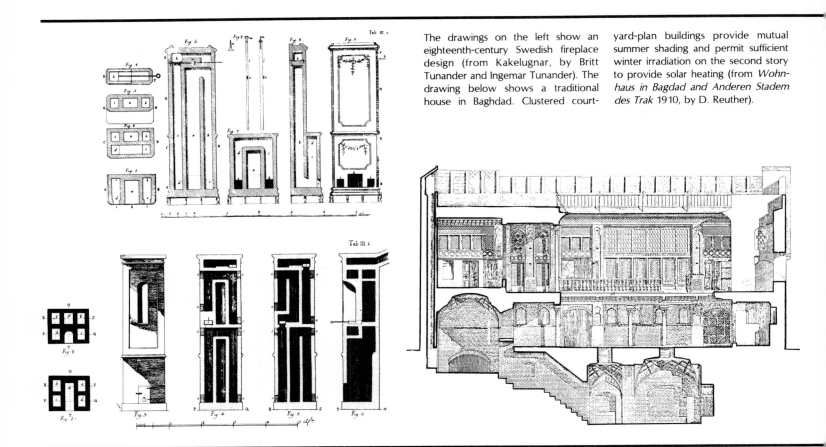

The drawings on the left show an eighteenth-century Swedish fireplace design (from Kakelugnar, by Britt Tunander and Ingemar Tunander). The drawing below shows a traditional house in Baghdad. Clustered court-yard-plan buildings provide mutual summer shading and permit sufficient winter irradiation on the second story to provide solar heating (from *Wohnhaus in Bagdad and Anderen Stadem des Trak* 1910, by D. Reuther).

a Btu saved is worth two Btu's produced, or, put in other terms, a dollar spent in energy conservation at the building scale could very well save twice the energy produced by an equivalent investment in power supply and production capacity.

The implications of the conservation alternative are thus enormously important to the design professions, as well as to the entire building industry. They are all the more so because, as coherent as the arguments for conservation may be, relatively little has actually been done to implement energy conservation practices compared to the range and magnitude of possibilities that already do exist.

To put the promise of the conservation alternative in a realistic framework, the difficulties of actually carrying out a large energy-conservation program at the building scale need to be faced. For if energy-conserving building design is ethical, wise, and economical, then why is it not inevitable?

The reasons come down to the fact that it is extremely difficult to change one's habits. Energy conservation requires changes in the way buildings are financed, designed, built, and used.

The most common argument offered against energy conservation design is that it is too costly, it cannot be financed, it cannot be marketed, it doesn't "pay back" quickly enough. In many cases, this economic reasoning can be faulted, but in others it cannot. Energy conservation does involve improved building quality which requires a larger economic investment than the "build cheap now, pay later" approach. The question that needs to be discussed, however, each time

the economic criterion is applied, is what are we saving by not investing in energy conservation? If it is capital or cash liquidity, what will that capital buy instead? Isn't there an increased price that everyone is willing to pay for stability of energy costs, for improved environmental quality, for increased economic and social well-being?

The point is that the market costs of energy does not now reflect its real cost, whether to produce and supply energy in the first place (plant costs are partly subsidized by tax credits and allowances, and energy charges are lower for large energy consumers); to clean up the environmental pollution and waste that result when energy is converted and transported (environmental clean-up costs are indirectly passed on to the general public or to future generations); or to replace the energy resource once it is depleted (in which case the replacement cost must include the entire capital expenditure required to supply an alternate source for the equivalent energy).

We need mechanisms by which the true costs of energy are reflected in our design decisions, either by marketplace corrections, which inevitably mean higher energy costs or—and here the ultimate economic advantage of energy conservation needs to be made emphatic—by reducing energy waste and consumption by conservative design.

From another important perspective— the cultural one—the interrelationship between building design and environmental quality should be recognized; it connects the act of design directly to the quality of life.

In the face of specious arguments that energy saving must result in lower environ-

mental quality standards and reduced comfort and convenience, it needs to be clearly stated that the allocation of economic, energy, and environmental resources is part of the same solution to maintain and improve the quality of life. In this respect, the potential of design—to anticipate change, to correct imbalance, to prepare solutions that are efficient and elegant—is our most valuable resource. The question is whether we can, in fact, use and improve our design abilities to create and sustain our cultural choices. As put by M. King Hubert, a scientist now retired from a career in the Shell Oil Company and the U.S. Geological Survey and an early prognosticator of the current energy shortages:

The foremost problem confronting humanity today is how to make the transition from the precarious state we are now in to an optimum future state by the least catastrophic progression. Our principal impediments at present are neither lack of energy or material resources nor of essential physical and biological knowledge. Our principal constraints are cultural.[2]

But cultural change is difficult, the more so as it requires changes in the underlying social and institutional structures. In a 1970 lecture, "Environments at Risk," anthropologist Mary Douglas draws a parallel between the contemporary environmental movement and the movement that began a century earlier for the abolition of slavery. She sees it as one that is equally profound in its potential impact upon our economic and social assumptions and that can be expected to have overcome resistance to what is an equally but inevitable process of cultural evolution:

"Energy conservation does involve improved building quality, which requires a larger economic investment than the 'build cheap now, pay later' approach. But what are we saving by not investing in energy conservation?"

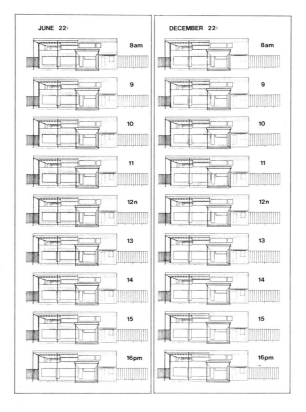

JUNE 22: DECEMBER 22:

8am 8am
9 9
10 10
11 11
12n 12n
13 13
14 14
15 15
16pm 16pm

Analysis of window wall shading on Walter Gropius's house in Lincoln, Massachusetts (from Nevin Summers, *AIA Journal,* February, 1977).

The abolitionists succeeded in revolutionizing the image of man. In the same way, the ecological movement will succeed in changing the idea of nature. It will succeed in raising a tide of opinion that will put abuses of the environment under close surveillance. Strong sanctions against particular pollutions will come into force. It will succeed in these necessary changes for the same reason as the slavery abolition movement, partly by sheer dedication and mostly because the time is ripe[3].

The energy issue has thus impelled design professionals into a perhaps unprecedented role as those most able to help solve resource and cultural problems by design. And rather than eliminate the esthetic component of design, the cultural perspective shows how necessary it is as the embodiment of our aspirations and commitments.

We know how to design energy-efficient buildings. It is at this moment only a matter of implementation.

We can conceive of this as requiring three steps. The first is relatively easy, that of utilizing technical-fix measures to reduce energy waste, with little cost or change in currently available building methods. The second is to address the fundamental patterns of energy use in the built environment by improved design of building and transport systems and other consumer products. Improved design alternatives depend on what changes can be made in institutional barriers in the building industry that act as disincentives to agreed-upon conservation goals. The third step—the most difficult, but an inevitable one if we are to meet our responsibility to ourselves, to the large segment of the world that is without even subsistence-level energy and other resources,

and to future generations—is a refocusing of our cultural values and social actions on a conservation ethic.

Viewing energy conservation efforts in terms of these steps—the technical, the institutional, and the ethical—helps to integrate technical invention with esthetically coherent and ethically appropriate design. Despite the apparent difficulties that await the necessary innovative program, there is a real basis for optimism and motivation in the renewed emphasis on quality. It provides the basis by which to make a distinction between those technologies that are disruptive to the environment and those that can help place us in balance with the ecological imperatives that ultimately bound our actions—ones that help connect us to our natural world and, through nature, to ourselves.

The quality of life, of the environment, of design, and of energy use are crucially interdependent. Just as energy requires a crossing of disciplines and of boundaries, it also serves to connect. The solution to the problems of energy and resources requires unprecedented cooperation between all segments of society, between private and public sectors, from local to national and international levels. We can improve our buildings, our cities, and our land by eliminating wasteful use of resources and by qualitative rather than quantitative goals in meeting technical and social needs.

Architects once studied the rules of proportion for the styles and orders of the classical temples of antiquity. The earth is now that temple: the rules are those of building and living within the limits of the earth's balance of resources and energy.

FOOTNOTES

1. This and the following historical paragraphs were written with the collaboration of Jeffrey Cook, to whom I am indebted for insights and examples and who allowed me to borrow freely from his manuscript, "History of Energy in Buildings."

2. As quoted in *The New York Times,* December 2, 1976.

3. Mary Douglas, "Environments at Risk" *Times Literary Supplement,* London, October 30, 1970.

ENERGY CONSERVATION: THE GROWING NEED, THE CHANGING INCENTIVES, THE NEW PRIORITIES . . . AND A SPLENDID RECORD OF ACCOMPLISHMENT

In October 1971, addressing his remarks to a pioneering Round Table on Energy Conservation sponsored by ARCHITECTURAL RECORD, then-Interior Assistant Secretary Hollis Dole said: "In a milieu that has been variously characterized as the affluent society, the throw-away economy, and the land of plenty, it is a novel experience to see attention focused on saving resources. . . . The truth is that for various reasons we are entering a period in which it will be increasingly difficult to supply our demands from domestic fuel resources of all kinds. The result of this failure of domestic energy supply will be increased dependence on foreign energy resources. If it is true that we are in for a long period of austere conditions relating to energy supply, then it makes eminent good sense to do what we can about conserving the supply that we have. . . . For years and years we have wasted unconscionable amounts of our nonrenewable resources just because the prices we paid did not reflect their true cost and we therefore thought them to be cheap and readily available. Now the discipline of scarcity is forcing us to husband and respect what we have wasted and abused. The reform is long overdue.

"Suffusing and permeating every other consideration is the impact that environmental considerations have upon the production and use of energy. The truth is that the statutes and regulations for protecting the environment that have and will come into existence will have an enormous impact upon the operations by which we produce, process, transport, and consume energy.

"I think it is abundantly clear that despite our best efforts, we are simply not going to be able—short of an all-out effort—to meet our essential minimum energy requirements from domestic sources within the next 15 years." (That said at a time, remember, when home heating oil was selling in New England for 15 cents a gallon!)

How far have we come in conserving energy? Today's state of the art is amazingly sophisticated. But we knew most of it all along.

The bulk of this book consists of case studies of energy-efficient building designs—through effective use of solar energy; through the fast-developing techniques of "underground architecture;" through more efficient heating, ventilating, and air-conditioning systems; through the design of higher-efficiency building envelopes; and (perhaps most effective of all, though not at all glamorous) through more efficient management and control of energy in a building. They add up to a bag of energy-conservation tools and techniques that, most experts agree, can result in energy savings of at least 30 per cent, and sometimes 40 per cent or more when applied in new building design or in the retrofitting of older buildings.

Siting and orientation of the building to the sun is one example of a basic design device that is receiving more attention from designers.

The proper orientation of a building on a site was once a beginning point of design—to orient the building properly to the sun, and to the prevailing breeze. Many custom houses are still given this kind of careful siting. But for other building types, routinely air-conditioned, considerations of siting became less and less important because we had learned that there was no design error that technology could not correct. But in the new drive for energy conservation, architects are returning to careful consideration of those basic lessons they learned at school. Where ten years ago sun loading on a building was generally ignored, today most architects would agree with solar expert John Yellott's admonition that "we must pay full attention to the impact of the sun on three sides—I leave the north out. The major problem is the south side of the building in the winter time—and unless you pay close attention to the problem of sun control you can wind up running the chillers in the coldest months." Engineer Frank Bridgers, a pioneer in solar energy, has pointed out in an ARCHITECTURAL RECORD article that: "If you take a rectangular building two and a half times longer than it is wide, with fifty per cent glass, and an east-west orientation, you can knock 30 per cent off the cooling load if you simply turn the building 90 degrees. If you plant shade trees all around, you get another 25 per cent saving. We have to remind people who site buildings and do planning about these basics. Too often, we engineers are given a building that is completely designed, with all the basic decisions made and the budget set—and then it is too late to get into consideration of the simple things like orientation and sun control that can save energy and save cost . . . ."

This return to design basics has been welcomed by most architects, for most would agree with this comment by Dick Wright of the National Bureau of Standards: "The most difficult design problems are those where there are no constraints: the flat site, the unlimited budget, the miracle material with ultimate tensile strength. In contrast, the most difficult site often produces the most exciting solution. Energy conservation has become such a useful constraint. Even though, right now, we are having to spend a bit more time and effort in design, a sense of order and priority is being established—criteria that the architect can work with from the start, that exclude a lot of erroneous options, and that may reduce design costs along with energy costs. . . ."

More careful design of glass area, and the use of more efficient glass and/or shading of the glass, has been an obvious response to energy conservation.

In the early days of energy conservation—in the early 1970s—there was what has to be described as an over-reaction to glass area. In a 1971 RECORD article, Connecticut architect Bruce Campbell Graham said: "We have been heavily involved with 'all-glass' buildings. And we have in those buildings ignored the realities of nature. Rather, we have overcome the realities of nature by massive mechanical systems—by brute force. I think this approach to design is going to have to be reconsidered in favor of a new esthetic involving less and/or higher quality glass and extensive sun-shading." Well, he was right of course—though at first there was what has to be described as an over-reaction to glass area. An early California law limited the total area of glass permitted in a house—without regard to any subtleties of glass quality or orientation.

But the all-glass esthetic has not in fact been abandoned, because it can produce some striking buildings, and because it can be made efficient: In recent all-glass buildings, the window area has indeed been reduced while the spandrel glass between rows of windows has been heavily insulated to approximate the performance of, say, masonry wall of similar glass area. (Needless to say, heavy insulation of all of the building envelope—walls and roof—is now totally accepted as an investment in any building design.)

It is also true that more architects and engineers have been specifying higher-quality, more-energy-efficient glass—since the higher costs of fuel have tipped the first-cost vs. operating-cost equation in the direction of higher-quality materials.

We also see fewer buildings with the same window treatment on all four walls. While this seems still to be mandatory in most high-rise office buildings, where windowless walls obviously create undesirable space for executive offices, more and more buildings are being designed that are essentially closed to the north weather, with sun control on the other sides. Various design techniques involving set-back of the windows, or utilizing various sunshades or fins or awnings, are seen—all devised to shade the windows from the hot summer sun and thus reduce the load on the air-conditioning, while at the same time admitting a controlled amount of winter sun to take advantage of solar heat. (This is, of course, a careful engineering job—because in the coldest months in the coldest cities, the southern sun can overheat offices and result in "running the coolers in January.")

Closely related to glass area, of course, are questions of energy conservation by means of solar gain and daylighting.

The National Bureau of Standards has undertaken considerable study on the effect of windows, and while the research is far from complete, it does show that (1) by orienting windows properly and (2) by covering them at night to reduce heat loss, the amount of energy saved by admitting useful solar heat in the cold months (while blocking it by sunshades in the summer) and the amount of energy saved by using daylighting instead of electric lighting during the daylight hours, "results in energy savings comparable to having no windows."

Architect and daylighting expert Ben Evans said in a RECORD article: "We're simply going back to where we were 25 years ago, when we designed for natural ventilation and daylighting and didn't use any energy all day. That approach would not be appropriate in a tall building in the middle of a big city, but we can make best use of what we have. There's no doubt that skylights in a one-story building save energy and costs on a life-cycle basis. So do properly handled windows. One of the problems is that most architects really don't know much about the daylight that is out there available to use, and so they use conservative figures. There are some exceedingly sophisticated techniques for calculating the amount of daylight that one might use in building design. But we need much more research, and it needs to be better disseminated."

John Honeycomb of IBM's Real Estate and Construction Division has pointed out that: "In Europe, architects make much more effective use of daylight. Our buildings there tend to be narrower—so that more people have a window; and they open those windows so our air-conditioning requirements are less. We've gone back and installed individual switching in the perimeter offices, and the savings on lighting are far more than we thought they would be because people like to work in natural daylight, and they *use* those switches. . . ."

"Waste heat" which used to be exhausted is now put to use heating the building—or put into storage.

Many industrial plants, and indeed many office buildings, have sources of unwanted heat—for example, lighting systems and (especially) computer rooms. Where once this heat was simply discharged from the building, it is often now directed to other parts of the building for use as heat. Canadian engineer Robert Tamblyn has pioneered the use of thermal storage systems which can pick up heat from process equipment or computers or other sources and store it—usually by heating water—for use when it is needed. One such system by Tamblyn is detailed on page KK. He reports: "If you engineer a solar heating system for an office building, you may find you have a ten-year payout. But if you look at the system carefully, you may well find out that the storage part of the system pays out in two years. So, when it comes to any building which generates a lot of its own internal heat, the concept of storage makes sense."

Engineers are wasting less energy bringing in and heating (or cooling) outside air.

Many engineers have long argued that the ventilation requirements in many buildings were arbitrary and probably excessive—and those standards have been under experimental study for some years. In several test cases, the supply of outside air was simply shut down, and very few people even noticed. Dr. Richard Wright of the National Bureau of Standards conducted an experiment in a New York City school in which the air-change rate was cut from four per hour to one. The difference was not noted by teachers or students. Engineer Robert Tamblyn has pointed out that lavatory exhaust requirements vary between 10 and 15 cubic feet per minute—but that that much leaks through the skin of most buildings. Dr. Wright's conclusion: "It seems as if there is a great deal of opportunity to examine the standards in this area. . . ."

Engineers—and the manufacturers who supply the equipment—have made enormous strides in improving the efficiency of hvac systems.

Most engineers no longer use reheat systems or constant volume systems—variable volume systems are now the rule. Suggestions by engineer Jack Beech: "You reclaim heat where you can, you tend to use heat for forced loading of chillers to obtain key efficiency. With oil at seven cents a gallon and electric power at one and a half cents a kilowatt, no one paid much attention to heat-pump systems—today they do. In recent years, we have been able to apply all the techniques we have known for years—but couldn't get into the job because they cost a few extra bucks."

A major reduction in energy usage has taken place because more and more engineers are designing to normal—rather than peak—conditions. As engineer Norman Kurtz has pointed out: "For years we designed the mechanical system to meet the peak conditions— and put in enough equipment to meet that peak. Today, we can design primarily for the in-between conditions—and come up with a much more energy-efficient system."

Lighting is such an obvious user of energy that it has gotten a lot of attention—but all the answers aren't in yet.

The new development that received the most attention in recent years was the so-called task ambient lighting built into furniture for open-office environments. Many of the leading manufacturers, with the design help of their own or consultant engineers, have produced an astonishing variety of lighting built-in— usually with lighting focused downward onto the work area—and upward to create general illumination by reflecting off the ceiling. These systems have proven to be enormously popular and extremely efficient, but to have some drawbacks—the most common complaint being that with the light so carefully (and efficiently) focused on the work surface, the employee is not as free to move around and still see well. For instance, it is difficult to sit back, put your feet up on the desk, and read.

Concurrent with this development was the broader-scale development of task lighting—very simply, putting enough light (but no more than that) on each of the tasks in any building. To be obvious about it, this concept would put less lighting in the hallways than in a drafting room or shop where detailed work was done—or the kitchen. This task lighting—as opposed to the uniform lighting levels (even luminous ceilings) so common just a few years ago—has proven appealing to architects not just because of the energy conservation, but because it tends to create a successful architectural environment.

At the same time as new design "systems" have been in development, the lamp manufacturers have been hard at work designing new sources—new driving mechanisms for fluorescents that increase their efficiency by 20 per cent, new and more efficient lamps, even

new shapes of luminaires that create a better quality of light on a workplace.

And, again at the same time that the development of new and more efficient lighting "systems" went into high gear, generally reducing the quantity of light (or at least the quantity of energy required), research into the quality of light accelerated. Research on the quality of light has been going on for at least 40 years, but few engineers have involved themselves deeply enough in this somewhat complex area of research to take advantage of the research. Most, as lighting expert Steve Squillace has said, "found that the easiest way to design lighting was to hide behind 'the authorities' "—that is, simply to follow the generally accepted standards.

But in the last few years, both the quantity and sophistication of lighting research has clearly accelerated—delving into not just the quantity of light required to perform a given task, but also the quality of light and its effect upon people. Lighting expert David DiLaura of Smith Hinchman & Grylls said in a recent RECORD article: "There are three basic considerations in setting lighting criteria. The first is cost-benefit analysis, what does a certain level of lighting 'buy you' in terms of employee productivity, attitudes, safety. This is relatively easy to answer: We can relate photometric properties to how well people do visual work—how quickly, how well, how efficiently, how error-free. But working with new techniques (specifically, a new standard called 'visibility level') we are approaching being able to measure much more complex variables: How does a certain level of lighting affect the way we feel—the question of human preference; and what does a certain level of lighting do to our emotional response—what makes a certain place beautiful, or attractive, or exciting.

"The human variances involved," DiLaura argued, "are not the problem they are sometimes thought to be. The fact that you have a bell curve of human response to almost any stimulus does not mean 'gosh, we don't know anything.' Human variance can be dealt with very precisely. We can tell, for example, that if we establish a certain lighting level and quality, half the people who have normal eyes and are between 20 and 30 years of age will be able to perform a given task. Those same levels will work for 40 per cent of the 30- to 40-year olds; perhaps 30 per cent of those over 40. The point is that we have the information; we have a hard fix on human variation and reaction to lighting stimuli. It is then simply a matter of deciding what level to use. . . ." Engineer John Flynn said in the same article: "We are always going to have some people who think there is not enough light or that 'it is too bright in here!'; just as there are those who are too cold and those who are too hot; those who think it is too noisy. Yet we must make decisions that can satisfy only, say, 70 per cent—which means we have made a conscious decision to discriminate against 30 per cent of the people. The solution is to recognize who they are and make some special provisions. . . ."

Similarly, in the cause of energy conservation, our "standards of comfort" have come in for reexamination.

The standards for thermal comfort established by ASHRAE (the American Society of Heating, Refrigerating, and Air-Conditioning Engineers) have been on the books a long time and were based on years of research into the conditions that people said they preferred. But the drive for energy conservation called them into question. Some engineers have argued for more sophisticated research. For example, engineer Gershon Meckler has argued that: "It is not enough to be concerned just with temperature and humidity—we are really concerned with the heat released from the body by conduction, by convection, and by respiration. A single number like 68 or 75, or a given relative humidity, is not necessarily the proper criterion for measuring human comfort; there is also the matter of air velocity, mean radiant temperature, and so on. These other variables have not been explored effectively."

But most of the "research" so far has been empirical—what people will accept. For years, office workers have been led to expect a temperature of 72 to 74 degrees, and a relatively low (about 50 per cent) relative humidity. Of course, people are not instruments—and they really don't mind variations of these accepted standards until they feel uncomfortable. And then the question is, how many people feel uncomfortable? As one architect put it: "I have always thought the 74 degree standard was where half the people were too hot and half were too cold. . . ."

Many building owners are experimenting with the temperatures that people will accept. Rockefeller Center in New York conducted a carefully controlled experiment, and found that there was no big increase in complaints until summer temperatures in the buildings got beyond 76 degrees to 77 or 78 degrees. On the winter side, complaints started as soon as the temperature dropped below 70. An NBS official, describing similar experiments in federal buildings, reported that: "The number of complaints in federal office buildings relates to three things: temperature, humidity, and distance from Washington. One of the things that has let us operate at higher temperatures in summer and lower temperatures in winter is a change in the dress code—no ties required, summer dresses allowed, sweaters encouraged in winter. Our summer temperatures are now allowed to rise to 78 to 80 degrees . . . for the winter, 65." The 78-65 combination became a requirement by Presidential order in 1979, of course.

Meanwhile, more sophisticated research continues. . . .

Building operation—the management and control of the building—is probably the least dramatic energy-conservation measure, but is considered by many to be the most effective.

Engineer Larry Spielvogel has written persuasively in RECORD and other professional magazines that—above everything else—careful operation of buildings is the single most effective way to conserve energy, and that the "single most effective tool for energy conservation is a screwdriver in the hands of an intelligent man . . . And the second most cost-effective technique, with pay-backs measured in terms of months, is improved controls. You cannot operate an energy-efficient building unless the designer incorporates the means of control—especially the switches to let you turn off what you don't need when you don't need it, and the metering that lets you know how much energy is going for what purpose in your buildings. . . ."

The question has been, until very recently, that if we know so much about how to save energy, why haven't we?

As long ago as the first concerns about energy—in the early 1970s—energy conservation seemed a *desirable* thing to do. It seemed a *moral* thing to do. But it has not been, generally, an *economic* thing to do—until recently.

The goal, for advocates of energy conservation from the early days, was to try to help solve our nation's energy problems while at the same time building higher-quality buildings that would return to their owners lower operating costs. For a few, the idealistic argument was even stronger: If we build buildings that are wasteful of energy today, they are going to continue to waste energy for 20 or 50 or 100 years—and that is an accumulation of a lot of energy that we must pump or mine out of the ground.

The trouble was—until very recently—that the economics, the cost-benefit (or any other real incentive) was just not there.

For one thing, lenders were (and still are) slow to reflect much in the way of higher first costs in the mortgage, even if operating costs are lowered. Their argument goes like this: Mortgage loans are based on

11

economic value, and value is based on net income. If you are able to prove an increased value (in terms of net income), higher first costs to conserve energy can be reflected with an increased loan. But the question arises as to whether the saving involved is really completely economical. To the extent that it is not, then the owner has to bear the expense.

Thus, mortgaging any increased first costs for energy conservation is still a tough argument for an architect or engineer to win, and still a deterrent to the construction of highly energy-efficient buildings.

But a lot has changed in recent years: The cost equations have changed, and the economic incentive is growing.

In the early 1970s, professionals were guessing at what could happen to energy costs. For example, utility expert Jack Shannahan said back in 1971: "Right now, there is little practical incentive to conserve energy. If there is an energy crisis, then it itself suggests that the price is out of whack. And that is exactly what is happening. . . . There have been tremendous increases in every element of cost that goes into the generation of power. Fuel costs are skyrocketing. And there are a whole series of new costs that have come into the power generation picture that are not yet factored into rates: pollution control, added costs in plant siting, and plant-siting delays. A whole new range of costs in research and development. . . . When these are factored into power costs—and this will take time—I think you are going to see substantial increases in the cost of energy. And this in itself might be enough to provide some of the incentive for the conservation of energy." Well, how right Mr. Shannahan was!

Bertram Goldberg, a top executive of New York City's major utility, Consolidated Edison, was equally farsighted: "There's no doubt the rates for electric service will increase. For one thing, the new capacity we are now building will cost about 50 per cent more per unit of capacity (megawatt) compared with the average costs of our existing system. This is going to have to be paid for in increased rates. . . . Additionally, our operating costs are increasing. The most significant impact on operating costs—that is, the costs of fuel—have risen gigantically in the past year and a half. In 1969, our average cost of residual fuel was 34 cents per million Btu. It was 48 cents in the first six months of 1971, and it was about 52 cents in October (of 1971). I expect it will average around 60 cents in 1972 and go to the high 60s when we begin burning only low-sulphur oil." Well, how right Mr. Goldberg was. Today's fuel costs have obviously changed the cost equation a great deal!

What about standards? While the government "fiddled" with a national energy policy, the building industry made considerable progress.

No one, of course, likes the idea of standards being imposed. But when architects and engineers (and even building owners) get together to talk about energy, there is less opposition than one might imagine.

Many developers and owners are not opposed to standards because they create an important competitive consideration: Standards would put everyone at the same starting point, force everyone to play by the same rules. Unspoken, but fairly clear, is the idea that responsible developers—anxious "to do the right thing" in energy conservation—consider that standards, by setting at least minimum requirements, might permit the developers to make the extra investment in time and money to build an energy-conserving building without being placed at a competitive disadvantage. The so-called minimum-cost, minimum-quality developers would be left out of the running.

Architect Lew Davis has spoken of "liking standards" from a strongly philosophical point of view: "How much energy does this country have, and how are we going to distribute the energy? That is the basic question. What we need as architects is input. Given an energy shortage, I would like to know exactly what is expected of me. If we were told to use so much energy per square foot, I think we could work to that and design a building. Then we could learn (within the constraints) to produce beautiful and vigorous buildings. And then the public would become conditioned to that type of building. Energy conservation can affect architecture—and it can affect architecture in a very positive way." Said a major building owner in a RECORD article: "I am in sympathy with what the government is trying to do in establishing some energy usage base. . . . Once we had some figures, based on investigations of many, many buildings, I think just knowing what the maximums and averages and minimums are would encourage conservation. If, as a building owner, I saw that I was way above the maximum, I would call in my technical staff or an outside consultant to analyze what was going on. I would want to know what is happening, what could be done to bring consumption down, and what it would cost to make the correction. Then I could weigh the economics. . . . Certainly it is to our advantage to operate our buildings as economically as possible, because we are competitors and we want to be able to offer a lower rental rate than the fellow down the street."

The first standard to gain acceptance was ASHRAE 90—far from perfect (indeed, in many ways controversial)—but a strong and understandable first step.

In 1973, NCSBCS (National Conference of States on Building Codes and Standards) requested the National Bureau of Standards to develop a document which could be used as a basis for state codes. NBS did—with a great deal of professional and industry input—produce a draft proposal in February of 1974. A few months later, ASHRAE took over this document and began revising it through its well-established consensus process toward a national consensus standard. The bulk of the document (all but a controversial section dealing with evaluating energy use at its source instead of at the building line) was approved by the ASHRAE committee.

This standard, from the beginning, has been criticized by some as "prescriptive"—requiring specific standards for various sections and components of the building instead of allowing the designer to meet, as he or she finds it most efficient to do so, an overall energy budget. But, generally speaking, that standard was quickly accepted as the best available tool—and has now been adopted as code in almost all of the states.

More importantly, perhaps, many architects, engineers, and owners have begun to use these standards as a guideline on a strictly voluntary (and cost-effective) basis.

A digest of this standard prepared by consulting engineer William Tao for his clients can be found on page 16—though it should be noted that ASHRAE 90 is constantly being updated and any design work should be based on a complete and current copy.

While ASHRAE 90 is the most widely used standard, attempts to create a budget standard for energy use are progressing—mostly under pressure from the federal government.

From the beginning of the effort to set standards, most professionals have preferred the idea of a budget standard—establishing an amount of energy that could be "spent" on a given building and then using that as a design goal with some kind of "penalty" for failure to meet that goal in practice. The trouble has been—how to establish those budgets. The first "energy-budget" standard—the famous "55,000 Btu per square foot per year"—was established by architect Wally Meisen, an assistant commissioner of the General Services Administration in the mid-1970s. He once described the not-altogether-technical method by which he established that standard (for federal office buildings): "Everyone told me we didn't have the necessary data, and didn't know how to find it. I simply asked them to come up with numbers for our existing buildings—and we got figures around 100,000 to 250,000. When I asked how much we could save, they said around 50 per cent. And I said, let us set the standard at 55,000 Btu per square foot per year. Everyone asked me how I knew that was right, and I told them that I didn't . . . but we would find out in a hurry.

"The intent was simply to make the people who are paying for energy aware of how much they are spending."

The advantage of a budget approach is, of course, that it permits a great deal of flexibility; it offers architect and engineer a full range of design options. But there are complications and problems—and those that still trouble the professions were expressed at a 1975 Round Table by engineer and energy consultant Larry Spielvogel: "There are two philosophical questions: doesn't a budget or performance approach permit a great deal of buckpassing? And what would be the incentive to keep eliminating inefficient systems once the budget had been met? Wouldn't it be better if you made everything efficient?"

He also hit on the weakness that, despite extensive research in the late 1970s, still seems the biggest problem of performance standards: We don't know enough to set standards we're sure are good and fair and accurate. "There is a great lack of data that is meaningful, because there are so many things that go on in a building. Our buildings today are so incredibly complicated that just to meter the various uses of energy would create an enormous economic and technical problem, even forgetting the changes that inevitably take place. How do you take into account complications like computer rooms; or buildings that are partially owner-occupied and partially tenant-occupied? What happens when you go to two shifts in the building, or work six days a week, or want to move into a building that is already a small energy-intensive lab? The way people *use* a building is really the key in determining how much energy they use. . . . We really don't know enough to set good standards."

In 1976, with the Energy Conservation Standards for New Buildings Act, Congress mandated that energy performance standards for all types of buildings be established—and be implemented by 1980. Under that mandate, a unique, $8-million research project, conducted by the AIA Research Corporation for the Department of Housing and Urban Development, was carried out. That program, the most important of the 1970s in establishing reliable standards, is detailed in an article on page 20.

When the Department of Energy issued its proposal for energy performance standards based on the research mentioned above and a host of other studies by design professionals and many professional bodies, the standard was published in the form of an Advance Notice of Proposed Rulemaking which appeared in the *Federal Register*—quite a formal action—and it stirred up a good deal of concern among many professionals who felt the proposed standards would be difficult to implement. The standards—and the concerns that surround them—are detailed in an article beginning on page 24, and represent "the current state of the art."

The question that is still being asked—but that will be answered given the federal government's obvious wish to *have* energy standards—is this: Should we make into law and enforce the 1979—1980 version of performance standards, with their undoubted weaknesses and difficulties of implementation; or shall we proceed with deliberate speed to enact a better standard at a later date?

Finally, looming behind all of the efforts to design more energy-efficient buildings, and all of the debate about standards, is the fundamental moral issue: We simply should not continue to squander irreplaceable natural resources.

A number of top industry leaders have produced some memorable quotes on that subject:

Ted Peck of Owens-Corning Fiberglas, and one of the pioneers and most thoughtful advocates of energy conservation: "Even if heating and cooling and lighting costs are not the major costs in a building, where we have the technology this does not excuse us from following wasteful practices or non-economic practices."

Stanley Gilman of Penn State: "We simply do not have the right anymore to waste the energy we have left—just as we do not have the right to continue to pollute our air and water. The time has come to stop bickering and get down to the business of exercising our professional responsibilities to design buildings and systems that will keep the lights on for our descendants as long as possible."

Colorado architect John Anderson, a leader in the design of solar-heated buildings: "The problem is right now. There is no substitute for natural gas. Right now we don't have enough natural gas to produce ammonium-based fertilizers, and our productivity of food could go down. . . . Whether or not we can make energy conservation pay off is not as important as the fact that our fuels are going to run out. We have a moral responsibility to get on with exploring alternatives."

Architect Earl Flansburgh: "This is not the first time our society has faced an energy crisis. You may remember that England switched from wood to coal not because of foresight on anyone's part; they switched because they ran out of trees."

And Will Rogers said in 1927: "We Americans think we are pretty good! We want to build a house, we cut down some trees. We want to build a fire, we dig a little coal. But when we run out of all these things, then we will find out just how good we really are. ..."

On the next pages. . .

THE ASHRAE ENERGY STANDARD FOR NEW BUILDINGS:
A DIGEST

ENERGY STANDARDS PROJECT TESTS
DESIGNERS' CONSERVATION SKILLS:
THE DEVELOPMENT OF STANDARDS

A FIRST LOOK AT THE PROPOSED
FEDERAL ENERGY PERFORMANCE STANDARDS

THAT ASHRAE ENERGY STANDARD FOR NEW BUILDINGS: A DIGEST

This digest (the standard's requirements in convenient tabular and condensed form) was prepared originally by consulting engineer William Tao to aid his clients in understanding the various mechanical and electrical requirements of ASHRAE Standard 90-75. Most states have adopted codes based upon standard 90-75. This standard is constantly under revision and study—a full copy should be obtained for any calculations.

1-3. PURPOSE, SCOPE AND DEFINITIONS
This standard is to provide design requirements which will improve utilization of energy in new buildings, with general scope in Section 2 and technical definitions in Section 3.

4. EXTERIOR ENVELOPE
Design elements—Energy-efficient design shall be based on evaluation of building orientation, shape, aspect ratio, number of stories, thermal mass, color, shading and reflections based on adjacent structures, natural ventilation and wind. Design criteria are summarized below.

Heating/cooling criteria—Maximum thermal transmittance (U_o and minimum insulation resistance (R) for component assemblies (walls, floors, roof/ceilings) are summarized in Table A. The U_o values of some assemblies may be increased and others decreased, provided the over-all heat gain or loss for the entire "building envelope" does not exceed the total which would result from conformance to the stated U_o values.

TABLE A. THERMAL COEFFICIENTS

Annual Heating Degree Days	Maximum Transmittance U_o = Btu/h·ft2·F					Min. Insulation[†] R (h·ft2·F/Btu)	
	Gross Wall			FLOOR over Unheated Space	ROOF & CEILING	For Slab-on-Grade	
	Over 3 Stories	3 Stories & Under	1-2 Family Dwelling			Heated	Un-heated
12,000						11.5*	8.8*
11,000		.20	.16			10.7*	8.2*
10,000	.28				.060	10.0	7.5
9,000		.22	.18			9.3	6.8
8,000		.24	.19	.08		8.5	6.2
7,000	.31	.26	.21		.068	7.8	5.5
6,000	.33	.28	.22		.076	7.0	4.8
5,000	.36	.30	.23		.084	6.3	4.2
4,000	.38	.32	.25	.11	.092	5.5	3.5
3,000	.41	.33	.27	.19		4.8	2.8
2,000	.43	.35	.28	.26	.100	4.0	2.2
1,000	.46	.37	.29	.33		3.3	1.5*
500	.47	.38	.30	.36		2.9	0.8*

*Extrapolation from Figure 2 of Standard.
[†]Total insulation length to be 24 inches minimum.

OTTV—Overall Thermal Transfer Value (for walls in Type "B" buildings) shall not exceed Table B. This table, which applies to the cooling-load situation, also includes Solar Factor (SF) for fenestration and Equivalent Temperature Difference (TD_{eq}) for walls, which relates to the "mass" of the exterior enclosure.

TABLE B. COOLING CRITERIA AND FACTORS

North Latitude	25°	30°	35°	40°	45°	50°	55°
Max. OTTV (Btu/h·ft2)	29.3	30.7	32.1	33.5	34.9	36.3	37.7
SF (Btu/h·ft2)	118	121	124	127	133	138	144

WALL	mass/area (lb/ft2)	0-25	26-40	41-70	> 70
	TD_{EQ} (F)	44	37	30	23

Air leakage—shall not exceed values in Table C.

TABLE C. AIR LEAKAGE LIMITATION

Type of Window/Door	Residential	Non-Residential
Windows	0.5 cfm/L.ft	0.5 cfm/L.ft
Sliding Doors	0.5 cfm/ft2	11.0 cfm/L.ft
Swinging Doors	1.25 cfm/ft2	11.0 cfm/L.ft
Revolving Doors	—	11.0 cfm/L.ft

5. HVAC SYSTEMS
Exceptions—Special applications, such as hospitals, laboratories, special equipment, etc., are exempt from requirements of this section.

Indoor design conditions—(winter) 72 F db at 30% max. RH; (summer) 78 F db with RH selected to minimize energy usage, within limits of ASHRAE Standard 55-74.

Outdoor design conditions—Selected from climatic conditions listed in 1972 ASHRAE Handbook of Fundamentals under 97.5% column for winter, and 2.5% column for summer.

Ventilation—shall conform to ASHRAE Standard 62-73. For recirculation systems, outdoor air may be reduced to 33% of the specified minimum, but not less than 5 cfm per person.

Temperature & humidity—Thermostats and humidistats shall be provided for each system (or zone). Humidistat shall prevent use of new energy to produce a space RH above 30% or below 60%. Controls shall be readily accessible for shutoff, setback or volume reduction during non-use or alternate-use periods.

Simultaneous heating & cooling—within a zoned space, and the reheating or recooling of supply air are discouraged except as delineated.

Cooling with outdoor air (economizer cycle)—shall be used when-

16

ever it will result in lower usage of new energy. Exceptions will be permitted for small systems (less than 5,000 cfm or 134,000 Btu/h), poor outdoor air quality, requirement of more new energy for humidity control or other systems, and systems designed for interzone energy recovery.

Air transport factor (ATF)—the ratio of sensible heat removal rate to fan power input. Shall not be less than 4.0 based on design conditions.

Energy recovery systems—recommended to conserve new energy.

Piping Insulation—shall be in accordance with Table D for thermal resistances (R) of 4.0 to 4.6 h·F·ft²/Btu/inch. For other insulation material, thickness shall vary in inverse proportion to R.

TABLE D. MINIMUM PIPE INSULATION THICKNESS (INCHES)							
Piping System Types	Fluid Temp. Range (F)	Pipe Sizes (inches)					
		Runouts ≤ 2	≤ 1	1¼-2	2½-4	5-6	≥ 8
Steam & Hot Water	306-450	1.5	1.5	2.0	2.5	3.5	3.5
	251-305	1.5	1.5	2.0	2.5	3.0	3.0
	201-250	1.0	1.0	1.5	1.5	2.0	2.0
	120-200	0.5	0.75	1.0	1.0	1.0	1.5
	Any	1.0	1.0	1.0	1.5	1.5	2.0
Chilled Water	40-55	0.5	0.5	0.75	1.0	1.0	1.0
Refrigerant/brine	<40	1.0	1.0	1.5	1.5	1.5	1.5

Ductwork—All ductwork (except ducts installed in unventilated basements, within HVAC equipment, exhausts, or having Δt less than 25F) shall be insulated if it would require additional energy otherwise. Insulation shall have thermal resistance (R) greater than 0.067 x Δt (F). (See para. 5.11)

6. HVAC EQUIPMENT

Performance responsibility—Supplier shall provide equipment performance data and maintenance manual upon request. System designer shall determine compliance of unitary equipment provided by more than one component supplier.

Standard rating conditions and COP—are summarized in Table E for various equipment and components.

TABLE E. STANDARD RATING CONDITION & MIN. COP OF HVAC SYSTEMS						
Type		Standard Rating Condition			Min. COP 1977	1980
Heating Equipment	Heat* Pump	Air Entering Outdoor Section ·········· 47 db/43 wb, F			2.2	2.5
		Air Entering Outdoor Section ·········· 17 db/15 wb. F			1.2	1.5
		Water Entering Outdoor Section ·········· 60 F			2.2	2.5
Cooling Equipment	Electrically Operated	Air Entering Temp.: 80 db/67 wb, F	< 65,000 Btu/h		1.8	2.0
			≥ 65,000 Btu/h		2.0	2.2
	Heat Operated	Direct Fired (Gas or Oil) ··········			0.40	0.48
		Indirect Fired (Steam or Hot Water) ··········			0.65	0.68
Cooling Components	Electric Water Chiller	Leaving Chilled Water ······· 44 F	Self-Contained	Air	2.2	2.3
		Entering Chilled Water ······ 54 F	Centrifugal	Water	3.8	4.0
		Leaving Condenser ·········· 95 F Entering Condenser ·········· 85 F	Self-Contained	Air	2.1	2.2
		Fouling Factor: Non-Ferrous Tubes······ 0.0005	Reciprocating	Water	3.2	3.4
		Steel Tubes ············ 0.0010	Condenserless	Air	2.6	2.8
	Compressor & Condensing Units (≥ 65,000 Btu/h)	Condenser Ambient (Air or Evap. Cooled), 95 db/75 wb, F	Reciprocating	Water	3.2	3.4
		Compr. Sat. Discharge:	Recip. (air Cooled)		2.3	2.5
		Water or Evap. Cooled , 105 F	Recip. (Evap. Cooled)		3.3	3.5
		Air Cooled ·········· 120 F	Recip. (Water Cooled)		3.3	3.5
*Based on 70 F db air entering indoor section on heating mode.						

Operation of heating equipment—minimum 75% combustion efficiency at maximum rated output; supplementary heater shall be cut off when the load can be met by heat pump alone.

7. SERVICE WATER HEATING

Scope—This section is to provide criteria for design and equipment selection that will produce energy savings when applied to service water heating for domestic, sanitary and swimming pool purposes.

Equipment and system performance—The maximum standby loss and continuous loss for water heaters, storage tanks and piping shall not exceed the values given in Table F.

TABLE F. MAXIMUM LOSS OF HEATERS & PIPING			
EQUIPMENT	MAXIMUM STANDBY LOSS		
	Unit	1976	1977
Elec. Storage Heaters	Watt/ft² of Tank Surface	6	4
Gas/Oil Storage Heaters	Percent (%)	43 + 67/V	23 + 67/V
Combination Service/ Space Heating Boilers	Btu/h	$\frac{25\text{pmd} + 250}{n}$	$\frac{13.3\text{pmd} + 400}{n}$

Notes: V = Rated volume of tank, Gallon
 n = Fraction of year when outdoor daily mean temp. > 64.9 F
 pmd = Probable maximum demand, Gallon/h

EQUIPMENT or PIPING		MAX. CONTINUOUS LOSS (Btu/h·ft²)
Unfired Storage Tanks		15
Piping of Recirculating Systems	Above-ground	25
	Underground	35

Recovery efficiency (E_r)—All gas and oil-fired automatic storage heaters shall have a recovery efficiency not less than 70% for 1976, and not less than 75% for 1977 and thereafter.

Operations and controls—Adjustable automatic temperature controls shall be provided for all service water heating systems. Switches and valves shall be provided to turn off the heaters, burners and/or circulating pumps when the system is not in operation.

Showers, lavatories and swimming pools—shall comply with the criteria given in Table G. Pools used for therapeutic purposes are exempt from this requirement.

TABLE G. SHOWERS, LAVATORIES & SWIMMING POOLS		
EQUIPMENT	DESCRIPTION	CRITERIA
Shower Heads	Max. Flow Rate	3.0 GPM
Faucets (in public restrooms)	Type of Faucet	Self-closing
	Max. Flow Rate	0.5 GPM
	Max. Hot Water Temp.	110 F
Heated Swimming Pools	Max. Water Temp.	80 F
	Min. Outdoor Temp. for Heating Uncovered Pools	60 F

TABLE H. CRITERIA FOR ELECTRICAL SYSTEM DESIGN		
Minimum Power Factor	Utilization Equipments >1000 W	85%
	Lighting Equipments >15 W	85%
	To Correct Util. Equipment w/PF < 85%	90%
Maximum Voltage Drop	Branch Circuits and Feeders	3%
	Total System	5%
Service Voltage	To be selected for least energy loss	
Lighting Circuits	To be switched by area, & by use	

8. ELECTRICAL DISTRIBUTION SYSTEMS

Scope—Electrical distribution systems shall be designed for efficient distribution of electrical energy from the service entrance to the points of use.

Criteria—Shall comply with Table H.

Energy determination—In any multi-tenant residential buildings, except hotels, college dormitories and other transient facilities, provisions shall be made to separately determine the energy consumed by each tenant.

9. LIGHTING POWER BUDGET DETERMINATION PROCEDURE

General—Power budget procedure is not a design procedure. Its purpose is solely for determining the maximum power limit for the lighting. The designer should strive to develop the actual lighting system to provide an effective and pleasing visual environment and is encouraged to use less power than the limit allows.

Reference—The 5th Edition of Illuminating Engineering Society Lighting Handbook (IES/HB) is used as the source for technical information and calculation procedures.

Budget For Building Interiors—shall be calculated from the criteria given in Table I.

TABLE I. INTERIOR POWER CALCULATION CRITERIA		
ILLUMINATION (E)		
1	FOR TASK AREA (E_{TA})	From IES/HB Fig.9-80
2	FOR GENERAL AREA (E_{GA})	1/3 E_{TA},< 20 FC
3	FOR NON-CRITICAL AREA (E_{NCA})	1/9 E_{TA},< 10 FC
DETERMINATION OF AREAS		
4	Task Area (TA)	Actual or 50 SF/Sta.
5	Non-Task Area(NTA)	Room Area — TA
6	General Area (GA)	up to TA
7	Non-Critical Area (NCA)	NTA — GA
MINIMUM LAMP EFFICACIES		
8	Moderate Color Rendition	55 Lm/W
9	Good Color Rendition Required	40 Lm/W
10	High Color Rendition Required	25 Lm/W
11	Space Smaller Than 50 SF	25 Lm/W
12	Where the use of HID Lamps < 250W or Fluorescent Lamps < 40W is appropriate.	25 Lm/W
MINIMUM COEF. OF UTILIZATION (CU @ RCR = 1)		
13	Task subject to Veiling Reflection	0.55
14	Task not subject to Veiling Reflection	0.63
15	Without specific Tasks	0.70
MINIMUM REFLECTANCES & LIGHT LOSS FACTOR		
16	Ceiling Cavity Reflectance	0.80
17	Wall Reflectance	0.50
18	Floor Cavity Reflectance	0.20
19	Light Loss Factor (LLF)	0.70

Dirty Atmosphere—Expected values of reflectances and light loss factors shall be used in power budget calculations for spaces where they are impractical to control.

Building Areas Exempted—The following building areas are exempted from the power determination procedures:
a) Residences and apartments other than kitchens, bathrooms, laundry areas, and public spaces.
b) Residential type spaces in institutions (hospitals, hotels, churches, museums, etc.).
c) Theater auditoriums, entertainment, audio-visual presentation spaces.

Lamps and Luminaires Exempted
a) For medical and dental purposes
b) For highlighting applications, exhibits, displays
c) Special applications—color matching, electrical interference, etc.

Budget For Building Exteriors—shall be based on the following:
a) Overhead lighting—use same procedure as interior lighting
b) Floodlighting—use beam lumen method and 0.75 as coefficient of beam utilization (CBU)
c) Facade lighting not to exceed 2 per cent of interior power budget.

Lighting Design and Controls
a) Design—consider non-uniform lighting pattern related to task locations, select luminaires with proper distribution pattern, better light-loss factor based on carefully evaluated cleaning and relamping schedule.

b) Controls—capable to reduce illumination by at least one-half when task is not being performed in any task areas greater than 100 sq ft; light in any space must be turned off when not in use or when daylight is adequate.

Guidelines and Forms—are provided to assist the designers to reduce the effort for determining the power budget of a building.
a) Part 1 Building interiors or exteriors—lumen method procedure
b) Part 2 Special task lighting—point calculation procedure
c) Part 3 Building floodlighting—beam-lumen method procedure
d) Part 4 Summary.

Simplified Procedures
a) Spaces with similar size and requirement—only need to be calculated once.
b) Spaces smaller than 150 sq ft may be consolidated into one equivalent large space having equal illumination requirements (using room cavity ratio (RCR) of a square space equivalent to the average space size).
c) Spaces without specific visual tasks—may be consolidated into one large space using RCR=1, 55Lm/W and 10 FC (or use 0.5W/ft² as power density)
d) Spaces with more than two tasks—may be combined into two equivalent tasks weighted average illumination.

Power Calculations—for the spaces shall be calculated from the following formula:

$$W = \frac{A \times FC}{CU \times LE \times LLF}$$

where W = Lighting power for the space, watts
A = Size of task area, general area, etc., sq ft
FC = Illumination level (E), footcandles
CU = Coefficient of utilization
LE = Lamp efficacy, lumens/watt
LLF = Light loss factor; use 0.70 unless otherwise justified

10. ENERGY REQUIREMENTS FOR BUILDING DESIGN ON SYSTEMS ANALYSIS

Scope—This section is included to provide an opportunity to deviate from the specific standard design criteria of Sections 4 through 9 by demonstrating that such deviations will result in annual energy consumption equal to or less than that resulting from compliance with these criteria. If any proposed alternate design deviates from the specified criteria of Sections 4 through 9, the annual energy consumption of the proposed design shall be compared with the "standard design" using the same heating and cooling energy sources.

Energy Analysis—Annual energy consumed by standard and alternate systems shall be based on same building area and environmental requirements, and shall be of sufficient detail to permit the evaluation of the effect of system design, climate factors, operational characteristics, and mechanical equipment. The calculation shall be based on ASHRAE recommended techniques and procedures for 8,760 hours of operation of the building and its service systems. Detached residential buildings and light commercial structures having the indoor temperature controlled from a single point may use simplified energy analysis procedure, such as bin or degree-day methods.

Documentation—Analysis and report shall be made by a registered professional engineer and shall provide sufficient technical details to verify that the alternate system will result in equal or less annual energy consumption.

11. REQUIREMENTS FOR BUILDINGS UTILIZING SOLAR, GEOTHERMAL, WIND OR OTHER NON-DEPLETING ENERGY SOURCES

General—Non-depletable energy (including nocturnal cooling) supplied to the building shall be excluded from the total energy chargeable to the proposed alternative design.

Solar Energy—To qualify for energy exclusion, solar energy must be derived from a specific collection, storage, and distribution system, or passing through windows when the windows are: 1) provided with operable insulating shutters or other devices to limit the maximum U_o values of gross wall (see Table A), and 2) shaded or otherwise protected from direct solar radiation during cooling periods.

Documentation—The energy savings derived from non-depletable sources and nocturnal cooling, supported by documentation prepared by a registered professional engineer, shall be separately identified from the over-all building energy consumption.

Exceptions—Proposed alternative design for residential and light commercial structures (less than 20,000 sq ft) that derive a significant portion (greater than 30 per cent) of their total annual energy consumption from non-depletable sources shall be exempt from the requirements of a full-year energy system analysis. For other structures that derive over 50 per cent of their "annual thermal" requirements (heating, cooling, service water heating) or over 30 per cent of their "annual total" energy requirement from non-depletable sources shall be exempt from comparing the proposed alternative design to a standard design.

MAXIMUM U_o AND OTTV FOR MAJOR U.S. AND CANADIAN CITIES (*Data from Airport Station)

CITY & STATE	Annual Heating Degree Days	Latitude (Degree North)	Over 3 Stories	3 Stories & Under	1-2 Family Dwelling	Floor Over Unheated Space	Roof & Ceiling	Maximum OTTV (Btu/h·ft²)	CITY & STATE	Annual Heating Degree Days	Latitude (Degree North)	Over 3 Stories	3 Stories & Under	1-2 Family Dwelling	Floor Over Unheated Space	Roof & Ceiling	Maximum OTTV (Btu/h·ft²)
Anchorage, AK	10,900	61.2	.28	.20	.16	.08	.060	39.4	Memphis, TN	3,200	35.0	.40	.33	.26	.17	.098	32.1
Atlanta, GA	3,000	33.7	.41	.33	.27	.19	.100	31.7	Miami, FL	200	25.8	.48	.39	.30	.38	.100	29.5
Birmingham, AL	2,600	33.5	.42	.34	.27	.21	.100	31.7	Milwaukee, WI	7,600	43.0	.29	.25	.20	.08	.063	34.4
Bismarck, ND	8,900	46.8	.28	.22	.18	.08	.060	35.4	Minneapolis, MN	8,400	44.8	.28	.23	.18	.08	.060	34.9
Boise, ID	5,800	43.5	.34	.28	.22	.08	.077	34.5	Montreal, Quebec	8,200	45.5	.28	.23	.19	.08	.060	35.0
Boston, MA	5,600	42.3	.34	.28	.23	.08	.079	34.2	New Orleans, LA	1,400	30.0	.45	.36	.29	.30	.100	30.7
Burlington, VT	8,300	44.5	.28	.23	.19	.08	.060	34.8	New York, NY	5,200	40.7	.35	.29	.23	.08	.082	33.7
Charleston, SC	2,000	32.8	.43	.35	.28	.26	.100	31.5	Oklahoma City, OK	3,700	35.3	.39	.32	.25	.14	.094	32.2
Chicago, IL	6,600	42.0	.31	.27	.21	.08	.071	34.1	Philadelphia, PA	5,100	39.8	.35	.29	.23	.08	.083	33.5
Dallas, TX	2,400	32.5	.42	.35	.27	.23	.100	31.4	Phoenix, AZ	1,800	33.5	.44	.36	.28	.27	.100	31.7
Denver, CO	6,300	39.8	.32	.27	.21	.08	.073	33.5	Portland, ME	7,500	43.7	.29	.25	.20	.08	.064	34.5
Des Moines, IA	6,600	41.5	.31	.27	.21	.08	.071	33.9	Richmond, VA	3,900	37.5	.39	.32	.25	.12	.093	32.8
Detroit, MI	6,200	42.3	.33	.27	.22	.08	.074	34.1	Salt Lake City, UT	6,100	40.8	.33	.28	.22	.08	.075	33.7
El Paso, TX	2,700	31.8	.41	.34	.27	.21	.100	31.2	San Francisco, CA	3,000	37.7	.41	.33	.27	.19	.100	30.7
Fairbanks, AK	14,300	64.8	.28	.20	.16	.08	.060	40.5	Seattle, WA	4,400	43.5	.37	.31	.24	.09	.088	34.5
Great Falls, MT	7,800	47.5	.29	.24	.19	.08	.061	35.6	Sheridan, WY	7,700	44.8	.29	.24	.20	.08	.062	34.9
Honolulu, HI	0	21.3	.48	.39	.31	.40	.100	28.3	Sioux Falls, SD	7,800	43.7	.29	.24	.19	.08	.061	34.5
Houston, TX	1,400	29.7	.45	.36	.29	.30	.100	30.6	St. Louis, MO	4,900	38.8	.36	.30	.24	.08	.084	33.1
Indianapolis, IN	5,700	39.4	.34	.28	.22	.08	.078	35.3	Tampa, FL	700	28.0	.47	.38	.30	.35	.100	30.1
Jacksonville, FL	1,200	30.5	.45	.37	.29	.31	.100	30.9	Toronto, Ontario	6,800	43.7	.31	.26	.21	.08	.069	34.5
Lincoln, NE	5,900	40.8	.33	.28	.22	.08	.077	35.7	Vancouver, B.C.	5,500	49.2	.34	.29	.23	.08	.080	37.7
Los Angeles, CA	2,100	34.0	.43	.35	.28	.25	.100	31.3	Wichita, KS	4,600	37.7	.37	.30	.24	.08	.087	35.2

$$U_o = \frac{U_{wall}A_{wall} + U_{window}A_{window} + U_{door}A_{door}}{A_o}$$

where

U_o = the average thermal transmittance of the gross wall area. Btu/h • ft² • F

A_o = the gross area of exterior walls, ft²

$$OTTV = \frac{(U_w \times A_w \times TD_{EQ}) + (A_f \times SF \times SC) + (U_f \times A_f \times T)}{A_o}$$

OTTV = over-all thermal transfer value

where

U_w = the thermal transmittance of all elements of the opaque wall area Btu/h • ft² • F

A_w = opaque wall area, ft²

U_f = the thermal transmittance of the fenestration area Btu/h • ft² • F

A_f = fenestration area, ft²

TD_{EQ} = a temperature value varying from 23 F to 44 F depending upon the mass of the construction

SC = shading coefficient of the fenestration

T = temperature difference between exterior and interior design conditions

SF = solar factor value given in Btu/h • ft²

A_o = gross area of exterior walls, ft²

ENERGY STANDARDS PROJECT TESTS DESIGNERS' CONSERVATION SKILLS: THE DEVELOPMENT OF STANDARDS

In a research project recently concluded, sponsored by HUD/DOE and conducted by AIA Research Corporation, 168 architect-engineer teams "redesigned" buildings of theirs constructed two to three years previously to get an idea of just how much energy savings they could achieve. What the project comprised, and what the results were (as exemplified by six of the 168 redesigns), follows.

In late 1978, the AIA Research Corporation turned over to the Department of Housing and Urban Development the results of an $8-million project designed to provide the basis for the energy performance standards for new buildings that Congress mandated be implemented by 1980. The project is unique in the annals of architectural practice: 168 architect/engineer teams were paid $4.3 million to participate in a program of education and design review that culminated in the redesign of 168 buildings built in 1975 and 1976 in an effort to achieve "maximum levels of energy conservation." Six of these projects—typical of the innovative solutions submitted are illustrated and briefly described here.

While the prime objective of the project, begun in May of 1977, was to give a basis for developing energy performance standards, it had several important corollary benefits: 1) it indicated the current level of a cross-section of architect/engineer expertise in energy-conserving design; 2) it convincingly demonstrated that energy consumption should be considered at the start of design, and that early architect/engineer collaboration is imperative; 3) it showed that there are numerous opportunities for energy reductions when this approach is taken; 4) it suggested that the resulting designs can be good architecture.

To a large extent the redesigns relied on architectural techniques. Skylights, clerestories, natural ventilation and "passive" techniques such as berms, sod roofs and Trombe walls were abundant in the redesigns. Also they were more responsive to site and microclimatic conditions than before.

Some designs included photo-cell-controlled circuits for integration of daylight and electric light, but little innovation was evident in the electric lighting designs. In fact, consultants to the project agreed that this was the weakest area of the redesigns. Some a/e teams, though, did show non-uniform distribution of luminaires and different luminaire types to suit a variety of tasks within the same general area of the building. The hvac

systems, too, though generally energy-effective, were not novel, employing heat pumps and variable air-volume (VAV) air distribution—used for some time by progressive engineers.

Quality of the redesigns followed a bell-curve distribution, managers of the project report—some teams were very imaginative, others gave only minimal attention to opportunities, but most were somewhere in between. Many of the redesigns failed to quantify seasonal energy performance of the daylighting and passive techniques they used. Calculations sometimes were skimpy, and occasionally not provided at all. In this respect, the design teams were handicapped in a number of these areas by the unavailability of practical design tools.

The 168 building redesigns constituted Phase Two of a three-phase program stipulated by HUD for the development of the performance-type energy standards to be promulgated by the Department of Energy (DOE). Trial standards were published in the Federal Register in November 1978, and final standards are due in 1980.

The first phase called for an assessment of how much energy buildings currently have been designed to use. The second phase—the 168 building redesigns—was intended to determine how much reduction in energy consumption from current practice could reasonably be accomplished. These first two phases were conducted by the AIA Research Corporation. In Phase Three, HUD will work with architects, engineers and building officials in field-testing and implementing the standards.

In Phase One, more than 3,200 questionnaires were mailed to architects of 12 different basic types of non-residential buildings located in 37 cities, on which construction had begun in 1975 and 1976, as identified by *Dodge Reports*. Over 1,800 questionnaires were completed and returned on a voluntary basis but with assistance and prompting by teams from 14 different architectural schools. Of the returned questionnaires, 1,661 were sufficiently complete for energy consumptions of the buildings to be estimated through use of a short-form version of the AXCESS energy-analysis computer program developed by consulting engineers Syska & Hennessy, who also monitored the returns, along with AIA/RC, and supervised the data processing. In Phase One, also, information on low-rise housing was obtained from a survey conducted by the National Association of Home Builders. Approximately 5,000 forms were

returned, representing some 175,000 single and multi-family homes and a like number of mobile homes.

For Phase Two, AIA Research Corporation invited the 1,800 respondents to the initial questionnaire to submit proposals for compensation for their potential participation in this phase. It was understood that about 200 buildings would be randomly selected from those firms whose proposals were close enough to AIA/RC's budget target, and which would provide an evenly divided sample for 16 building categories and seven climatic regions.

Immediately after they were selected, the 168 design teams engaged in a 12-15 week charette to produce redesigns for more effective energy usage. All teams were required to attend a one-day data-requirements workshop, a two-and-a-half day redesign information seminar, a one-day concept design review, and a one-day pre-final review. For buildings with more complicated requirements, such as hospitals and schools, a redesign midreview also was required. Finally, the design teams had to submit final documents for the redesigned buildings.

In Phase One, energy use was estimated for the total of 1,661 buildings, on the basis of about 150 parameters using the short-form AXCESS method.

In Phase Two, energy use was determined by computer for 168 buildings by the long-form AXCESS method (over 1,000 parameters considered) before and after redesign. Syska & Hennessy reviewed and analyzed a number of different strategies such as passive heating and certain control mechanisms used in the redesigns that the AXCESS program could not handle, and made value judgments on how much energy these might save. Furthermore, a computer program was developed to convert data in the redesigns to ASHRAE standard 90 criteria so that energy use under these constraints also could be determined.

HUD/DOE intends to determine the budget members for the standards after a consideration of all of the values obtained by the above methods, selecting budget numbers somewhere between what is technically possible, and what can be done within reasonable cost and design-time constraints, and also somewhere between existing standards and the maximum possible. The *design (not operating)* budgets will be in the form of Btu per square foot per year, with different numbers for the different building types and for the seven different climatic zones.

Clinic
Maryland

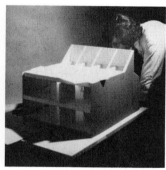

In the process of redesigning an ambulatory care facility, the architects built large-scale models of skylighted spaces to take illumination measurements with various combinations of louvers, reflectors and screens. For example, in a direct south summer sun situation, they simulated reflectors and/or louvers to produce indirect, cool light in the building. Using the results of the experiments, they wrote a brief computer program that compared the cost of natural light versus electric light. The results showed that skylights could be an asset if insulated louvers or screens were used to prevent night heat loss in winter, and heat gain in summer, and some type of movable shutter system to vary the amount of exposed glass.

The use of daylighting was estimated to have provided about 25 per cent of the total savings achieved. The other 75 per cent was attributed to heat pump systems for heating and cooling and for domestic hot water. Though waterloop type heat pumps were used in the original building, more optimum sizes were selected in the redesign for greater efficiency.

CLINIC, Maryland. Architects and engineers: *The VVKR Partnership.*

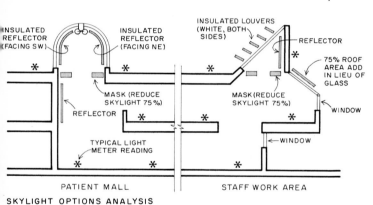

SKYLIGHT OPTIONS ANALYSIS

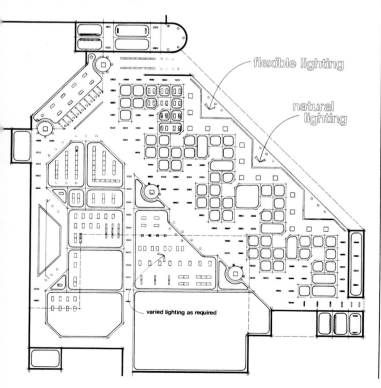

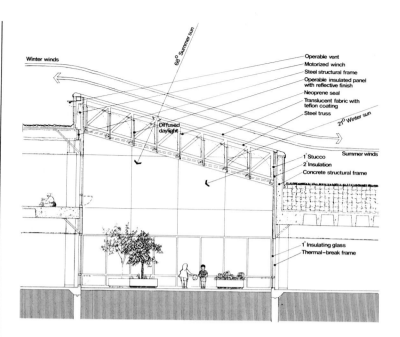

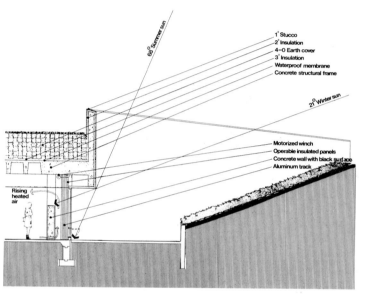

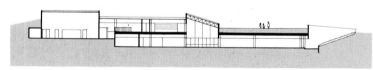

Elementary
School
Apple Valley,
Minnesota

Bermed walls, sod roofs, shaded glass, and a play court, which can be shaded by operable panels when the sun gets too warm, comprise the passive techniques for a Minnesota elementary school. The roof of the court is covered with *Teflon*-coated fabric to diffuse direct sun. The court also has vent windows at bottom and top for natural ventilation.

The overhang of a south-facing glazed wall shields it from sun in summer. A Trombe wall behind the glass provides warmed air for winter heating, and operable insulated panels block the sun's rays when heat is not needed.

Luminaires in classroom spaces next to the court and next to glass on the south facade of the building are connected to photocell control.

ELEMENTARY SCHOOL, Apple Valley, Minnesota. Architects and engineers: *Hammel Green & Abrahamson, Inc.*

Dormitory Washington, D.C.

Architects doing redesigns in the AIA Research Corporation performance-standards project were urged to take cognizance of, and exploit, microclimatic conditions—and this building reflects the advice. Because this dormitory was to be on a sloping site, it was bermed into the slope to utilize the insulating value of the earth and to block winter winds. Vertical louvers in front of the rear wall would be open in summer to expose the cool surface, but shut in winter to preclude a cold radiant effect.

All glazing is on the south side shielded by overhangs from summer sun. Natural ventilation is achieved by turbine-type ventilators on the roof, with air-foil shapes within the enclosure to encourage Venturi action so as to increase air speed.

The architects and their engineer also considered energy usage vis-a-vis hours of occupancy and concurrent outdoor air temperature and humidity conditions, and required occupant comfort.

DORMITORY, Washington, D.C. Architects: *HTB, Inc.* Engineer: *Alphatec, P.C.*

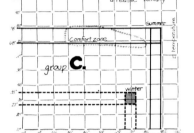

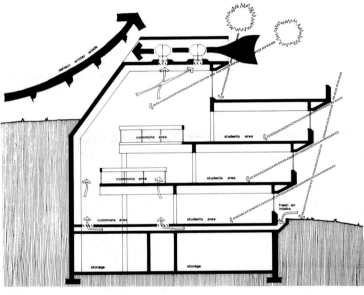

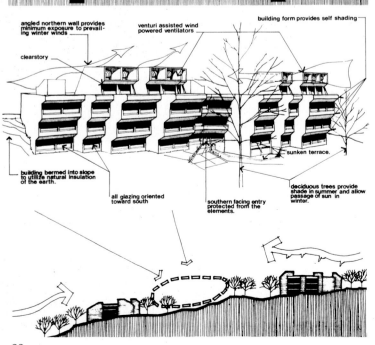

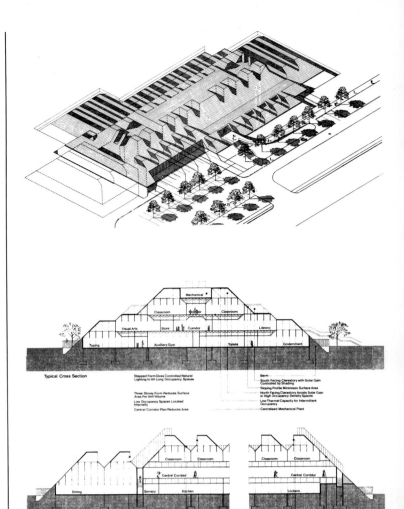

Secondary School Detroit, Michigan

The very unusual pyramidal massing of this school derived from the architects' desire to exploit daylighting and the sun's heat for a site that is basically oriented north-south. In order to have light/solar scoops for classrooms and gym and utilize either north or south light, the architects created the series of volumes shown. For high-occupancy spaces, with a higher heat load from people, glass faces north. For medium- and low-occupancy areas, glass faces south, but it has upward-tilting louvers to shut out sun in warmer weather. The louvers were given an inward slope to prevent entrapment of hot air under them; at the highest altitude of the sun in summer, the angle of the louvers prevents entry of sun, but daylight is allowed in.

A thick double-window arrangement at the clerestories provides for use of a Beadwall system in which polystyrene beads are vacuum-pumped at night from storage to between the glass to reduce nighttime heat loss. Solar studies were conducted to verify the performance of the shading provided by building forms and louvers.

SECONDARY SCHOOL, Detroit, Michigan. Architects: *Sims Varner & Assoc. Inc.* Engineers: *Detroit Public Schools T.P.D.; Sidney Dorb, P.E.*

Community Activities Building Oakland County, Michigan

The words "passive solar techniques" bring to mind images of sun scoops, skylights, clerestories, and Trombe walls. Here the architects have applied The Trombe principle not just to masonry walls, but to the roof as well. The metal roof is dark to absorb solar radiation. When heat is needed and is available from the roof, a damper at the bottom of the roof cavity is opened so that air moves by convection through the cavity to an opening at the top of the ceiling, whence "Casablanca" fans (the architect's terminology) push the air down to occupancy level. A Trombe wall on the inside face of the corridor, on the other hand, provides convected and radiated heat to locker rooms and racquetball courts.

Daylighting from narrow skylights and from a clerestory are relied on for much of the illumination. Suspended HID luminaires provide nighttime illumination, and the south row can be switched on during the day to supplement daylight on the south.

COMMUNITY ACTIVITIES BUILDING, Oakland County, Michigan. Architects and engineers: *TMP Associates*.

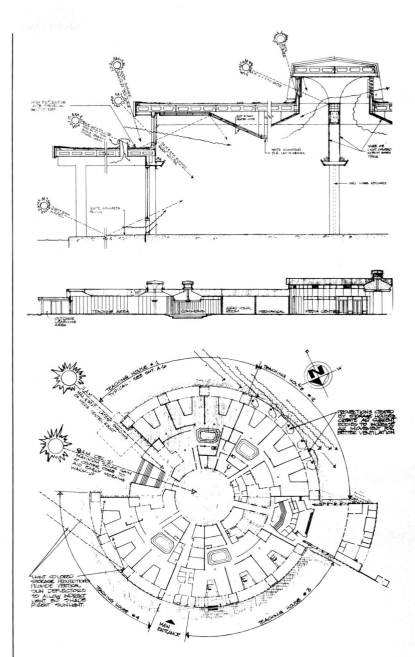

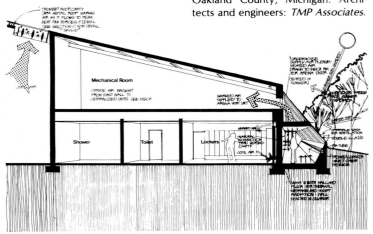

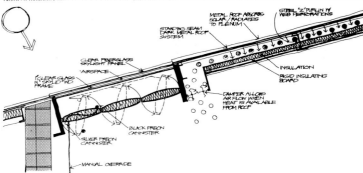

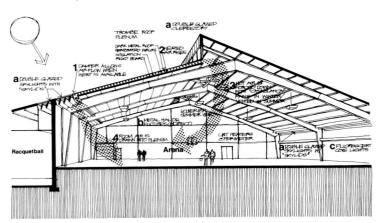

Elementary School Raleigh, North Carolina

Clerestories for daylighting for natural ventilation are the main energy-conserving features of this elementary school. Operable louvers behind the glass control the amount of sun and daylight admitted. The interior light well has operable, insulated louvers for relieving warm air that gathers at the cupola. Vent windows at the floor level admit outdoor air for ventilation. A ⅛-in. scale model of a pie-shape section of the building was used for daylighting studies. Light-meter readings were taken in teaching areas, the commons, and the media center for March 21 and December 21 at different times of day. Fluorescent lighting is provided in the area between the clerestories. Heating and cooling of the building is by a reciprocating-compressor heat pump with double-bundle condenser for building heating and cooling-tower circuits.

ELEMENTARY SCHOOL, Raleigh, North Carolina. Architect: *Owen F. Smith*. Engineer: *Shelton Y. Adcock*.

A FIRST LOOK AT THE PROPOSED FEDERAL ENERGY PERFORMANCE STANDARDS

The Department of Energy has issued its proposal for energy performance standards that are being studied and debated by design professionals and many professional bodies. This article describes the standards and the vast array of problems facing their implementation. The big question is: since energy conservation has become second nature to architects and engineers, should we press the government for more time to work out the technical problems and problems of compliance?

In November 1978, the Department of Energy published its first version of building energy performance standards for buildings (known to the cognoscenti as BEPS)—a step that could lead to final promulgation in 1980, followed by obligatory adoption of these standards (or their equivalent) by the states. That the Federal government had these standards in preparation came as a surprise to many in the building community—perhaps because more than 40 states have adopted, or are about to adopt, codes based on ASHRAE Standard 90, and because the timetable for developing them has been extremely short, considering how complex the problem is.

Performance standards were mandated by Congress in the Energy Conservation Standards for New Buildings Act passed in August, 1976, and the AIA actively encouraged passage of the Act in an effort to promote conservation, but also to put its authority behind the performance-standards approach. The Act provided for promulgation no later than 1981, but the Carter administration has advanced the timetable by one year.
In an unusual step, on November 21, 1978 the Department of Energy published the standards in an Advance Notice of Proposed Rulemaking (ANPR) in the Federal Register "...to make available to the public the form of the Standards as presently envisioned by the Department, as well as support information available at the time of publication, and to invite the public's review and comments on the standards." The actual Notice of Proposed Rulemaking was scheduled for publication in early 1979. Public meetings (not hearings) for the discussion and comment on the ANPR were held in Washington, Chicago and San Francisco in December 1978. For lack of publicity, they drew only limited audiences, not a spectrum of the building community except in San Francisco, where some spirited and helpful discussion took place. The

McGraw-Hill Information Systems Company presented meetings in New York City and Kansas City for building product manufacturers on the new Standards, at which DOE and HUD officials explained the basic proposals. The National Institute of Building Sciences sponsored a workshop in Washington at which these officials spoke, and for which an impressive workbook was prepared covering a dozen significant issues such as energy-budget format, state and local compliance, sanctions, and residential and commercial-building impacts.

Given an Administration anxious to have energy standards, and a building community—in particular the engineers and the code officials—with a vast number of concerns and reservations about them, DOE seems to be betwixt and between. And for this reason, perhaps, at the public meetings DOE's Dr. Maxine Savitz emphasized some of the alternatives DOE has asked Battelle Pacific Northwest Laboratories to evaluate in the environmental assessment of the BEPS required by law. The range of alternatives includes: 1) no action, or the repeal of the legislated mandate for the Standards; 2) design energy budgets set at three different levels, the first as chosen for the Standards, the second less stringent, and the third more stringent; 3) component performance standards instead of building performance standards; 4) the Standards with tax incentives; 5) prescriptive standards; 6) education and dissemination of information instead of the promulgation of standards; 7) different methods to encourage the use of renewable energy resources; and 8) energy pricing to effect conservation.

What are the proposed standards like, and how were they developed?
The energy performance standards (the BEPS) are "design energy budgets" for buildings over-all, rather than their parts, expressed in Btu per square foot per year that are applica-

ble at the design stage of the construction process. They were given in the ANPR for 16 different building classifications and for seven different climatic zones. They were not given for assembly buildings, which might need a finer breakdown in classification, for industrial buildings in which it is difficult to separate process and non-process energy, for restaurants where there is a high ratio of process to non-process energy, or for warehouses where there were some high, unexplained energy consumptions in the original data.

The design energy budgets in the ANPR are also source-energy related—through the use of multipliers known as resource utilization factors (RUFs) which are intended to account for the energy losses involved in delivering non-renewable resources to a building site.

With oil and gas, transportation results in a small loss from origin of the fuel to delivery at the building site; with electricity, losses inherent in the generation process (the largest percentage) and in distribution mean that for every Btu of fuel used at the power plant, about one-third of a Btu equivalent of electricity is delivered to the site.

The design energy budgets in the Advance Notice are not the numbers determined by evaluation of the statistical sample of 1,661 buildings, but are larger to the extent of the multiplication by the RUF factors. For purposes of presentation in the Advance Notice, the RUFs were based upon the original statistical sample. The RUFs are different for every building classification and also for the different climatic zones because of the typical fuel usages in the various regions. The individual RUFs in the Advance Notice for oil and gas were set at slightly over one, but the individual RUF for electricity is 3.0.

An example of how this was applied in the Advance Notice: The preliminary unadjusted design budget for a small office building (less than 50,000 sq ft) in Climatic Zone 2 was determined to be 55,000 Btu per sq ft per yr. The combined RUF for small office buildings in Zone 2 was set at 2.5—indicating that the energy usage is to a large extent electricity (for air conditioning and for lighting), with other fuels for heating. Multiplying 55,000 by 2.5 would give an allowable design energy budget of 137,500 Btu per sq ft per yr. The Advance Notice does not indicate what a building designer would do if he is using a different mix of energy sources than those assumed in the proposed standards. It is not clear whether or how building designers could determine their own RUFs.

The advance notice states that "Theoretically RUFs can be computed for individual sites, but the practical application of this theory is, in reality, quite complex." On the other hand, the ANPR also states that, "...ongoing studies relate to setting RUFs equal to or less than zero for renewable resources, in order to encourage their utilization. . . ." To account for sociological considerations (such as fuel availability, economics, health and environmental impacts, etc.) DOE is examining the effects of applying resource impact factors (RIFs), but this concept is still embryonic.

Three months after the energy act (Public Law 94-385) was passed, AIA and ASHRAE formed a Joint Energy Budget Committee to investigate the feasibility of energy performance standards. The committee considered a proposal for collecting actual energy usage by real buildings to provide a reference base, and also discussed the merits of developing prototypical buildings for different building types, with detailed calculations of energy requirements for specified operating conditions and schedules. Shortly thereafter the AIA Research Corporation, independently, began negotiations with HUD for a research contract to develop energy performance standards. Earlier HUD, which had the original responsibility for developing and implementing the standards, had asked for a proposal from the National Bureau of Standards, but this did not proceed, apparently because of time and cost factors. Meanwhile the Joint Committee had been expanded to include three more professional societies: American Consulting Engineers Council, Illuminating Engineers Society, and National Society of Professional Engineers (NSPE/PEPP). AIA/RC subsequently asked the committee to serve as a Technical Advisory Committee, and in the spring of 1978, the National Association of Home Builders and the Manufactured Housing Institute were added.

AIA/RC signed a contract with HUD in the spring of 1977 to conduct a study basic to the establishment of standards for energy consumption in buildings—a study that became known as the "Baseline Project." The first phase of the project, conducted from May through November of 1977, was designed to assess the amount of energy that buildings are currently designed to use. Though the AIA/RC's Technical Advisory Group (TAG) had hoped that actual operating data would be gathered for a reference base, and that prototypical buildings could be developed and analyzed in detail, AIA/RC decided against this approach because they said HUD did not want to consider buildings designed prior to the 1973 oil embargo. Further, it is reported that AIA/RC felt that use of actual consumption data would imply a consumption standard rather than a design standard, and thus aggravate liability concerns of design professionals.

For data collection in Phase I of the project, buildings were broadly divided into nonresidential (which included high-rise residential) and residential, which included single-family homes, low-rise multifamily housing, and mobile homes. Consultants to AIA/RC estimated that an average of 30 buildings of each building type in each climate region would produce summary estimates of sufficient accuracy for design consumption figures. This yielded a total sample of approximately 3,200 buildings which was obtained from *Dodge Construction Reports*. Of this total, 1,661 survey forms were returned sufficiently complete and consistent for analysis. This number, then, provided a representative sample of recent building designs, and a baseline for the evaluation of alternative energy standards.

For Phase II, AIA/RC selected 168 commercial/multifamily buildings out of the 1,661 and paid the architects and their consultants to do energy-conscious *redesigns* of their buildings to achieve the most feasible levels of energy conservation to arrive at realistic limits for energy efficiency.

To obtain energy consumption data for the 1,661 buildings in Phase I, a modified version of the AXCESS Short Form energy analysis computer program was used, with data requirements being on the order of 100 to 125 data points per building. Consulting engineers Syska & Hennessy processed the data and developed supplemental and default values as inputs where data on the survey forms were incomplete or missing. For

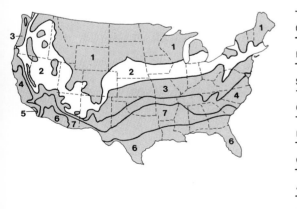

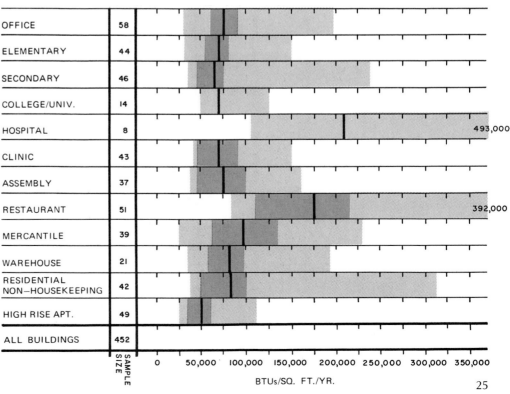

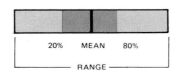

	SAMPLE SIZE	0	50,000	100,000	150,000	200,000	250,000	300,000	350,000
OFFICE	58								
ELEMENTARY	44								
SECONDARY	46								
COLLEGE/UNIV.	14								
HOSPITAL	8							493,000	
CLINIC	43								
ASSEMBLY	37								
RESTAURANT	51							392,000	
MERCANTILE	39								
WAREHOUSE	21								
RESIDENTIAL NON-HOUSEKEEPING	42								
HIGH RISE APT.	49								
ALL BUILDINGS	452								

BTUs/SQ. FT./YR.

20%   MEAN   80%
— RANGE —

the residential sample, data were collected from existing surveys representing 125,000 single-family homes, 45,000 multifamily low-rise units, and 175,000 mobile homes.

Who will be most affected by standards, and what problems loom for enforcement?
The groups that would be most affected by energy-budget type standards are architects, engineers and building code officials. The designers have to develop a building that meets the energy budget figure, proved through some type of simulation procedure, most probably a computer program. Building code officials have to find some way of assuring themselves that the energy consumption figures were calculated correctly.

The technical standards as presented in the Advance Notice were developed by DOE/HUD from the data presented to them by AIA/RC, and this is where most of the emphasis has been placed so far. But the standards cannot be more than voluntary, until their implementation has been worked out in the form of regulations that spell out what must be done to comply with the standards, and tell the states how to determine whether or not the standards they have in their codes are "equivalent" to the Federal standards.

The Energy Act of 1976 specified that the National Institute of Building Sciences provide advice and assistance to "identify procedural obstacles or technical constraints inhibiting implementation of such standards," and pursuant to this NIBS has conducted an "issues" study, a "code equivalency" study, and four case studies on states' experience with energy-conservation standards for build-ings, including California, Colorado, Massachusetts and Virginia.

Implications of the building energy performance standards as they now stand
NIBS analysis of the Advance Notice developed the following. . .
- The design-energy budget format represents a significant departure from the formats of existing energy standards;
- The simplicity of a "single goal" is complicated by the diverse nature and use of the nations's building stock;
- The BEPS are design standards, and actual energy usage may depart significantly from design goals;
- The assumptions associated with the design energy budgets (energy uses included/excluded, the distinction between process/non-process energy, and operating profiles) may be artificial or remote in regard to a particular project, causing the designer to design the project for one set of conditions and calculate it for another.
- The state of the art of energy-analysis techniques is such that it will cause problems in providing an accurate calculation of a building's design energy consumption;
- Existing computer programs do not always provide the same result when applied to a single building, which further compounds the problem of obtaining an accurate energy consumption level;
- The use of a computer program to do the energy analysis adds effort and, presumably, cost to design and construction;
- It is not clear whether energy analyses will have to be done for each change during construction;

- Problems of coming up with an accurate design level of energy consumption for a single building will certainly compound the problem of establishing equivalency between the BEPS and an existing standard that a state or locality wishes to have certified;
- There may be confusion between the BEPS as a design standard and the building owner's expectations of the building's total annual energy-consumption levels once the building is in use;
- The DOE Advance Notice does not compare the preliminary standards with design levels of energy consumption resulting from use of codes based upon ASHRAE 90-75R, and thus the magnitude of the code-equivalency problem is yet unknown;
- BEPS may lead to site inequities within a given climatic region because of the wide range of climates within the region;
- RUFs will markedly affect energy selections in new construction, which may or may not correspond to proper economic decisions;
- RUFs will require additional education at all levels of the design, contract and construction cycle;
- RUFs have far-reaching, long-term implications for utility planning, specifically in the areas of load management, capital expansion requirements, and rate structures;
- RUFs will tend to be a divisive factor among energy suppliers;
- BEPS will require an infusion of new financial and staffing support for many building code departments;
- The scheduled period of approximately four months for the public to review and comment on the standards and regulations may be too short for concerned groups to be

DESIGN ENERGY CONSUMPTION (MBTU/SQ. FT./YR)	CLIMATIC ZONE						
	1	2	3	4	5	6	7
20% BASELINE	50	49	49	47	47	54	47
30% BASELINE	56	55	55	53	53	60	55
50% BASELINE	56	64	64	62	62	70	64
80% TECHNICAL REDESIGN	49	47	47	46	46	52	47
LOWEST TECHNICAL REDESIGN	29	45	20	*	*	39	*

* - Not available.

CLIMATIC ZONE	1	2	3	4	5	6	7
PHASE II PARAMETRIC BASELINE BUILDING LINE DESIGN ENERGY CONSUMPTION (MBTU/SQ./YR)	56	55	55	53	53	60	55
COMBINED RUF	2.6	2.5	2.7	2.8	2.7	3.0	2.8
DESIGN ENERGY BUDGET (MBTU/SQ. FT./YR)	145.6	137.5	148.5	148.4	143.1	180.0	154.0

The source of numbers for the design energy budgets was the Baseline Study of the AIA Research Corporation on 1,661 buildings designed in 1975 and 1976, and the redesign of 168 of these to determine maximum feasible energy savings. The chart on page 25 shows the range of design energy consumptions for the buildings that were in Climatic Zone 2. For office buildings, these ranged from about 30,000 Btu per sq ft per yr minimum to 200,000 maximum. The chart includes the total population of office buildings. The design energy consumptions and energy budgets shown in the tables on this page are for small office buildings (i.e., under 50,000 sq. ft.) The top table shows that 20 per cent of these buildings in Climatic Zone 2 had design consumptions of 49,000 Btu per sq ft per yr. The 30th percentile was up to 55,000, and the 50th percentile was up to 64,000. DOE chose the 30th percentile figure for all the building types except where the 80th percentile of the redesigned buildings turned out to be higher, and in such cases the 80 per cent figure was used. The 30th percentile figure was felt to be low enough to encourage energy-conscious design, while still not imposing economic hardships. The design energy budgets were obtained by multiplying the design energy consumption numbers by resource utilization factors (RUFS) that account for energy losses between source of the energy and the building site. For example, for the small office buildings in Climate Zone 2, 55,000 Btu per sq ft per yr is multilied by a RUF of 2.5 to give 137,500.

both comprehensive and detailed enough to shape standards and regulations;
- Given the apparent technical complexity in formulating and administering the BEPS, it may be impossible for a number of states and local jurisdictions to achieve compliance by the scheduled date (February 1980);
- Widespread noncompliance resulting from an unrealistic implementation schedule could seriously undermine the BEPS program.

Engineers are concerned about the cost of proving compliance, and about liability

Government officials and others have suggested that administrative problems at the code-jurisdiction level might be mitigated if building designers certified that buildings designed with assumed operation and weather conditions would consume given Btus/sq ft/yr. This worries engineers familiar with the BEPS program, who say that their liability insurance will not allow them to "certify," and who envision nuisance suits from building owners who do not understand the difference between "design" and "operating" energy budgets, and who might have operated the building differently than assumed by the designers. Attorney/architect Arthur Kornblut, who writes for RECORD on legal matters, says that the law does not expect professionals to guarantee results, and that language might be used on the order of "to the best of our knowledge, information and belief," or "to the best of our professional experience, we certify that. . . ." A California engineer says that jurisdictions his firm has worked with have accepted the phraseology recommended by a West Coast insurance carrier somewhat to the effect that "the documents have been reviewed and are in substantial conformance with the regulations." The California energy code allows either a BEPS approach or a subsystem energy performance standards approach (SEPS) that has been based upon ASHRAE Standard 90-75R. A consulting engineer from the East says his insurance carrier states that by "certifying" performance, per se, the professional would have contracted away the carrier's rights, but that the professional can file an affidavit with acceptable language on the order of "to the best of our knowledge and belief. . . ."

Costs of demonstrating compliance are a moot question at this time since methods have not yet been specified by the government. Nonetheless, computer time plus the engineering firm's time is said to be at least $1,000 for a small multizone building. A Pennsylvania engineer states that preparation for and running the AXCESS Short Form for a large elementary school might cost $1,200 or more; preparation for and running the Long Form AXCESS might cost $3,000 to $4,000. These figures could represent from 10 to 25 per cent of the engineer's fee for this kind of building. One study reported by NIBS in its issues analyses indicated that an office building has to be over 220,000 gross square feet before the "commensurate design fee is adequate to support a computer analysis of two alternative mechanical designs, let alone

an analysis of a building's total estimated annual energy consumption." On the other hand, a computer services firm involved in building energy simulations believes that buildings with simple plans might be simulated for fees on the order of a few hundred dollars.

Engineering societies, the TAG and ad hoc groups say more work needs to be done

If building energy performance standards are going to be promulgated, ASHRAE feels that Standard 90-75R should be the vehicle, primarily because of the consensus approach employed, says ASHRAE president Morris Backer, not because it is "the ultimate refinement in energy conservation"—admittedly it is not, having gone through several revisions already, and ferment is developing for still further improvements. Of course this standard is a subsystem performance standard primarily with respect to the building envelope and lighting. Architects got behind the building energy performance standards approach in the beginning because they felt the building envelope was being unduly singled out. Section 10 of Standard 90-75R permits trade-offs between the envelope and interior systems as demonstrated by energy simulation analysis, but the building first has to be designed according to Sections 4 through 9. Architects apparently have relaxed a bit about Standard 90, if the experience in California is any measure. Given the option of either a BEPS approach or a SEPS (subsystem-oriented energy performance standards) approach in the state's energy code, building designers are reported to be taking the SEPS approach most of the time—though this could be because the SEPS approach is simpler and less costly to do. One California consulting engineer comments that for conventional design the SEPS approach does not pose unreasonable constraints. When his firm has done energy simulations of building designs, they generally have been for public-building clients.

The Technical Advisory Group gave kudos to the AIA/RC project in some areas, but also expressed some concerns. Among the positive results cited: 1) the project was an enlightening educational experience for a broad segment of design professionals, 2) the project indicates that energy can be saved through a cooperative effort of design professionals, 3) a broad base of valuable information has been accumulated on recently designed buildings, 4) the project should enlighten the government on the complexity of buildings and the difficulty in implementing a performance standard.

Some of their concerns were: 1) even though 1,661 teams of design professionals responded in Phase I, "this was a volunteer effort, and the quality of data collected left something to be desired," 2) process loads, including domestic hot water, elevators, office machines, computers, etc., were not considered in the energy calculations in Phase I, 3) the lack of an adequate reference base on actual energy use of existing buildings made it impossible to validate the computer

results in Phases 1 and 2.

Another group, the ad hoc Design Professional/Federal Agencies Conference on Energy Standards wrote a resolution that could be adopted by professional societies: ". . .this Society endorses the concept of energy performance standards and recognizes that the proposed design energy budgets, though tentative and incomplete, will provide guidelines for future improvements." But, "before design energy budgets can be considered as adequate performance standards, considerable sustained effort will be required to develop and resolve key technical issues and economic factors."

More complex than technical issues are those of compliance and equivalency.

The government has a number of options to ease assimilation of standards

The equivalency of state and local codes to the Federal Standards is likely to become an important issue because most states have adopted, or plan to adopt, codes derived from ASHRAE 90-75R which the Federal government helped finance under Public Law 94-163.

A study by NIBS says it appears that the Federal government could take any of a number of administrative approaches to equivalency, such as making an administrative determination that a state code is in compliance with the Federal Standards, or incorporating a code version of ASHRAE 90-75R into the Federal Standards.

Or the government could take technically-based approaches to equivalency. These are too numerous and the ramifications too involved to discuss here, but suffice it to say that one type is absolute equivalency, which means that any building designed under a local standard must consume an equal or smaller amount than under the Federal Standards, or statistical equivalency, which means that some acceptable portion of buildings designed under a local standard consumes an equal or smaller amount than the Federal Standards. It is doubtful that most localities could meet absolute equivalency without adopting the Federal Standards.

A still different approach the Federal government might take, according to the NIBS report, is a "multiple-path" approach under which it might promulgate both standards that establish Btu per sq ft goals and standards based on ASHRAE 90-75R. Under this "multiple-path" approach, states and localities would then have the option of which standard to follow.

And finally, the government might write the regulations that go with the Standards so that the program takes effect in steps over time, with SEPS-type standards (like ASHRAE 90-75R) in effect to start, and BEPS-type standards being made mandatory at some future date.

So the question becomes—shall we go ahead with performance standards with their greater flexibility but with their vast implementation problems, or shall we proceed with deliberate speed to arrive there at a later date?

2
SOLAR ENERGY: EXPERIMENTATION IN USING OUR ONLY ENDLESSLY RENEWABLE RESOURCE

In recent years, interest in making use of energy from the sun has accelerated enormously. It has attracted the attention of everyone: homeowners; clients for every kind of industrial, commercial, and institutional building; architects and engineers. Its lure is obvious: the sun delivers to the earth's surface—free—more energy than we could ever use. The problem is equally obvious: how to convert that energy—at reasonable cost—into a reliable, usable form for heating and cooling our buildings.

But if the interest in solar energy has accelerated recently, it has interested mankind for thousands of years. Some principles of using solar energy were well understood by the Romans and the Indians of the Southwest—and these and other early applications of solar energy are well described in the essay by solar expert Donald Watson, on page 2. This article, which puts a most helpful perspective on today's hardware-oriented efforts, is a good reminder of what many architects have said as they approach solar design: "We're going back to some of the ideas we learned in school, but never had to use. . . ."

Through interviews with architects who have made good use of solar energy, engineer Margaret Gaskie has summarized (see page 32) the current thinking of architects and their consultants as they approach solar design—some very useful perspectives on the availability and efficiency of existing technology, its place in the broader struggle for energy efficiency, the problems of orientation and massing of buildings to make solar more efficient, and the need for careful and detailed engineering. As architect John Anderson says: "With solar, you can't just pull it off the shelf."

Next, beginning on page 38, are shown four houses that are not only handsome and livable—but make the point that solar houses need not be limited to parts of the country (like Colorado) where the sun shines a lot. These houses are all in the Northeast, where the sky is grey a lot, and their solar systems, all different in approach and technology, are contributing major portions of the energy needed to heat the house in this difficult climate.

These are followed, on page 46, with another article by solar expert and architect Don Watson, on

"What size solar heating system is economical for a house?"

The first commercial building to have a solar heating system was built almost 25 years ago, in 1956. And there have not been many built since. But beginning on page 50, you will find descriptions of seven important buildings designed with solar systems— Community College of Denver, North Campus; the headquarters building for Famolare, Inc. in Vermont; two post offices in Houston; an Armed Forces Reserve Center in Connecticut; an Alabama Power Company office building; and an arts complex at Hampshire College in Massachusetts. They show how some very skillful architects and engineers, designing complex buildings of considerable size, have integrated solar collectors into their designs, combined active and passive systems, made solar work for cooling as well as heating, devised simple but effective (and handsome) systems of controlling solar energy and moving air around the buildings—and turned up some major (if not totally cost-effective) savings in energy use. If the savings vs. the added first cost of these systems would not make a speculator weep for joy, these buildings do explore the state of the art today—a major contribution to our understanding of how to use age-old principles and a brand-new technology.

Beginning on page 68, two articles take us back to that first solar-heated building—the Bridgers & Paxton office building in Albuquerque—and trace its development; for it not only worked on that first try over 20 years ago, but is still being studied and monitored. It is still state-of-the-art design.

It still must be said that the cost/benefit of solar-energy systems—their "time to pay off"—is not sufficient to cause everyone to rush to solar. But that cost/benefit ratio can and is changing, as we see changes in our social consciousness, government incentives and/or fiats, more emphasis on life-cycle costing, or the ability of building owners to pass along higher and higher operating costs. And it may be, in the not too distant future, that the rules will change altogether. For, as Richard Crowther of Crowther/Solar Group says in one of the articles that follow: "To me it is irrelevant whether solar energy can be made to show a profit at this moment—or shortly. The real question is whether we can afford to continue pulling all our resources out of the earth and burning them up, when the sun's energy is there and when we have so many higher priority uses for fossil fuels. Not to use the sun is immoral, unethical—and ultimately uneconomical. . . ."

NOTES FROM THE FIELD: HOW ARCHITECTS, AND THEIR CONSULTANTS, APPROACH SOLAR DESIGN

by Margaret F. Gaskie

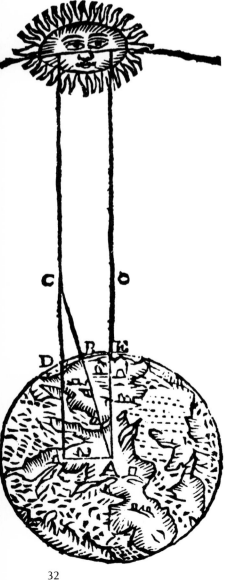

Colorado, as its boosters tirelessly affirm, basks year round in what less favored regions might consider more than its fair share of sunshine.

It has, as a result, harbored over the years a fair share of effort to harness that abundant energy, culminating recently in the location near Denver of the much-coveted Solar Energy Research Institute—a prize whose acquisition moved Governor Richard Lamm to proclaim Colorado on the spot "the solar energy capital of the world."

Well, maybe.

Certainly, the coincidence of climate and that aggregation of current events known as the energy crisis has lately spawned in the Denver area a comparatively high concentration of buildings utilizing solar energy, while raising to a high level the solar consciousness of its architectural community.

Designers' attitudes, explorations and experiences, as revealed in conversations with a small but thoughtful sampling of architects and mechanical engineers, presently engaged in solar projects, perhaps foreshadow those awaiting design professionals whose confrontation with the solar alternative has been postponed—until tomorrow.

"When we learned we couldn't get enough gas, we looked at every possibility we could think of—including capturing heat from the Platte River—before we went to solar."—Charles S. Sink, Charles S. Sink & Associates

Lest Denver's design community be credited with uncommon willingness to innovate—or charged with uncommon alacrity in experimenting at their clients' expense—be it said that the current boomlet in solar building is pragmatically based.

Natural gas, still the fuel of choice in the Denver area, is in short and uncertain supply—often not obtainable for new construction in the amount required or the time frame desired, and sometimes not obtainable at all.

Alternative energy sources, notably electricity, have not sky-rocketed in costs as they have in many parts of the country, but prices are rising steeply. Thus, given the region's highly favorable insolation rate, solar energy is seen by many here as a viable option despite comparatively favorable current fuel rates.

(The irony of recent studies predicting that solar energy for heating will compete economically with conventional fuels in such unlikely places as Maine and Minnesota before the same is true in Colorado is not lost on local architects. "We can collect a lot more Btus," muses John Anderson of John B. Anderson and Associates. "But theirs are worth a lot more.")

Attempts to generalize about the long-range economics of solar energy on a national or even regional scale lead quickly into a morass of "ifs" and "buts." Such attempts are also, practitioners agree, unhelpful.

The feasibility, economic and otherwise, of solar energy applications can only be explored validly on a project-by-project basis, they argue, and even then there are quite enough variables to challenge the computers often employed to sort them out. But however formidable in execution, feasibility determinations devolve as a basically simple process of weighing the proportion of total heating (and/or cooling) load that the solar system can be expected to meet, and the resulting savings in alternate sources of energy over time, against the cost of the system itself. Presto: the magic number, "years-to-payout."

What constitutes a reasonable payout period, of course, depends largely on who is doing the paying. "If you show a developer a balance sheet that says he's going to be lucky to save enough on his utility bills to cover the interest on the money he had to borrow to put in the solar system in the first place," notes architect John Rog-

Paired office buildings display a compendium of passive solar devices

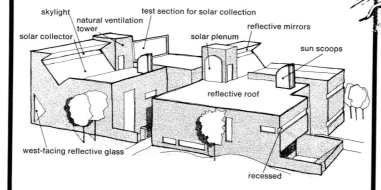

skylight · natural ventilation tower · test section for solar collection · reflective mirrors · solar collector · solar plenum · sun scoops · reflective roof · west-facing reflective glass · recessed

reflective mirrors
skylight
solar collector
reflective roof
rock heat storage beyond

Although the small collector area produces less than 20 per cent of total heating required, energy conserving techniques—ranging from wood foundations through controlled reflectances to induced ventilation—bring combined energy savings close to 80 per cent. Cherry Creek Office Buildings, Denver, Colorado. Architects and engineers: Architects Group, affiliated with Crowther/Solar group.

ers of RNL, Inc., "that man is not going to be too enthusiastic."

In many instances, however, clients—particularly public or institutional clients—who will themselves accrue the operating savings over an anticipated building-life of up to 50 years, can readily justify the payout periods of ten to fifteen years (in some cases, less) which are now well within reach.

Then, too, there is a strong current of opinion among the public as well as professionals which holds that dollars and cents should not be the only or even the most compelling motive for the use of solar energy.

Richard Crowther of Crowther/Solar Group minces no words: "To me it is irrelevant whether solar energy can be made to show a profit at this moment—or shortly. The real question is whether we can afford to continue pulling all our resources out of the earth and burning them up, when the sun's energy is there and when we have so many higher priority uses for fossil fuels. Not to use the sun is immoral, unethical—and ultimately uneconomical."

John Anderson, whose views are similar, adds that he finds clients disinclined to argue the proposition that at some point over the life of a building there may simply be *no* acceptable alternative to solar energy for building heating. "They can see that if you spend a little more money now, whether or not it ever pays off in terms of today's dollars, it certainly will turn out to be an economical step to have taken when somewhere down the road everyone's scrambling to retrofit at a much greater cost because there's no longer any real choice."

In addition, several architects cited solar projects undertaken for reasons of social consciousness, or prestige, or customer goodwill. And others suggest a number of factors—government incentives (or fiats); shifts to life-cycle costing; limits, by the market or by taxation, on building owners' ability to pass through operating costs—that could change the economic picture over time. Mean-

while, though, most agree that premium first costs for solar energy undeniably—and from the buyer's point of view quite logically—inhibit its application in commercial and industrial buildings.

"Let's face facts," says mechanical engineer Frank Bridgers, whose experience with solar systems dates back to 1956, when Bridgers and Paxton designed and built a solar-heated office building for their firm's own use. "An awful lot of solar applications we're seeing today are Federally funded or state funded or municipally funded, so the people's tax money is subsidizing them one way or another—through grants, or appropriations, or low-interest rates, or what have you. I'm not saying this isn't a good thing, just that it's a little different situation for the guy who's borrowing money at 10 per cent."

Or maybe not so very different. "I don't think people should get so hung up on costs," says Donald More of More Combs Burch. "I can remember when the only air-conditioned building in town was the movie. Then suddenly air conditioning became a necessity—but there's still no way to justify it in terms of cost. Solar's a real necessity, and people are going to wake up to that."

"On almost every project these days, the client wants to discuss the implications of solar energy."
—William C. Muchow, Muchow Associates

Whether inspired by soaring fuel bills, a record cold winter, or the recent media barrage of information and misinformation about solar energy, clients increasingly are taking the lead in probing the possibilities of solar systems—an initiative design professionals greet with mixed feelings.

"We've come to feel that if we don't encourage clients to consider solar energy, we're shirking our professional responsibility," asserts John Anderson. "So we're delighted when they raise the question."

Other architects, like John Rogers, are less sanguine about the public interest in solar energy: "Sure, people want to talk about it because they think it's exotic and exciting, but they don't want to talk about the price. You've got to be reasonable about giving the client alternatives: solar energy is just one more tool. I think energy conservation and passive systems are going to have a bigger impact faster."

James D. McFall of the me-

chanical engineering firm McFall and Konkel, Inc., expresses a similar concern that eventual full acceptance of solar technology may be retarded by "too much being promised that can't be delivered."

"Those people who are willing to say that their deep-rooted concern is to 'witness' for a technology we truly need are probably more comfortable with solar energy than those who try to rationalize it on the basis of payback. So we're cautious about making sure our clients recognize that solar energy is still largely a demonstration effort."

Frank Bridgers, too, believes there is a danger of solar energy being oversold, especially in residential applications. "It's not free energy as people would like to believe," he cautions, "and it's got some shortcomings people will have to learn to live with. If they expect to just plug in a solar system like they would a furnace and walk away while it coins them money, consumers are going to be disappointed. It's more complicated than that."

"Solar energy has been looked on by the public, and architects too, as an essentially experimental technology limited to small-scale applications. This is a myth. The existing technology is immediately applicable, and we've been able to convince clients that it's just as feasible for large projects as for smaller ones."
—John Anderson, John B. Anderson and Associates

Anderson's views are perhaps colored by his experiences in planning the mini-megastructure that will house the North Campus of the Community College of Denver, which at 300,000 sq ft is the largest solar application in the Denver area. (page 50).

But most practitioners agree that while scale is a significant factor in determining the feasibility of solar energy for a particular project, it is not size in itself that

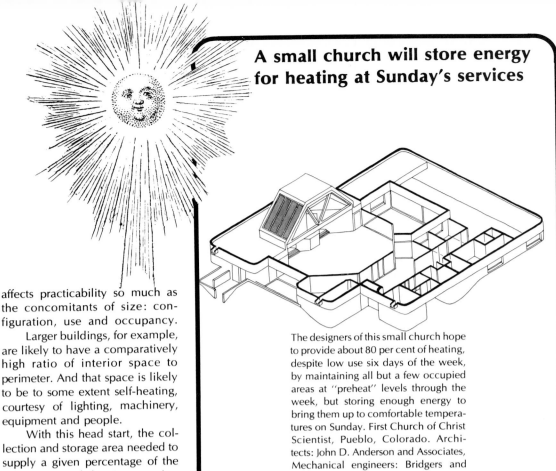

A small church will store energy for heating at Sunday's services

The designers of this small church hope to provide about 80 per cent of heating, despite low use six days of the week, by maintaining all but a few occupied areas at "preheat" levels through the week, but storing enough energy to bring them up to comfortable temperatures on Sunday. First Church of Christ Scientist, Pueblo, Colorado. Architects: John D. Anderson and Associates, Mechanical engineers: Bridgers and Paxton.

affects practicability so much as the concomitants of size: configuration, use and occupancy.

Larger buildings, for example, are likely to have a comparatively high ratio of interior space to perimeter. And that space is likely to be to some extent self-heating, courtesy of lighting, machinery, equipment and people.

With this head start, the collection and storage area needed to supply a given percentage of the building's total heating requirement may be reduced—or a solar system of given size may be able to satisfy a greater proportion of the over-all demand.

The same factors also have a clear impact on cost, much of which is fixed. As buildings get smaller (assuming an increase in perimeter ratio), the ratio of collector area to building area needed to supply the same percentage of energy demand goes up. So does system cost in relation to total project cost. And so do unit costs for the system, which tend also to vary inversely with collector area.

But building use is an equally critical consideration in solar applications. "If you use a lot of energy," says Frank Bridgers, "you have a better chance of saving a lot with a solar system. And the more energy you save, the more money you can afford to spend to do it."

To illustrate, he posits as a near-ideal user of solar energy a hospital. "That's about the most energy-intensive operation you can get. They've got a lot of load; they need a lot of outside air, which has to be heated; they operate 24 hours a day, seven days a week, 365 days a year."

At the other end of the spectrum? A church. (Though the Anderson-Bridgers team expects to meet even that challenge in the case of the proposed First Church of Christ Scientist in Pueblo, Colorado, by taking advantage of a

long collection week, with relatively little heating demand except in carefully zoned areas, to store energy for Sunday's peak use.)

"In terms of its impact on architecture, I think solar energy has to be looked at as only one means of addressing the larger issue, which is energy conservation."—Richard Crowther, Crowther/Solar Group

In discussing the myriad design considerations surrounding the effective use of solar energy, architects regard a thermally efficient building envelope as the *sine qua non* of an effective solar installation.

"You can't even start talking about solar heating until you've buttoned up the building as tight as you can. But by the time you've run the gamut of passive measures—proper orientation, good insulation, weatherproofing, double glazing and the rest—that next step to an active solar system can look pretty small," says John Anderson.

John Rogers emphasizes, in addition to "a good envelope," intelligent operation and load management, and "a reasonable attitude to what you really need" in terms of, for example, inside

temperature tolerances or outdoor air supply.

"Any real energy savings have to start with energy efficiency," he asserts. "Without it, solar will never work."

Richard Crowther goes a step further. The most promising path to fruitful use of solar energy, he believes, lies not in active systems but in enlarging the concept of energy conservation to include what might be called the active use of passive solar energy.

"By making the building itself—the site, the structure, the people, the equipment—a solar collector, and by using various kinds of applied passive systems, you get the most results with the least expense" says Crowther. "A collector gives you better control of solar energy—but it comes last."

It is perhaps worth noting that much of Crowther's work in solar design has been on small-scale projects—principally residences, for which the solar premium is often particularly high in relation to total building cost. By following his own dictum of first exploiting available natural energies, however, he is able to aim for a seven-year payback period on active systems—which he does not recommend at all if estimated payback is more than ten years.

The design foundation for solar applications, Crowther maintains, is basically no different from that which should be employed in the design of any building. "It is a matter of orchestrating all the building elements—placement, shape, form, materials, fenestration, location of entries—to control and integrate internal and external energies so that there is real correspondence between the building and its climate."

The point is echoed by other architects who express concern that as solar technologies become more feasible, they may be seized on as a renewed license to bottle building environments, rather than as an extended means of working with natural forces to control climate.

And some feel that while energy conservation is a clearly necessary goal, whether or not it entails the use of solar energy, a misunderstanding of its implications may invite solutions too simplistic, or too single-minded.

The designer's arsenal includes both defensive and offensive modes of achieving energy conservation, and both are needed to achieve a right balance between economic and human values.

"If you design strictly from the standpoint of not wasting heat—bury the building underground, do away with windows, and so on—you can create a wonderful situation for a solar collector," says William Muchow, "but I'm not sure how efficient you're being in human terms."

Muchow goes on to cite as a contrasting approach the creative work being done in school design some 25 years ago, in the Dark Ages before school programs were written with one eye on security and the other on air conditioning. Architects at that time, he recalls, were exhibiting considerable ingenuity in manipulating building orientation, configuration and fenestration to provide effective classroom lighting and cooling by natural means—surely no less valid a form of energy conserva-

Solar-assisted heat pump system for suburban city hall

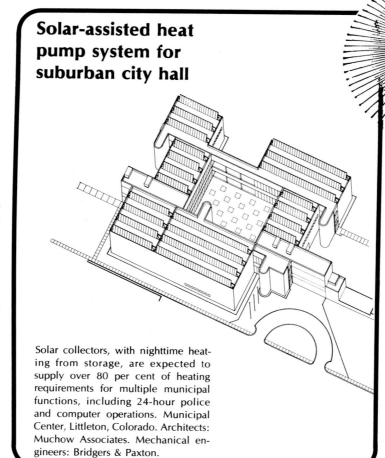

Solar collectors, with nighttime heating from storage, are expected to supply over 80 per cent of heating requirements for multiple municipal functions, including 24-hour police and computer operations. Municipal Center, Littleton, Colorado. Architects: Muchow Associates. Mechanical engineers: Bridgers & Paxton.

tion than the later impulse to make schools virtually indistinguishable from bunkers to lighten the burden on their mechanical systems.

The recollection is of an approach to energy saving design that many architects find both sympathetic and familiar. "If you go back," says Cabell Childress of Childress/Livaudais, "conservation in the sense of being sensitive to and working with the natural environment is what we were all trained for."

"Remember good old ventilation?" echoes John Anderson. "Most of us learned what we need to know to use solar energy passively long ago, and then just put it in the closet when we thought we had an endless supply of cheap energy. What we've got to do now is pull it out and dust it off and use it."

Richard Crowther, however, believes this may be more difficult than it sounds for architects whose practical experience has been acquired within a framework of throwaway energy. Most designers, he says, can deal handily with passive and active solar systems in an additive, linear sense, but few are trained in the "holistic" approach he believes necessary to exploit natural energies fully. The best solutions, in his admittedly somewhat evangelical view, emerge when designers "look at the building itself, with the things around and in it, as a total, unified energy system."

"We're just on the threshold of learning how to design for solar. It's anybody's guess what future buildings will look like, but it's certain they won't look the same once energy conservation gets a really high priority."—Donald C. More, More Combs Burch

Most architects have the idea that once they pass the hurdle of designing for energy efficiency, the addition of active solar systems will have comparatively little impact on building design.

Where they differ sharply is in the degree to which they perceive "energy efficiency" as including the deliberate exploitation of solar and other natural energies, apart from the essentially defensive mode of thermal conservation that John Anderson refers to as "buttoning up the building."

The several designers whose solar projects to date have been virtually retrofit, in the sense that design was well along before the decision was made to employ solar energy, would clearly have preferred a better opportunity to integrate the systems.

Yet, by and large, the last-hour addition of a roof-full of collectors is greeted as equally as would be, say, the addition of a roof-top cooling tower.

Charles Sink, for example, says of the belated solar installation on his recently completed garage-maintenance facility for Denver's Regional Transportation District, "We were glad we had that huge flat roof to make it feasible."

Similarly, in the case of the solar-heated municipal building now under construction in the Denver suburb of Littleton, William Muchow notes, "We discussed the possibilities of solar heating in the early stages, so the building was designed from the start to accept the system if the client decided to go ahead. But I wouldn't say the architecture changed much as a result."

In solar-conscious Denver, such briefs are increasingly common from clients who, while reluctant to commit themselves to a solar system at the outset, are nonetheless anxious that the building be designed to accommodate it later.

Some architects, indeed, routinely urge such provision on their clients, at least in mechanical system design, believing it short-sighted at best to plan present-day buildings without reference to solar energy.

Certainly "just-in-case" design can guarantee a neater job of solar retrofit, both mechanically and architecturally. But it rarely inspires the extra effort required for the seamless weaving of active and passive solar elements into building fabric.

For that reason, a few designers take exception to "advance retrofit," believing it reinforces what they see as an already present tendency of architects and clients alike to think of solar energy as additive rather than integral to the building design.

The approach of Denver architects to planning for solar energy is perhaps typified by William Muchow's description of the Little-

ton project as an attempt to design "a good energy conscious building that would work well with or without solar energy"—understanding "solar energy" to mean only the active system.

With a few notable exceptions, architects appear to have given little thought to what one writer has called "the conscious articulation of the sun by architecture."

As a result, solar design is viewed primarily as a practical matter of making optimum use of an added energy source—the active system—within the context of basically conventional (however thermally efficient) building configurations.

"Integrating" the system, in the sense of a tidy and pleasing disposition of the collectors that are its most conspicuous component, is recognized as a design desideratum but rejected as a design determinant.

The intelligent planning of the project as a whole is still the overriding consideration, the reasoning goes. If that dictates that collectors be arrayed on the roof, or up a wall, or over a parking lot—or down the block—so be it.

Which is not to say that architects are not acutely aware of the difficulties often encountered in handling the sheer bulk of collectors in large systems. On the Littleton City Hall, for example, William Muchow initially hoped the collectors could form a trellis over the building courtyard, doubling as a sun shield. "But we couldn't get enough surface," he says.

As Donald More points out, "Architects have to work solar into present-day budgets, methods, and technologies," and few are inclined to let the solar tail wag the architectural dog.

At the same time, designers reveal an underlying acceptance that the use of solar energy, in its broad ramifications, is ultimately not compatible with "building as usual."

Richard Crowther perhaps sums up the position by observing that an energy-short society can

35

Collectors "by the acre" provide heat for bus storage and maintenance building

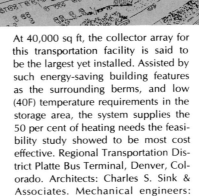

no longer afford many otherwise esthetically valid architectural approaches. "The architect has to accept a more limited palette, which means that he will have to be more ingenious in using it." (Bach, he adds, worked with a limited palette, too.)

"Present-day technology is certainly adequate, but I'm sure we'll eventually develop more sophisticated ways of capturing solar heat. Much of the equipment is still pretty crude."—Charles Sink, Charles S. Sink & Associates

As mechanical engineer James McFall asserts, flat-plate technology (which for all practical purposes is synonymous with "available" technology) is very old, very simple—and produces energy of very low quality. Nevertheless, the verdict of the design community is that such systems are the Model-Ts of solar energy—efficient enough and reliable enough for immediate application with relatively few butterflies about performance.

Because the most efficient panels are already nearing the upper reaches of their theoretical potential, given the limiting factor of the sun as a diffuse, low-level energy source, most professionals agree with John Anderson that "future increments of improvement are likely to be very small. You can't catch what isn't there."

Moreover, for space and hot water heating, there is no particular advantage to be gained from painfully boosting attainable temperatures much above the present range.

As a result, dramatic technological advances are not expected to suddenly confront today's buyer with an obsolete system, as some fear. "I don't think that's a danger," says Frank Bridgers. "As long as you're talking about low-temperature heating applications, today's flat plate will still be good twenty years from now."

At the same time, practitioners are following closely such

At 40,000 sq ft, the collector array for this transportation facility is said to be the largest yet installed. Assisted by such energy-saving building features as the surrounding berms, and low (40F) temperature requirements in the storage area, the system supplies the 50 per cent of heating needs the feasibility study showed to be most cost effective. Regional Transportation District Platte Bus Terminal, Denver, Colorado. Architects: Charles S. Sink & Associates. Mechanical engineers: Swanson-Rink & Associates.

emerging technologies as high-performance collection, which is anticipated as a potential key to increasing the feasibility of solar cooling as well as the flexibility and efficiency of solar heating systems.

Concentrating collectors in particular hold promise of producing the high energy levels needed for absorption cooling. To do so, however, most must directly face the sun, and must therefore be equipped with tracking mechanisms. As Frank Bridgers says mildly, such systems "need more work." Practical applications, he believes, are still a number of years off, and will probably be feasible first in regions like the South and Southwest, where heating requirements are very small compared to cooling, and where solar systems best suited to heating have been slow to gain a foothold.

Denver architects await with equal interest further improvements—and cost reductions—in absorption cooling units designed to operate efficiently at relatively low temperatures, thus making it more feasible to cool as well as heat with a flat-plate collector system.

Second to cooling in the balloting for technology most-needed comes better storage capability, at least partly in the hope that break-

throughs in storage may ultimately make possible self-sufficient solar systems.

(Solar energy advocates' ambivalence toward the need for back-up systems is reflected in the use of the term itself: it is more usually the solar systems, which at present supply only a greater or lesser percentage of total energy demand, that back up 100 per cent mechanical systems.)

Stand-alone systems can be designed now. (And, in fact, as Frank Bridgers notes, the solar-assisted heat pump system he designed 20 years ago for his own firm's offices was originally installed without heating back-up.)

But under most conditions, the size of the system required—collector area as well as storage—increases so drastically that self-sufficiency remains more a theoretical than a practical possibility.

Since, as James McFall says, the quality of collected energy is diluted at the instant of storage, with existing technology it is both difficult and costly to maintain stored heat at the desired temperatures for efficient operation for more than a day or two.

More efficient, cost-effective solar heating-cooling systems could reduce the *use* of back-up systems, but not the *need* for them,

so long as there are nights and cloudy days when the sun declines to make itself available for collection.

Thus most designers believe that any real possibility of dispensing with dual systems will wait—probably for a long time—on the development of storage technologies efficient enough to bridge the gaps between collection periods without an inordinate increase in size and cost.

Short of that perhaps impossible dream, however, many designers note that improved storage capability could greatly increase the options in system design, and contribute to more effective—and cost-effective—solutions.

Meanwhile, Frank Bridgers suggests, storage capacities verging on the stand-alone may come to be required simply to reduce the back-up demand on utilities.

"Most solar systems now use the utilities only when they're in trouble," he says, which results for utilities in an increase in their demand loads, and corresponding need for increased production capacity without consistent offsetting revenue. In response, they are rapidly turning to rate structures that exact heavy penalties from users—like solar installations—whose peak loads are high in relation to their base loads.

The obvious defense for solar users is to use their back-up systems when rates are most favorable to store heat against the need to run them when rates are highest. Such strategies can reduce over-all energy use as well as utility costs, but, according to Frank Bridgers, "it's going to take a lot of storage."

"We've seen changes take place just in the short time between design work on the community college and the projects we're doing now." —John Anderson, John D. Anderson and Associates

One barometer of the solar industry's evolution from an art of high uncertainty to something approaching building industry norms

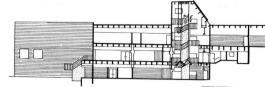

Solar system will meet 80 per cent of community college's heating needs

In the 300,000 sq ft structure designed for Denver's community college, the potential disadvantage of extensive perimeter, dictated by program demands for outside access, is offset by substantial internal heat gains from relatively high levels of occupancy and such heat-producing areas as vocational shops. The solar-assisted heat pump system is expected to meet about 80 per cent of heating needs, augmented by ambient heat. Community College of Denver/North Campus, Denver, Colorado. Architects: John D. Anderson and Associates. Mechanical engineers: Bridgers and Paxton.

is the level of caution designers find necessary in specification and bidding procedures.

On his first solar project, for example, John Anderson backed performance specifications with performance testing of the systems submitted as meeting them—which was just as well, as the low-bid system proved not to meet the specifications. On two recent school projects, by contrast, "We knew pretty well what we could expect from various systems, so we could specify on an 'or equal' basis among those we considered acceptable."

Despite agreement that both the products and the information supplied by manufacturers have become much more reliable in recent years, few architects are yet prepared to specify on a product basis. The common practice is to issue performance specifications requiring certified tests.

Moreover, design professionals uniformly assert that changes for the better in collector performance and reliability are by no means matched by improvements in the composite systems of which they are a part.

Most would support James McFall's contention that solar energy now is in an interface stage between development and application that is new to the building industry, in that the two are being pursued simultaneously rather than sequentially. The attempt, he believes, is both slowing development and multiplying "debugging" problems in the field.

"We feel that solar energy is now basically in the first generation of application experience," he says.

The cautionary tales circulating among Denver's design community focus on (1) the assembly of individual panels into the collector array, (2) the attachment of the collector units to building surfaces, and (3) the integration of the solar collection and storage system with the back-up mechanical system.

Some pages from Frank Bridger's notebook illustrate:

Underscoring Charles Sink's description of solar systems as a "plumber's paradise," Bridgers notes that plumbing is a larger component of installed system cost than the collectors. An efficient piping design, therefore, is crucial. At the Community College of Denver, he says, a 10 per cent reduction in the number of field connections, with allied system revisions, contributed to a cut in mechanical-electrical cost of almost $400,000 under first estimates.

In similar vein, Bridgers recalls an instance in which the low-bid collectors required side coupling and could not be installed flush together as planned. Result: a reduction in the number of collectors that could be accommodated in the "billboard space" provided by the supports.

And again: if the back of a roof-mounted, side-to-side collector array is exposed, wind can produce a strong sail effect which must be accommodated in the design of the supports and attachments, and possibly also in the structural design requirements for negative wind load.

Such details, some obvious and some not, no doubt explain the unanimous advice of Denver architects to others considering the plunge into solar design: "Get a good mechanical engineer."

Cabell Childress, whose experience with solar projects so far comprises a near-miss and a maybe, finds this piece of advice a bit hollow.

Five years ago, he recounts, "We had a client who knew the energy crisis was about to break, and wanted to make a 'statement.' So we called mechanical engineers from Chicago to California, but we couldn't get technical support for a solar design. The building was too big, the equipment wasn't available. . . . One actually gave us a collector area of something like five acres for 20,000 sq ft of building.

"The client would pay," he says. "But we couldn't make sense of it."

On a more recent project (the maybe), the chilling factor was an additional cost for a solar system estimated at almost 20 per cent of total project cost—compounded by a doubled fee for mechanical engineering.

Not surprisingly, Childress's present view is that while solar energy may be "no big deal technically," the difficulties of encompassing it within the norms of practice are daunting.

"Solar," he concludes, "has just got to be easier."

Easy it is not. A few Denver architects have apparently been able to confine their involvement in the nitty-gritty of solar projects to following their own advice on the hiring of able technical help. But the majority have felt constrained to undertake an arduous program of self-education, on top of the extra investment in design time.

Nor is the situation different for mechanical engineers. As Frank Bridgers says, "Unfortunately, there are no real short cuts to becoming competent in solar design. You can't become competent just by studying; you have to get out and see first-hand what works and what doesn't. People doing solar work for the first time are going to make mistakes."

James McFall, whose firm is among those regarding solar design as premium work, points out that usual fee structures assume a conversancy with the systems and the supporting industry that cannot obtain in the case of a developing technology like solar energy, adding, "We haven't—on any solar job—fully recovered costs."

"There's pressure in today's economic situation," sums up John Anderson, "to pull stuff out of a drawer. With solar, you just can't do it."

---

*The 17th-century drawing on page 32, taken from a book by the German scientist Athanasius Kircher, illustrates sunlight and its distribution over the earth. Although he erred in having the sun revolve around the earth, Kircher, using geometry, determined accurately which parts of the globe would be dark at a given time of the year. (From the book *Weather*, Life Science Library, 1965.)

SOLAR HOUSES FOR FOUR ALL-WEATHER SITES IN THE NORTHEAST

Robert Perron photos

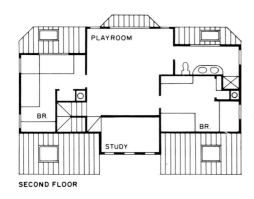

PLAYROOM

BR.

STUDY

BR.

SECOND FLOOR

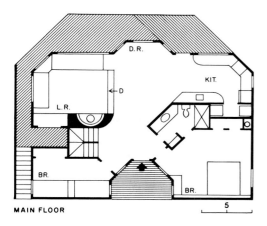

D.R.

KIT.

L.R.

D

BR.

BR.

MAIN FLOOR

5

Private Residence
Ludlow, Vermont

Okemo Mountain, in Ludlow, Vermont, has an elevation of 3700 feet, winter temperatures that sometimes do not rise above 15 F for periods as long as 21 days, and a winter sunshine factor in the range of 40-45 per cent. These chilling conditions make the mountain a magnet for weekend skiers, like the owners of this house, but sorely challenge the solar designer. Architects Ric Weinshenk and Martha Poole of *Sunshine Design* accepted the challenge and designed this strong-massed, 3000-square-foot weekend house in a birch grove on this gently sloping, windswept site.

The solar collection system is integral to the design rather than imposed on it. Backed by a layer of insulating foam, the system is a grid of ¾-inch copper pipe and ⅜-inch refrigeration tubing shielded on the outside by two ¹⁄₁₆-inch thicknesses of fiber glass with a ¾-inch airspace between. The visual result is the series of opaque panels that are the predominant feature of the south elevation. The whole collector surface is about 1000 square feet (or ⅓ the floor area of the house) and it faces just east of due south to take advantage of the morning sun. Water, passing through the col-

lector, is heated then returned to a 1000 gallon storage tank where it awaits circulation to the boiler by way of the heat exchanger.

Because the principal view is to the north, more than the minimum number of openings occur on this elevation, but all windows are double glazed and fitted with custom-designed, almost airtight insulating curtains that can be drawn to trap heat at night or when the house is not in use. This window treatment, combined with six inches of insulation in the stud walls and 12 inches at the roof, produces an R factor of ± 20 for walls and 30 for roof.

Additional heat is provided by a fireplace—not just by radiation but by a heavy heating coil that serves as an andiron and keeps a flow of heated water going to the storage tank whenever the fireplace is in use.

Beyond its mechanical invention, this Vermont house is spatially lively and fresh in its graphic images. It was built at a cost of $32 per square foot (p176) including furnishings, equipment and sitework.

PRIVATE RESIDENCE, Ludlow, Vermont. Architects and builders: *Sunshine Design*—Ric Weinshenk, partner-in-charge.

House
New Castle, New York

This house, now nearing completion at a site 30 miles north of New York City, is interesting because it indicates how a conventional developer's plan can be remassed and adapted for solar heating. The need to appeal to a broad market of potential buyers led to a program that includes four bedrooms, separate living and dining rooms, family room and two-and-a-half baths. This program produced about 2400 square feet plus basement and a two-car garage.

The decision to use solar collectors, together with the sloping site, suggested to architects Raymond, Rado, Caddy & Bonington a compact volume and a stacking of elements. Six inches of glass fiber insulation fill the wall cavities and 12 inches are applied at the ceiling of the second floor and at the first floor under the deck. This heavy insulation, coupled with a modest use of glass, keeps heat loss to about 100,000 Btus per hour—this in a region with an average winter temperature of 42F and approximately 4900 degree days.

The deeply-sloping roof faces just west of due south and is inclined at 50 degrees—an angle assumed to be optimal for solar collection at this latitude. This roof is fitted with a system of flat plate aluminum collectors with a surface area equal to nearly one half the square footage of floor space to be heated. The liquid medium (water treated with an antifreeze solution) is picked up in manifold pipes between the collectors, then conveyed to a heat ex-changer in the basement. Here the heat is transferred to a conventional forced-air distribution system before being recirculated to the collector system on the roof. To protect against a protracted period of overcast or rainy weather, a standby oil-fired heater trips on automatically when the water temperature in the storage tank has dropped below useable levels for space heating. Both solar and conventionally-generated heat are of course distributed by the same system of ducts.

Domestic hot water demands are also met by a solar system and backed up by an electric heater. The two backup systems might theoretically have been unified but, in this instance, discrete systems were more economical.

Apart from the solar-heating collectors, their mechanical adjuncts, and the heavier level of insulation, the construction and selection of finishes is typical of the better quality built-for-sale housing in this region. The roof is finished in asphalt shingles, the walls are clad in textured plywood siding except at the foundation, where ribbed concrete blocks were used. The site had no special treatment except the removal of a few close-in trees that otherwise would have filtered the sunlight before it reached the collectors.

HOUSE in New Castle, New York. Architects: *Raymond, Rado, Caddy & Bonington;* structural engineers: *Weidlinger Associates;* solar energy collection system: *General Energy Devices, Inc.;* Builders: *John Reventas and Carlo Ventimiglia.*

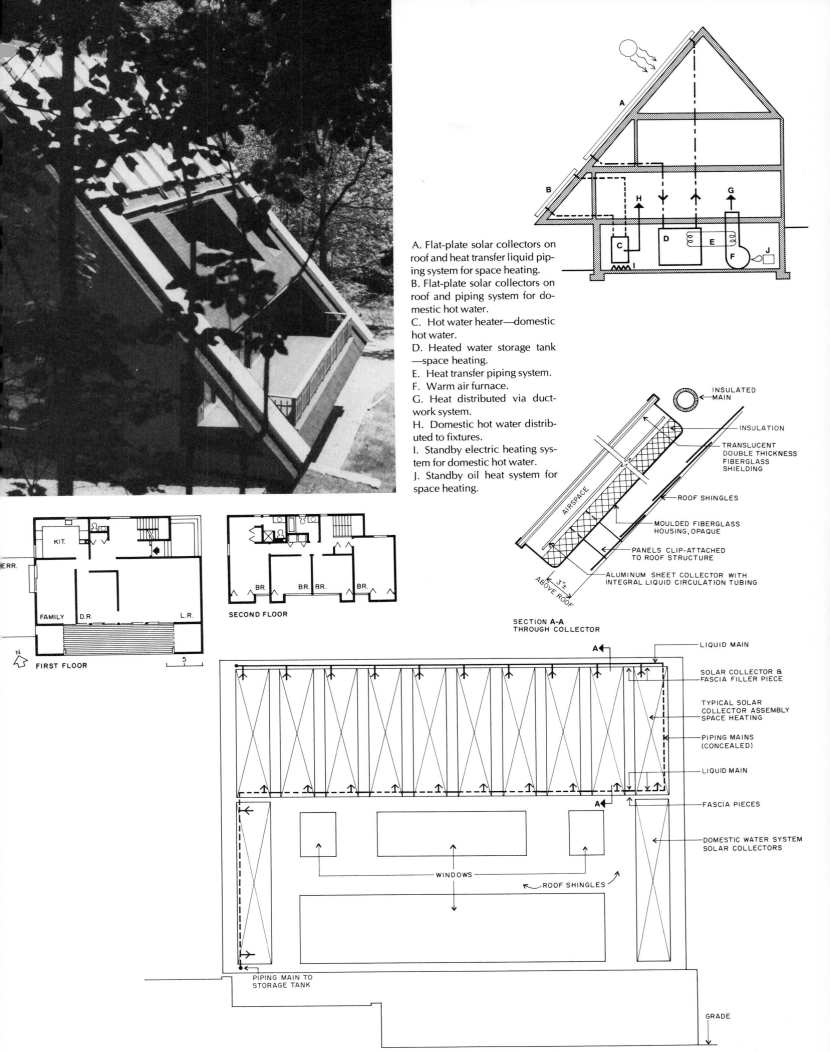

A. Flat-plate solar collectors on roof and heat transfer liquid piping system for space heating.
B. Flat-plate solar collectors on roof and piping system for domestic hot water.
C. Hot water heater—domestic hot water.
D. Heated water storage tank —space heating.
E. Heat transfer piping system.
F. Warm air furnace.
G. Heat distributed via ductwork system.
H. Domestic hot water distributed to fixtures.
I. Standby electric heating system for domestic hot water.
J. Standby oil heat system for space heating.

INSULATED MAIN

INSULATION

TRANSLUCENT DOUBLE THICKNESS FIBERGLASS SHIELDING

AIRSPACE

ROOF SHINGLES

MOULDED FIBERGLASS HOUSING, OPAQUE

PANELS CLIP-ATTACHED TO ROOF STRUCTURE

ALUMINUM SHEET COLLECTOR WITH INTEGRAL LIQUID CIRCULATION TUBING

3" ± ABOVE ROOF

SECTION A-A THROUGH COLLECTOR

KIT.

ERR.

FAMILY   D.R.   L.R.

N

FIRST FLOOR   5

BR.   BR. BR.   BR.

SECOND FLOOR

A

LIQUID MAIN

SOLAR COLLECTOR & FASCIA FILLER PIECE

TYPICAL SOLAR COLLECTOR ASSEMBLY SPACE HEATING

PIPING MAINS (CONCEALED)

LIQUID MAIN

A

FASCIA PIECES

DOMESTIC WATER SYSTEM SOLAR COLLECTORS

WINDOWS

ROOF SHINGLES

PIPING MAIN TO STORAGE TANK

GRADE

DIAGRAMMATIC ILLUSTRATION OF ROOF SOLAR COLLECTION SYSTEM

Kelbaugh House
Princeton, New Jersey

The Kelbaugh house is a 2100-square-foot, year-round residence in suburban Princeton, a community with a 40 degree north latitude, a climate that typically includes 5100 heating degree days, and a 50-55 per cent sunshine factor during the winter.

By obtaining a zoning variance, the Kelbaughs were able to push the house to the northern boundary of their 60- by 100-foot lot, thus clearing the pattern of shadows cast by neighboring houses and at the same time, giving the lot an ample outdoor space instead of the usual mishmash of shallow yards.

The key to the solar capabilities of the design is the massive concrete wall, an adaptation of the "Trombe wall" (see section drawing) set back six inches from the glass curtain wall that faces south. The 600-square-foot concrete surface absorbs and stores heat from the sun and radiates it continually into living spaces that are nearly uninterrupted spatially both upstairs and down. Back-up space heating has been provided by a gas-fired, hot air system, independent of the house's solar capabilities, but with ductwork cast into the concrete wall.

During its first winter (a mild one with about 4500 degree days), the Kelbaugh house performed well. With the thermostat for the back up system set in the 60-64 F range (58 F at night), only 338 cubic feet of natural gas was consumed. This represented a saving of nearly 75 per cent when compared with the estimated 1220 cubic feet of gas that would have been required to maintain a 65 F daytime temperature by conventional heating. And these savings came at little sacrifice to comfort. The temperatures inside were allowed to swing 3-6 degrees during the 24-hour cycle to allow the concrete wall to collect and discharge its heat. Auxiliary 250-watt infrared heaters were installed in the bathroom but seldom needed and the fireplace was used several times a week for localized comfort.

Insulation, of course, is critical. Kelbaugh provided an average 4-inch wall insulation of cellulosic fiber (recycled newspaper) and a 9½-inch roof insulation that achieved an R factor of 40. In addition, he used a one-inch thickness of polystyrene (two inches would have been better, he reports) on the perimeter foundation wall to a depth of two feet. The re-

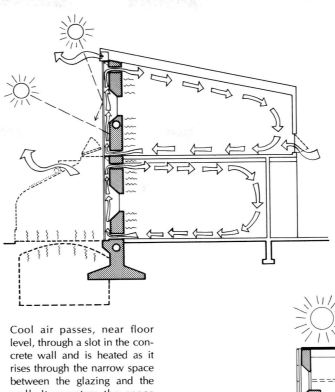

Cool air passes, near floor level, through a slot in the concrete wall and is heated as it rises through the narrow space between the glazing and the wall. It re-enters the space through slots at ceiling height. Circulation through the room is by gravity convection. In summer, the narrow space is vented at the eave. When gravity convection does not suffice, four small fans are employed.

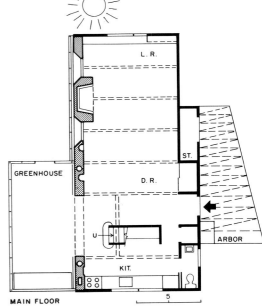

MAIN FLOOR

sultant heat loss, by conventional analysis is about 75,000 Btu per hour—32,000 of which is lost to the small greenhouse on the south face of the building. After double glazing this greenhouse, and fitting it with rolling shades, the loss should be considerably less next winter. Other adjustments and fine tuning will follow to balance temperature differentials between upstairs and down. With refreshing candor, Kelbaugh says that if he was beginning again, he would enlarge the eave vents and/or install operable windows in the south wall to increase cross ventilation.

As the photos amply indicate, the Kelbaugh house is much more than just a struggle for energy efficiency. Though it is frankly experimental, it is nonetheless a tightly disciplined piece of design with the kind of apparent simplicity that only comes with close study and careful refinement. Questions raised by its presence among the more indulgent residential forms of the past must be measured against the lessons it can yield to those interested in a less energy-extravagant future.

KELBAUGH HOUSE, Princeton, New Jersey. Architect: *Douglas Kelbaugh.* Contractor: *Nathan Bard.*

Robert Perron photos

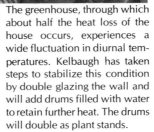

The greenhouse, through which about half the heat loss of the house occurs, experiences a wide fluctuation in diurnal temperatures. Kelbaugh has taken steps to stabilize this condition by double glazing the wall and will add drums filled with water to retain further heat. The drums will double as plant stands.

Eddy House, Little Compton, Rhode Island

Performance of this 1500-sq-ft house addition in Little Compton, Rhode Island late this winter indicates that architect Travis Price could have achieved his goal of a system that requires no backup, save for a small wood-burning stove. The addition allows the Eddy family to close off the main house in winter and rely on the "free" heat from the sun.

Space heating is provided by 18 air-type solar collectors from which heat is picked up by a small ½-hp fan and circulated either directly to the house or to a 10- by 18- by 8-ft deep insulated storage bin filled with 4-in. rocks. Summer collection will give as much as nine days' storage for winter.

The sun's heat also penetrates the double-glazed southerly fa-

cade, adding 20-30 per cent of the heat needed. (Andersen Corporation plans to assist in data collection on over-all performance).

Domestic hot water is provided by three water-type collectors at ground level. A system of self-powered Sky Lids behind the greenhouse windows open during the day to let in sun and shut at night to keep out cold.

Sky lids, looking like miniature airplane wings have a black-colored Freon-filled cylinder on the leading edge and a light-colored cylinder on the trailing edge. Heat vaporizes the Freon, and a cooler environment condenses it, tipping the louver to the coolest side.

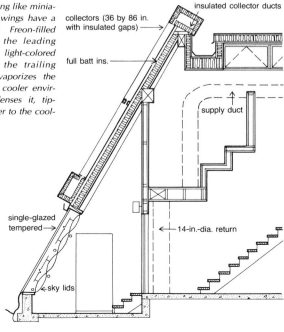

WHAT SIZE SOLAR HEATING SYSTEM IS ECONOMICAL FOR A HOUSE?

by Donald Watson, AIA and Fred N. Broberg, P.E.

The practicality of solar heating for houses depends, first of all, upon climatic factors and the anticipated cost of conventional fuels. The most favorable locations are cold, clear climates where the heating requirements are high and where there is ample winter sunshine—the more so if local fuel rates are high.

Some degree of solar heating is economical now for northern climates. The most critical variable in determining how much solar heating the owner of a house can afford is the rate of escalation of conventional fuel costs: the higher the rate, the more practical are larger-capacity solar-heating systems.

Climate, too, is an important variable. While Pittsburgh and Denver are both near 40° north latitude, they receive quite different amounts of sunshine because of differences in cloud cover, sky clearness, and altitude. And while Williston, North Dakota is much farther north than Denver or Pittsburgh, and has a much greater space-heating requirement, its excellent winter sunshine makes it as viable a location for solar heating as Denver. Hartford is included as a representative New England location, with moderately high heating requirements, but only moderate winter sunshine availability.

In this article, the economics of six approaches to solar house heating are compared for these representative northern climates. For these economic evaluations, it was assumed that the additional costs of the solar systems are amortized over the life of a 20-year mortgage at 8½ per cent interest, and that savings

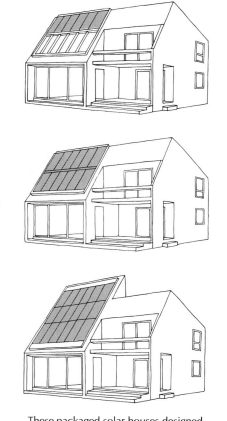

These packaged solar houses designed by Donald Watson for American Timber Homes offer three capacities: auxiliary, medium (with heat pump) and large.

in conventional energy are averaged for the 20-year period and divided into monthly-saving increments. Average monthly paybacks in the first table, and in the graphs that follow, are determined by subtracting monthly amortization costs from the monthly energy savings.

Systems range from domestic hot water, to window heat recovery, to space heating

Alternative A: Solar Domestic Water Heating. A small solar collector area (two or three collectors) can supply a major proportion of the year-round requirement for domestic water heating. Solar domestic hot water equipment, now available from many manufacturers throughout the United States, imposes few if any restrictions on the building design.

Alternative B: Window Heat Recovery. An approach to solar heating that is often neglected is the utilization of heat gain from solar-oriented windows, skylights, greenhouses and sun rooms. Window heat, of itself, has the effect of overheating the sunny side of a building while the colder side still calls for heat. Window heat can be recovered, however, and more evenly distributed by an air circulation system that removes heated air from windows, sun rooms and/or upper portions of the house and passes it through rock storage—in effect cooling the house when it is overheated during winter days and storing the heat for some nighttime carryover. Installation costs of windows are part of the normal house construction and rock storage can be built within typical foundations. Sun rooms or greenhouses

MONTHLY PAYBACKS FOR SIX ALTERNATIVES	HARTFORD					PITTSBURGH					WILLISTON					DENVER				
		% fuel increase					% fuel increase					% fuel increase					% fuel increase			
	% sol	0	8	12	16	% sol	0	8	12	16	% sol	0	8	12	16	% sol	0	8	12	16
ALTERNATIVE A domestic hot water	11	4	21	40	72	11	3	19	36	65	8	5	25	46	81	15	7	29	52	92
ALTERNATIVE B window heat recovery	24	-2	10	23	45	21	-4	5	15	31	22	1	16	33	62	36	1	18	35	65
ALTERNATIVE C auxiliary solar space heating	18	-1	24	50	94	17	3	17	38	75	14	1	27	55	103	25	1	28	57	106
ALTERNATIVE D combined alternatives B and C	40	-4	31	69	134	37	-8	21	53	106	34	-1	40	83	156	58	1	43	88	164
ALTERNATIVE E large capacity solar 20% CA/FA	51	-24	15	57	127	44	-30	0	32	86	42	-20	24	71	151	74	-17	32	84	172
ALTERNATIVE F large capacity solar 40% CA/FA	70	-41	6	58	145	60	-49	-13	27	93	57	-37	18	76	176	95	-34	24	87	194

Monthly dollar paybacks are tabulated for six different solar-heating alternatives for a 1200-sq-ft- house in four different climates. The values were derived by subtracting the monthly amortization (over 20 years) of additional cost of the solar equipment from the monthly savings in conventional energy, averaged for the same period. Energy assumed for conventional domestic hot water was electric at 4¢/kWh; and, for space heating, oil at 42¢/gallon. Systems range from domestic hot water, only, to large-scale solar space heating. CA/FA is the ratio of solar collector area to the "heated" floor area.

can gain solar heat without overheating the residence itself.

Alternative C: Auxiliary Solar Heating. Auxiliary solar heating, like window heat recovery, involves only a small investment for partial solar heating. As first suggested to the authors by Everett Barber, Jr., auxiliary solar heating is a system that uses the same components as a solar domestic water installation (Alternative A, above) adding only a few more solar panels to increase collection area, and a heating coil to pipe excess heat into the conventional space heating system. Other than increasing the size of domestic hot water storage slightly, no other heat storage or controls are involved, and thus installed cost and construction requirements are small. The control sequence used—whether to supply domestic hot water first with the excess to space heating, or the reverse—depends upon engineering decisions related to climate and comparative fuel cost. In this article, the former control sequence was assumed.

Alternative D: Auxiliary Solar Heating and Window Heat Recovery. This option combines previous Alternatives B and C. If a window heat recovery system did not have the rock-type heat storage component, then it would be redundant to combine it with the auxiliary space heating system since both would provide space heating on sunny days only. However with heat storage, the daytime heat recovered from the house can be carried over into nighttime hours.

Alternative E: Solar Space Heating with Relatively Small Collector Area. In this option, the collector area is held to less than 20 per cent of the heated floor area and thus imposes little constraint on architectural design while providing sufficient heat to a storage unit for partial carry-over. The solar panels also supply domestic hot water.

Alternative F: Large Capacity Solar Space Heating. This is the same as Alternative E, but with more collectors (approximately 40 per cent of the heated floor area). Of the solar alternatives compared, this option requires the largest construction cost but also contributes the largest percentage of solar heating.

In evaluating solar alternatives such as those just described, the architect and engineer must first of all assess their performance and their esthetic impact. But whether a particular approach is viable or not is determined by the projected energy-cost saving. Life-cycle costing is important to the economics of solar house-heating approaches; and, yet, it. involves judgmental decisions about fuel cost increases that directly affect the relative economic merit of the various alternatives being evaluated.

High quality solar equipment was assumed in projecting system installation costs

The same building plan, a one-family 1200-sq-ft house, is used for the tables and graphs, with construction costs and present fuel costs assumed to be equal in all four locations. Housing is a good candidate for solar heating because of its steady demand for relatively low-temperature heating, including a year-round demand for domestic hot water, and generally detached or low-density construction which

The potential dollar savings (and optimum size of system) depend upon cost of fuel and amount of sun available

Two series of graphs show how the savings from house solar heating in four different northern climates are affected by the relative costs of conventional energy sources (top), and by the extensiveness of the solar-heating systems (bottom).

Curves at the top show how increases in assumed cost of conventional fuel affect the economics of different-sized solar-energy systems. At the greater increases, the larger systems generally become more and more economical.

From the bottom series of graphs one can determine the optimum percentage of solar-system contribution (the curve peaks) for different assumed fuel-cost increases—0, 8, 12 and 16 per cent.

Climate is a very significant factor. Hartford, for example, has a moderately-high heating requirement, but only moderate sunshine. Pittsburgh is not as cold as Hartford, but has more cloudy days. Denver is colder than Pittsburgh, but its weather and altitude give it good sunshine. Williston, N.D. is near the Canadian border, but it gets a lot of clear days.

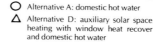
○ Alternative A: domestic hot water
△ Alternative D: auxiliary solar space heating with window heat recover and domestic hot water
□ Alternative F: large capacity solar heating (40 per cent CA/FA)

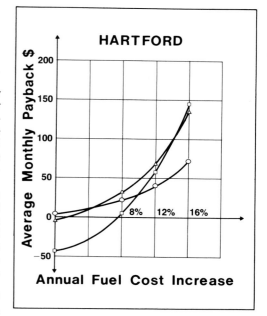
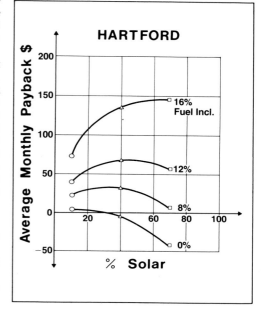

offers a large surface area exposed to the sun.

While cost and performance breakthroughs in solar technology can be anticipated, these are not considered in the estimates. The performance and costs of the solar equipment, and the installation costs used in the comparisons represent state-of-the-art estimates. The installation costs used are relatively high, compared to costs claimed by other sources, but the solar-system performance assumed in the calculations also represents high-quality solar equipment. Lower installation costs and lower system efficiencies appear to be directly related at this time.

The heating load of the house in the example is greatly reduced by following high-insulation standards, with the result that the total energy contribution of the solar heating systems is smaller (see graph at bottom of page 48). The solar heating payback would look better than the results reported if a higher heat loss due to poorer insulation characteristics were assumed.

The cost effectiveness of improved insula-

tion standards is so apparent, however, that an architect or engineer would obviously use heat saving techniques first, and *then* compare solar heating alternatives. The intent of the comparisons is to show what the relative economic merit might be of different solar approaches *after* everything had been done by practical construction and design methods to reduce the fuel requirement.

The table at the top of page 49 summarizes the heating-load calculations of the example house design in the four locations. The design heat losses shown are in the range of 40 per cent less than average, reflecting higher insulation standards and reduced infiltration heat loss that good planning and construction achieves.

The table on page 46 show the average monthly fuel cost savings, less finance charges, for each of the six alternatives for assumed annual fuel cost increases of 0, 8, 12, and 16 per cent. The negative numbers in the 0 per cent fuel escalation rate column show that if fuels do not increase in cost, the solar investment in

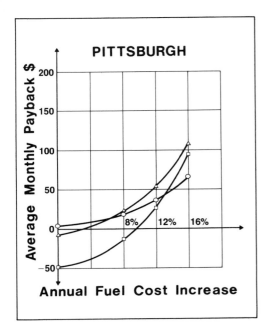

PITTSBURGH

Average Monthly Payback $ vs Annual Fuel Cost Increase (8%, 12%, 16%)

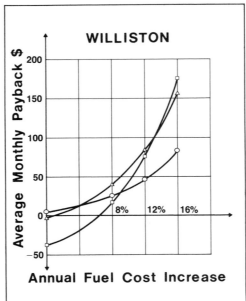

WILLISTON

Average Monthly Payback $ vs Annual Fuel Cost Increase (8%, 12%, 16%)

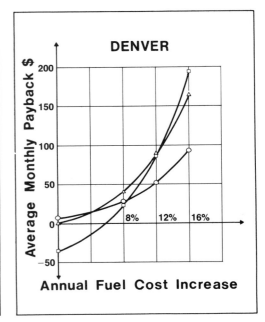

DENVER

Average Monthly Payback $ vs Annual Fuel Cost Increase (8%, 12%, 16%)

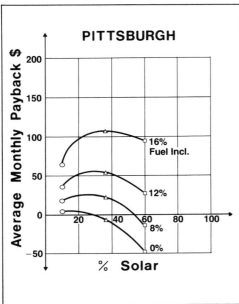

PITTSBURGH

Average Monthly Payback $ vs % Solar
16% Fuel Incl., 12%, 8%, 0%

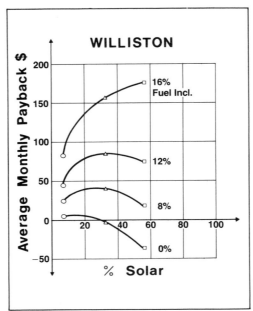

WILLISTON

Average Monthly Payback $ vs % Solar
16% Fuel Incl., 12%, 8%, 0%

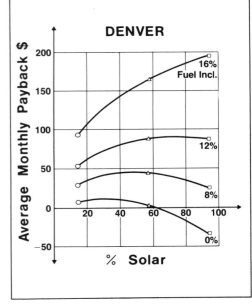

DENVER

Average Monthly Payback $ vs % Solar
16% Fuel Incl., 12%, 8%, 0%

some cases does not pay back within the 20-year mortgage period. But, a projection of 8 per cent fuel escalation is the consensus of both private and government forecasts.

Higher-cost systems may save more money when climate is favorable and fuel expensive
Of particular interest in the payback results is the fact that the order of merit of the six alternatives does not follow the relative order of their initial cost. It varies considerably according to climate and assumed fuel cost escalation. For example, the large-capacity solar-heating approach, *Alternative F,* is among the least economical of the six choices at the present time, even though it may rank highest in "environmental merit" by greatly reducing the reliance on nonrenewable and polluting fuels. But if fuel escalation increases above 12 per cent per year, the economic merit of *Alternatives D* and *E* is highest in nearly every case, except for Pittsburgh where local cloudiness makes a large investment in solar heating still unattractive. And if escalation were to rise to

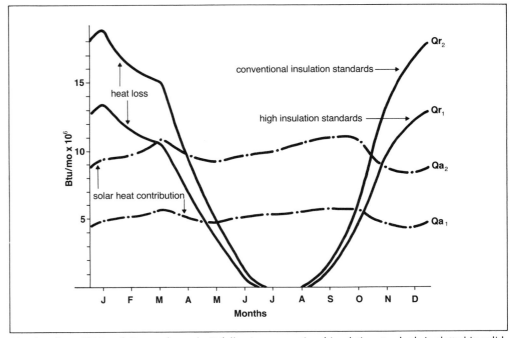

Heat loss for a 1200-sq-ft Denver house built following conventional insulation standards is plotted in solid curve Qr_2, and following high-insulation standards, in solid curve Qr_1. The comparative solar-heat contribution of a solar collector with an area equal to 20 per cent of the floor area is plotted in the dash-dot curve Qa_1, and equal to 40 per cent of the floor area, in curve Qa_2. Although solar energy contributes more heat proportionately to the house with conventional insulation, the investment, over-all, is not as cost-effective.

LOCATION	LAT	ELEV	t_0	DD	DHL (MBH)	YEARLY ENERGY 10^6 X Btu		
						DHW	HTG	TOT
HARTFORD, CT.	42	15	5	6235	35	13	83	96
PITTSBURGH, PA.	40	749	11	5053	33	13	67	81
WILLISTON, N.D.	48	1877	-17	9243	47	14	123	138
DENVER, CO.	40	5283	3	5524	36	13	74	87

	DHW		SPACE HEATING				INSTALLATION	
	CA	tank size	AUX	WA	CA	STO	Cost$	$ mo.
ALTERNATIVE A domestic hot water	56 S.F.	60 gal.					$900	$8
ALTERNATIVE B window heat recovery				300		X	1200	10
ALTERNATIVE C auxiliary solar space heat	93	80	X				2000	17
ALTERNATIVE D combined alternates B and C	93	80	X	300		X	3200	28
ALTERNATIVE E large capacity solar 20% CA/FA	56	60		150	223	X	5800	50
ALTERNATIVE F large capacity solar 40% CA/FA	56	60		150	427	X	8500	74

Solar heating adds a cost that can be recovered from savings in fuel

The top table lists the geographic and weather characteristics of four northern cities, and itemizes the heat-load characteristics of a 1200-sq-ft, well-insulated house located in each city. DHL is the heat loss of the house at outdoor design temperature. Yearly heating loads are given for domestic hot water, for space heating, and for the two combined.

The bottom table lists the areas of solar collectors (CA), sizes of domestic hot water tanks, the larger dhw tank used for auxiliary space heating, and window areas (WA) for the assumed example. Storage (STO) is required for space-heating alternatives (except alternative C) and for window heat recovery.

The costs listed are the dollars required to pay for the additional cost of the alternative systems over that of conventional domestic hot water and space heating systems. The monthly cost is the additional monthly mortgage payment for 20 years at a finance charge of 8½ per cent.

16 per cent, the largest-capacity system would yield the largest monthly payback. And though *Alternatives A, B* and *C* rank low when fuel escalation is above 8 per cent, the table on page 46 shows that when combined (*Alternative D)*, and the escalation is between 8 and 12 per cent, this *Alternative* is the most economical option in all four of the climates. The top series of graphs on pages 48 and 47 shows the approximate crossover points of economic merit of various alternatives as a function of changing fuel escalation rates. The bottom series of graphs have the same data plotted in another format to show the optimum percentage of solar capacity for given installation and fuel costs.

The example is limited to a single, though typical, case—that of a house financed under conventional mortgage terms. The economics, however, look poorer than if compared with standard house construction, in which case the paybacks would appear more favorable. Installation and financing costs also depend on individual circumstances. Many individuals are able to undertake a solar installation on different financial terms than used in the example through low-interest building loans. Tax incentives are being considered on the state and Federal level that may further change current economics in favor of solar heating. System cost breakthroughs or performance improvements may result in more cost effective solar installations. Finally, the calculation methods used are monthly averages and result in only

general results. Nonetheless, the *relative order* or economic merit of the various alternatives shown in the example would not change.

The study takes a moderate, if not overly conservative, view of solar installation and fuel costs in order to represent the typical case for solar heating with the options that it presents now. The results, in fact, suggest that—in the almost certain event that fuel costs will increase—some sort of solar heating is justified in any northern climate. If only solar domestic water heating and auxiliary space heating systems were to find the place in the residential market, the increase in production of solar equipment would make possible substantial economics of scale which would lead in turn to lower costs for the larger capacity systems. Even now, a middle-range solution might be adopted—an incremental approach to solar heating in which a building is constructed with only a small solar installation at first, such as *Alternates A through D*, with provisions made in the design for adding more capacity in the future, as the economic variables change in favor of increased solar heating. Other factors that could help lower installation costs include "one-contract" supply, installation and servicing; solar building and equipment packaging; and various subsidized economic incentives. In any case, the need is obvious for close coordination between architect, engineer, manufacturer and builder to ensure that a solar installation is appropriate for a building in terms of climate, heat requirement and financing.

APPLICATIONS IN LARGER BUILDINGS: DESIGNING FOR THE SUN, WHETHER HARVESTING IT OR SHUTTING IT OUT, CAN BE ENERGY CONSERVING, FORM-GIVING, AND FUN

It is clear from the examples following that architects are beginning to take solar seriously. Though paybacks on collector systems may not exactly thrill business clients, some systems do offer quite respectable paybacks. In any case, we should all be thankful to those clients, both public and private, willing to take the plunge and allow the rest of us to learn from their design and operating experience. Architects for some of the buildings shown here found that, with energy-saving techniques and economical building materials, total costs could be made comparable to those of like buildings.

But just as important, other examples demonstrate some inventive ideas for the use of solar heat and light through windows. Architects must recognize that this "passive" approach can lead to good design—and that more and more clients will be asking for it.

Reginald Wade Richey

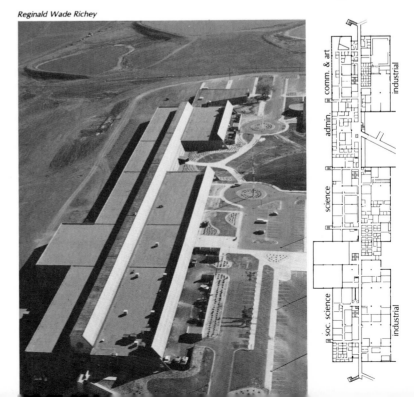

Community College of Denver, North Campus Denver, Colorado

COMMUNITY COLLEGE OF DENVER-NORTH CAMPUS, Denver, Colo rado. Architects: *John D. Anderson and Associates.* Engineers: *KKBNA, Inc. (structural); Bridgers and Paxton (mechanical, energy conservation and solar energy); Sol Flax & Associates (electrical); Chen & Associates (soils).* Landscape: *Alan Rollinger.* General contractor, construction manager: *Pinkard Construction Co.*

The mini-megastructure that is the North Campus of Denver's Community College flaunts its solar collectors with an architectural aplomb rarely manifested by mechanical systems.

Early planning meetings for new quarters to replace the college's bursting temporary facilities took place in the summer of 1973, when warnings of impending shortages were given substance by long lines of motorists haunting still-pumping gas stations.

Thus alerted, architect John Anderson and the client commissioned the Albuquerque mechanical engineering firm of Bridgers and Paxton, pioneers in work with solar energy, to prepare a feasibility study including a solar option. The choice—later rendered moot when the local utility served notice of a cutoff of new natural gas allocations—narrowed quickly to conventional gas-heating and cooling versus solar-assisted heat pump system. The solar system commanded an

initial premium at 8.5 per cent over the original budget but was deemed a viable long-term option because of the relatively short payback period— 11 years on the conservative assumption of a 300 per cent increase in natural gas prices between 1973 and 1990.

The system as installed (comfortably within the revised budget) is, as Anderson notes, "nothing trailblazing." Playing safe with a fledgling technology, it employs 35,000 sq ft of steel flat-plate liquid collectors and water storage. Two centrifugal chillers needed for cooling serve as heat pumps to boost stored water temperature when it falls below the 100F required for the air-handling system. Back-up is provided by the domestic hot water boiler. In a typical insolation year, the system is expected to supply some 80 per cent of heating requirements.

The designers expect in addition a substantial bonus through use of the heat pumps to redistribute ambient heat gener-

Slope and framing of collector array supported by monitor structure is continued at main entrance by window wall which admits daylight to lobby and adjacent corridor-cum-"street" and, via a balconied light well, to a student lounge area below. Structure, exposed throughout, combines cast-in-place and precast concrete and concrete block. Precast double-tee roof framing members, supported elsewhere by beams, are carried at the monitor by massive concrete panels with sloping ends slotted to receive them.

Reginald Wade Richey

ated by people, lights and machinery, buttressed by a full gamut of heat-recovery devices. The resulting heavy heat traffic flow is directed by sophisticated control and monitoring instrumentation that Anderson and Bridgers agree is the *sine qua non* of successful system operation.

Anderson further stresses the thermal "buttoning-up" of the building as the essential point of departure for solar heating.

Particularly stringent constraints were imposed by a curriculum weighted heavily to occupational education.

On the south, flanking the main entrance, are single-story units housing shops whose requirements for loading access and heavy equipment loads mandated their placement on grade. On the north a parallel element, two stories stair-stepping to three, contains additional academic spaces, with administrative, service and support areas.

Linking the two is a 28-ft-wide central spine that serves as a continuous interior street running the length of the building, and doubles as a buffer isolating the noise and vibration of the shops from areas opposite. Its elevated roof, angled at 53 degrees on the north side, provides surface support for the north bank of solar collectors and encloses eight fan rooms containing the bulk of the building's air handling equipment. The 10-in.-thick precast panels that span the monitor section at each bay transmit lateral loads across discontinuous roof diaphragms to concrete block shear walls. Where not occupied by fan rooms, the elevated monitor provides clerestory light and dramatic vertical space to the wide "places in the road" that punctuate the structure's length and serve as student gathering places.

But it is the use of the "unused" areas of the highly—and multi—functional monitor to create the building's soaring, climactic spaces that perhaps best exemplifies Anderson's efforts to add spice without resort to prettifying or pretense.

Portholes on north wall of monitor supplement lighting from industrial-style fixtures in cafeteria area—the campus's Great Hall. Repeated in transverse panels, portholes minimize their bulk visually as well as physically.

Freestanding collectors are supported by steel frames every 9 ft and by a space-frame section (above and left) spanning 84 ft. Frames are anchored to double tees with flanges beefed up to handle wind loads.

Skylit, barn-red "silos" at building ends form playful enclosures for access stairs to roof between monitor and south bank of collectors. Indented circle on end facade of monitor echoes interior porthole motif.

Famolare Headquarters
Brattleboro, Vermont

FAMOLARE HEADQUARTERS, Brattleboro, Vermont. Owner: *Famolare Inc.* Architects: *Banwell, White & Arnold.* Consulting engineers: *R.D. Kimball (mechanical/electrical); Carroll Lawes (structural).* Solar consultant: *A.O. Converse.* General contractor: *O'Bryan Construction Co., Inc.*

The positive effect of pleasant work space on worker productivity and morale has not been lost on Joe Famolare, the exacting president of Famolare Shoes Inc. When Famolare decided to move operations from leased warehouse space in New Jersey to the mountains of Vermont, he requested attractive work space with a sharp eye kept on energy consumption.

After preliminary designs for an elaborate high-technology solar collector system were declared not cost-effective, the architects created a passive solar system for the new headquarters, using sun scoops, skylights, and special window shutters to take

Robert Perron photos

maximum advantage of natural light and sun.

Set amid farms in mountainous Vermont, the office building is topped by a large sun scoop yawning open to the south. Manually-adjusted fiberglass panels bounce sun into the scoop in winter, flooding the offices with light, and are turned to deflect sun in summer. Several smaller skylights brighten showroom areas of the office building and movable fiberglass panels hung inside the skylights can be used to deflect sun.

A system of monitors on the adjoining warehouse roof admits sun in winter for direct solar gain, and excludes sun in summer by use of overhangs. The monitors provide sufficient warehouse lighting about 80 per cent of the time; high-pressure sodium fixtures are used only in recessed areas or on overcast winter days.

Office building windows on the south are fitted inside with special sliding shutters of translucent fiberglass. The shutters are closed when the building is unoccupied to insulate the glass, and are used to exclude direct sun from offices facing south. When the shutters are closed, solar-heated air in the space between the shutter and window is collected and transferred in winter to the north side of the building. The window shutter system is estimated, conservatively, to reduce the building's heating and air conditioning load by 10-15 per cent annually.

To encourage communication between the office and warehouse personnel, even in harsh Vermont winters, a suspended tunnel of bronze-tinted acrylic plastic is used to connect the buildings. Heated air in the tunnel is collected for circulation throughout the rest of the building.

Energy conserving measures extend to the use of 6-inch thick fiberglass insulation in the office building walls, and an insulation of 2.35-inch thick isocyanurate foam board in the roof. Task-ambient lighting in the offices is designed to use only 2.2 Watts per sq ft.

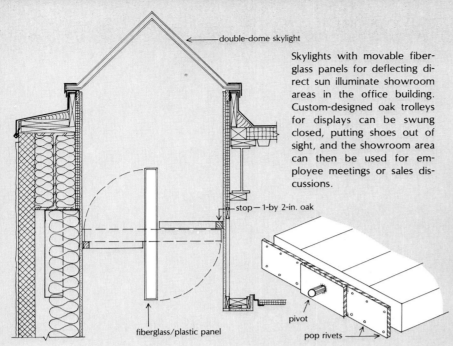

double-dome skylight

stop—1-by 2-in. oak

fiberglass/plastic panel

pivot

pop rivets

Skylights with movable fiber-glass panels for deflecting direct sun illuminate showroom areas in the office building. Custom-designed oak trolleys for displays can be swung closed, putting shoes out of sight, and the showroom area can then be used for employee meetings or sales discussions.

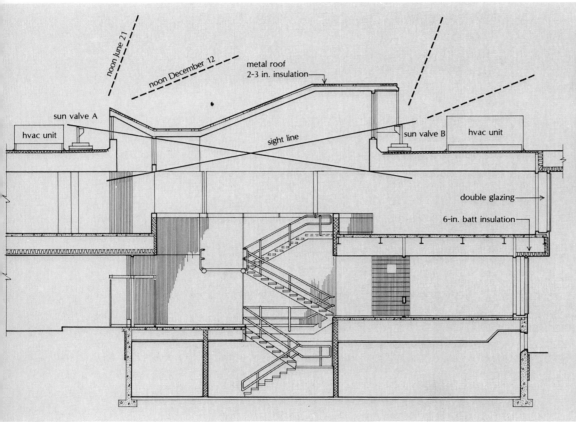

noon June 21

noon December 12

metal roof 2-3 in. insulation

sun valve A

hvac unit

sun valve B

hvac unit

sight line

double glazing

6-in. batt insulation

Movable rooftop panels (called "sun valves" by solar consultant Professor A.O. Converse of Dartmouth) tip sun through a large scoop into the office building, creating a bright center well and airy open office space (photo below far right). Hvac units on the roof near the scoop are placed so as to be out of sight from inside the building.

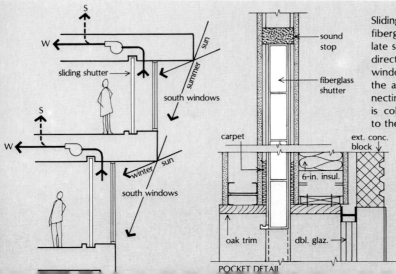

S

W

sliding shutter

south windows

summer sun

S

W

winter sun

south windows

sound stop

fiberglass shutter

carpet

6-in. insul.

ext. conc. block

oak trim

dbl. glaz.

POCKET DETAIL

Sliding shutters of translucent fiberglass trimmed in oak insulate south windows and block direct sun. Heated air between windows and shutters, and in the acrylic plastic tunnel connecting office and warehouse, is collected and redistributed to the north side.

Robert Perron photos

Memorial Station
Houston, Texas

MEMORIAL STATION, Houston, Texas. Owner: *U.S. Postal Service—Bill Wright, Gordon Steger, John Wright, liaison.* Architects: *Clovis Heimsath Associates—Ray Wobbe, project architect; Harold Carlson, supervising architect.* Engineers: Nat Krahl & Associates (structural); Timmerman Engineers, Inc. (mechanical). *Contractor: Westpark Construction Company.*

Because this postal facility is in a large shopping center visible from the Southwest Freeway in Houston, thought of by many as the energy capital of the country, and because he was encouraged by the Postal Service to stress energy conservation, architect Clovis Heimsath felt that the inclusion of a solar system would be an appropriate symbol, and that patriotic colors would provide an appropriate palette.

Two major considerations dominated the design: First, only off-the-shelf technology could be considered for solar because the building had to be kept on schedule. Secondly, the solar system was possible from cost and size standpoints only through substantial reduction in load derived from energy-conservation techniques. These included: 1) reducing makeup air; 2) zoning spaces so the workroom could be substantially closed down much of the workday; 3) facing all glass north, and using it only for the lockbox lobby; 4) using a square plan to reduce exterior wall area; 5) using mercury HID lamps for the workroom; 6) using insulated metal wall roof panels to reduce heat flow.

By saving money on the building exterior and simplifying every element of design, including exposing the structure, lights and ducts, the designers could afford the additional first cost of solar, while still bringing in the building at about $40 per sq ft (less site) which was under budget. Premium for the solar energy addition was $130,000 (using a central station water-cooled-condenser system for comparison). With a $6,144 per year estimated operating cost savings, the payback at current energy costs would be 21 years. Projected increases in energy costs would reduce this payback to nine years. The solar collector system is designed to provide 80 per cent of the cooling requirements.

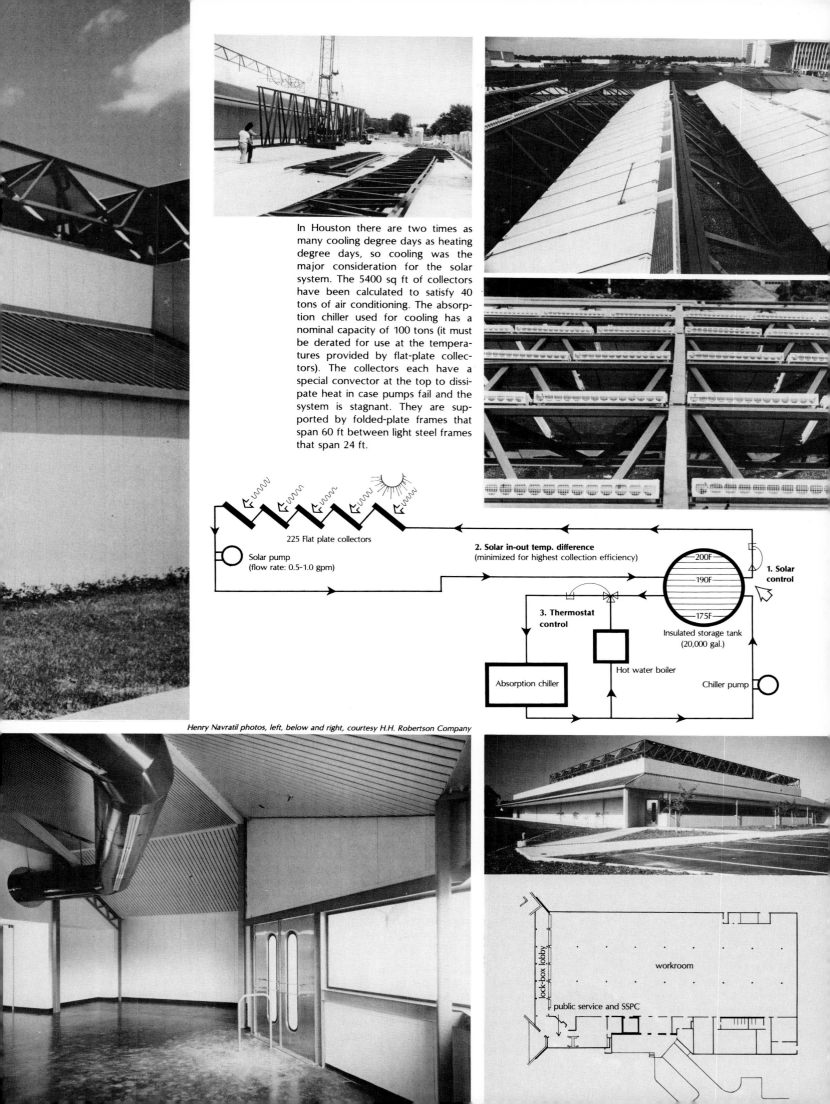

In Houston there are two times as many cooling degree days as heating degree days, so cooling was the major consideration for the solar system. The 5400 sq ft of collectors have been calculated to satisfy 40 tons of air conditioning. The absorption chiller used for cooling has a nominal capacity of 100 tons (it must be derated for use at the temperatures provided by flat-plate collectors). The collectors each have a special convector at the top to dissipate heat in case pumps fail and the system is stagnant. They are supported by folded-plate frames that span 60 ft between light steel frames that span 24 ft.

225 Flat plate collectors

Solar pump
(flow rate: 0.5-1.0 gpm)

2. Solar in-out temp. difference
(minimized for highest collection efficiency)

1. Solar control

200F
190F
175F

Insulated storage tank
(20,000 gal.)

3. Thermostat control

Hot water boiler

Absorption chiller

Chiller pump

Henry Navratil photos, left, below and right, courtesy H.H. Robertson Company

lock-box lobby

workroom

public service and SSPC

Armed Forces Reserve Center Norwich, Connecticut

ARMED FORCES RESERVE CENTER, Norwich, Connecticut. Owner: *State of Connecticut Department of Public Works and Connecticut Military Department—Major General John F. Freund.* Architects: *Moore Grover Harper, PC—Robert L. Harper, William H. Grover, Glenn W. Arbonies, Jefferson B. Riley, Charles W. Moore.* Engineers: *Besier and Gibble (structural); Helenski Associates (mechanical).* Consultants: *Arthur D. Little Company (solar).* Contractor: *F. W. Brown Co.*

It is clear upon examining this armory in eastern Connecticut that, when architects stop to think about it, energy-conserving features can evolve as a very natural part of building design. Here Moore Grover Harper have disposed spaces naturally by function and size in a way that assists energy conservation, and that leads to logical application of both active and passive solar heating techniques. For instance, the main building steps up in three tiers, allowing logical placement of solar collectors overhanging three walls so they act as sunshades in summer. And at the far corner, the architects, in a droll step, designed a quoined tower that heralds the entrance while also serving as a chimney.

Both the State of Connecticut (which financed 25 per cent of the project and pays the operating costs) and the military wanted energy-conserving techniques, including so-

lar. The 10-acre site in Norwich Industrial Park was selected because it was clear of trees to the south, but had woods on the north to serve as a windbreak. The project comprises an Armory Building with offices, drill shed, classrooms and rifle range and a separate Organization Maintenance Shop (OMS) for vehicle maintenance and repair. Because the offices and OMS building are in continuous use, while the drill hall and ancillary spaces are used only occasionally, the solar-heating systems are functionally separate. Only the office-section solar system utilizes storage (a 2000-gal. tank). The two other systems for the armory and for the OMS building feed directly to air-handling units.

The project cost $1,459,147 of which solar heating systems cost $88,489 and other energy-saving components, $54,600. It was 25 per cent under budget.

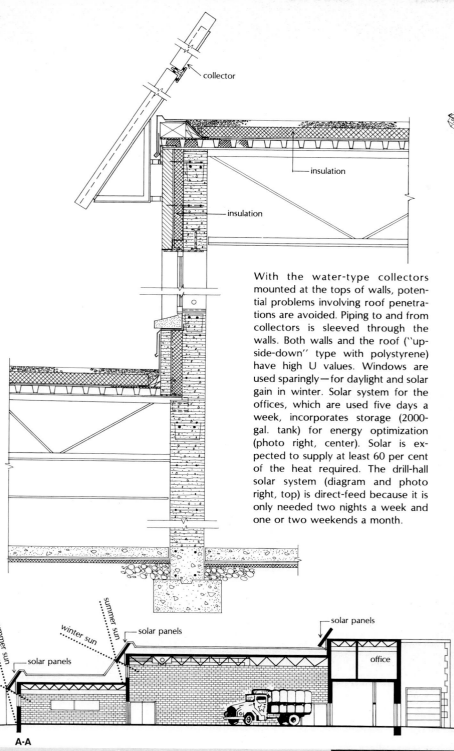

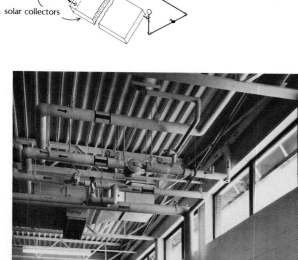

With the water-type collectors mounted at the tops of walls, potential problems involving roof penetrations are avoided. Piping to and from collectors is sleeved through the walls. Both walls and the roof (''upside-down'' type with polystyrene) have high U values. Windows are used sparingly—for daylight and solar gain in winter. Solar system for the offices, which are used five days a week, incorporates storage (2000-gal. tank) for energy optimization (photo right, center). Solar is expected to supply at least 60 per cent of the heat required. The drill-hall solar system (diagram and photo right, top) is direct-feed because it is only needed two nights a week and one or two weekends a month.

Norman McGrath photos

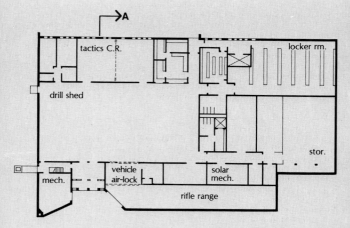

Ventilation load is reduced by air locks at entrances. An overhead door at the rifle range and one at the drill shed perform this function for vehicular movement. Temperature is allowed to float in the drill shed when it is not in use: heat is added when it drops below 50F, and exhaust fans go on above 75F. The masonry walls act as thermal storage.

Alabama Power Company District Office
Montevallo, Alabama

ALABAMA POWER COMPANY DISTRICT OFFICE, Montevallo, Alabama. Owner: *Alabama Power Company*. Architects: *Cobbs/Adams/Benton—Doyle L. Cobb, principal; Aubrey Garrison III, project architect.* Engineers: *Miller & Weaver, Inc. (mechanical); Cater & Parks, Inc. (electrical).* Consultant: *Vachon & Nix, Inc. (solar).* Contractor: *Andrew & Dawson.*

In their design of a 17,000-sq-ft office building near Birmingham for the Alabama Power Company, an energy-conservation demonstration project for the utility, the architects discovered not only that saving fossil fuels was not as forbidding as they had first thought, but also that they could develop a new esthetic in the process.

From a planning standpoint, the building was skewed at the front end of its long, narrow site so there would be room for a pedestrian plaza and for visitor parking, and so that the rear of the site where company vehicles are parked would be blocked from

view. The 2½-floor building has spaces for operation/marketing, accounting, display/auditorium and appliance repair.

With the building oriented so that the long wall faces directly south the rooftop solar collectors could be mounted parallel with the front. To keep sun from entering, however, was a challenge for the architects which they solved through a study of overhang and vertical-fin configurations, and with an awning for the entrance. The building was selected by ERDA (DOE) as one of the first 32 projects to be funded by the Solar Demonstration Act of 1975.

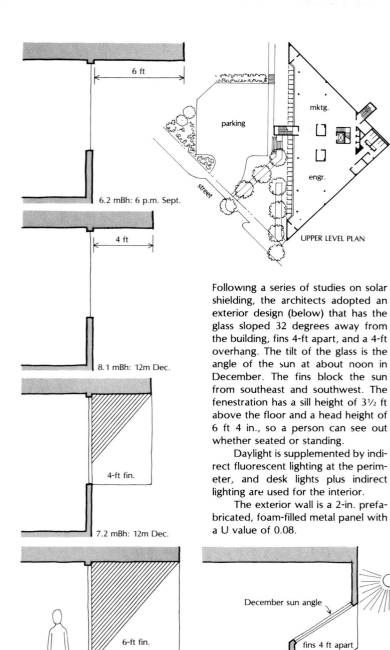

6 ft

6.2 mBh: 6 p.m. Sept.

4 ft

8.1 mBh: 12m Dec.

4-ft fin.

7.2 mBh: 12m Dec.

6-ft fin.

5.1 mBh: 4 p.m. July

parking

street

mktg.

engr.

UPPER LEVEL PLAN

December sun angle

fins 4 ft apart

FINAL DESIGN
.08 U-factor

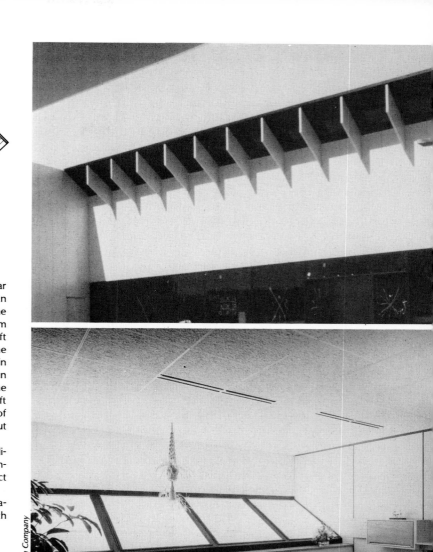

Following a series of studies on solar shielding, the architects adopted an exterior design (below) that has the glass sloped 32 degrees away from the building, fins 4-ft apart, and a 4-ft overhang. The tilt of the glass is the angle of the sun at about noon in December. The fins block the sun from southeast and southwest. The fenestration has a sill height of 3½ ft above the floor and a head height of 6 ft 4 in., so a person can see out whether seated or standing.

Daylight is supplemented by indirect fluorescent lighting at the perimeter, and desk lights plus indirect lighting are used for the interior.

The exterior wall is a 2-in. prefabricated, foam-filled metal panel with a U value of 0.08.

Henry Navratil photo, courtesy H. H. Robertson Company

The solar-assisted system comprises 2500 sq ft of flat-plate collectors using a black chrome finish, an 8000-gal. hot water storage tank, a nominal 25-ton absorption chiller, inert gas freeze-protection system, and control and data-monitoring equipment. To enhance the efficiency of the collectors for cooling, which are mounted at 30 deg., the system has 8-ft-high front mirrors set at 45 deg., and top mirrors, 2-ft high. Standby heating (100 per cent) is provided by an electric boiler. Solar cooling is available when the solar water temperature is above 170F. The remaining time, a 30-ton reciprocating water chiller is utilized which has an 8000-gal. tank, sized for offpeak storage of chilled water. Freeze protection is accomplished by draining the collectors and replacing the water with nitrogen gas. Premium for the solar was about $170,000.

Granville W. Elder Station (North Shore) Houston, Texas

GRANVILLE W. ELDER STATION (NORTH SHORE), Houston, Texas. Owner: *U.S. Postal Service—Bill Wright, Gordon Steger, John Wright, liaison.* Architects: *Clovis Heimsath Associates—design/production: Clovis Heimsath, Emmett White, Ray Wobbe, Jerry Mendehall, Harold Carlson.* Interiors: *Lacey Flagg.* Engineers: *Nat Krahl & Associates (structural); Timmerman Engineers, Inc. (mechanical).* Contractor: *Capellen Construction Company.*

When architects Clovis Heimsath Associates were commissioned to design a postal service facility for a rapidly developing area northeast of Houston, they were urged to make this a cost study in energy-saving opportunities. For the resulting building, the architects and their engineers predict an energy savings of close to 40 per cent plus a reduction in cooling demand of 39 per cent, when compared with a "baseline building model." They developed the baseline building from a plan type of the U.S. Postal Service and from its design guidelines. Systems specified by the Postal Service for this size building in Houston are air-cooled electric compression refrigeration and electric resistance heating.

Importantly too, the architects have achieved operational efficiencies in the layout of the facility, a more efficient lookout gallery, and much more pleasant spaces for the workers and customers.

The largest savings (16 per cent, of which 60 per cent is power for lights, and 40 per cent power for cooling) resulted from using improved-color mercury HID lighting in the workroom, and by shutting off some lights in the carriers' sorting area which are not needed for two-thirds of the time.

The next largest savings (10 per cent) came from ventilating the locker room and toilets with exhaust air from the workroom. Another 8 per cent was lopped off the baseline building by reducing the U value of the roof from 0.12 to 0.06 and the walls from 0.20 to 0.07. Savings were less for changes in fenestration, inasmuch as there was not much glass in the baseline building. Nonetheless, glass is used much more effectively here. All windows face north in sawtooth fashion along the lockbox lobby, and at the clerestory above the workroom, giving a more pleasant space plus daylight.

scale

vending

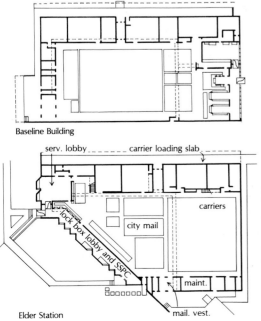

Baseline Building

serv. lobby   carrier loading slab

lock box lobby and SSPC

carriers

city mail

maint.

mail. vest.

Elder Station

Courtesy Butler Manufacturing Company

Arts Village
Hampshire College
Amherst, Massachusetts

ARTS VILLAGE, HAMPSHIRE COLLEGE, Amherst, Massachusetts. Owner: *Trustees of Hampshire College.* Architects: *Juster Pope Associates.* Consultants: *Cosentini Associates (mechanical engineering); Joseph Frissora (energy).* Landscape architect: *V. Michael Weinmayr.* Construction manager: *Edward J. O'Leary Co., Inc.*

High performance tubular solar collectors form graceful blue-canopied walkways linking simple but tastefully-detailed buildings of pre-engineered components in this new Arts Village at Hampshire College.

Architects for what eventually will be a five-building arts complex at the experimental college wanted the solar system to serve the entire complex, despite a phased construction schedule. At the same time, they wanted to incorporate the solar system as a major design feature of the complex in order to put the sometimes obtrusive collectors back in proportion to the buildings. Consequently, the rows of all-glass, selectively-coated evacuated tubular collectors were transformed into a string of canopies on a bright blue steel structure between buildings. The result was a functional but clean "environmental sculpture" overhead and large sheltered building walkways below.

The design solution solved several practical problems of building with the solar elements as well. Moving the collectors from building roofs eliminated extra load which could have prohibited use of the simple buildings of pre-engineered components, and allowed use of a standing-seam metal roof system.

The solar system, made possible largely by a $355,000 Federal grant, is expected to supply 95 per cent of the complex's cooling needs, 65 per cent of the space heating requirements, and all domestic hot water. Coordination of the solar system is done by a microprocessor. Additional energy not supplied by solar will be obtained from a central electric boiler in the complex.

Because of the build-as-funded nature of the project, and the need for flexible work space that could change with curriculum and teaching techniques, the architects used understated but well-detailed pre-engineered building components that are complemented with landscaping and the solar canopies.

Two of the five buildings have been completed to date, with the Painting Studio taking just 10 months from design to occupation, and the Music and Dance building requiring a similar construction timetable.

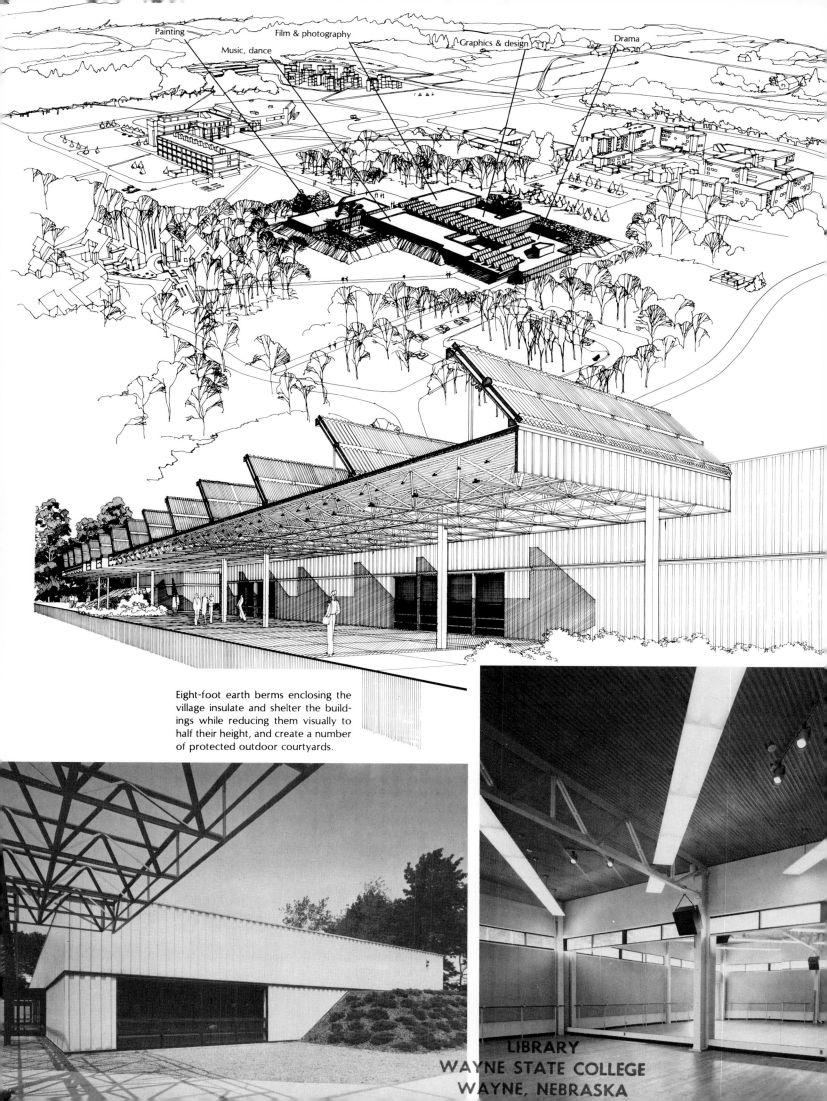

Painting

Music, dance

Film & photography

Graphics & design

Drama

Eight-foot earth berms enclosing the village insulate and shelter the buildings while reducing them visually to half their height, and create a number of protected outdoor courtyards.

SOME HISTORY: THE WORK OF PIONEERING ENGINEER FRANK BRIDGERS IN MAKING EFFECTIVE USE OF SOLAR ENERGY

Energy saving in buildings can be accomplished in design via brute-force techniques or finesse. The brute-force route is simple: use less lighting, less glass; reduce optimum temperature levels, etc. For the mechanical and electrical engineer, and the lighting designer, the finesse route means bringing to bear a greater depth and breadth of knowledge, putting in more time for investigation of alternatives for design (which the client should pay for), and embarking upon projects with some courage and conviction—and with the attitude that husbanding energy resources is the engineer's responsibility along with the architect's and the owner's.

Frank Bridgers of Bridgers & Paxton, consulting mechanical engineers of Albuquerque, has always had a deep interest and belief in energy-conserving systems—and his interest predates the start of his firm in 1951. Some of his interest undoubtedly stems from his graduate engineering work with F.W. Hutch-

Albuquerque, New Mexico, site of the Bridgers & Paxton office building, has a maximum of solar radiation in the winter—so it was an ideal situation to try out the concept. The building shape reflects an optimized angle for the collectors. The system includes storage and a heat pump for cooling as well as heating.

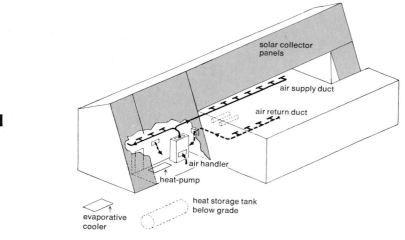

Frank Bridgers, past-president of ASHRAE, has been energy-conscious since he started his practice over 20 years ago. His own office building was designed for solar heating, and he is consultant for the largest solar-heating system proposed so far. He also has sought ways to make beneficial use of the sun that normally gets into buildings. His work exemplifies what competent, conscientious engineers can do by imaginatively using technical resources already at hand. This article is a profile of his work and attitudes. It also examines the implications of government response to the energy crisis.

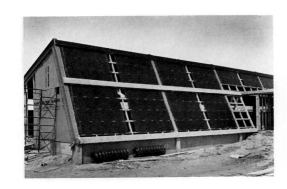

inson at Purdue University, who pioneered early mathematical analysis for radiant heating panel design; and also from his early experience in the consulting engineering firm of the late Charles S. Leopold of Philadelphia—who designed some of the earliest commercial installations of radiant-panel heating and radiant-panel cooling, and also the earliest test installations of water-cooled lighting fixtures.

Bridgers' concern with heating efficiency predates the energy crisis by 20 years

A reflection of Bridger's interest in energy conservation is the firm's own office building, designed in 1954 to use solar collectors for space heating. One whole side of the building was covered with solar collectors, and sloped for optimum solar energy recovery. A packaged water chiller, used for air-conditioning in summer is used as a heat pump during the heating season, combined as a system with the solar collectors and an underground storage tank. If heat from the sun is inadequate on cloudy or very cold days, heat is drawn from the stored water.

The building has been instrumented by Dr. Stanley Gilman of The Pennsylvania State University through a National Science Foundation grant, and data are being developed by Bridgers and Gilman to provide application guidance for other engineers.

Bridgers also was one of the first engineers in the country to design a heat-pump system for a high-rise office building—with the main objective being to pick up heat from one side of the building that required cooling and transferring it to another calling for heating.

Furthermore, the system included radiant heating-cooling panels in the perimeter ceiling and under the windows to reduce air-conditioning supply-air requirements—which was aided further by the novel sill air-return arrangement that helped minimize heat-transmission effect through the glass into the occupied space.

Since then, Bridgers has done a number of internal-source heat-pump designs, including the use of large unitary (packaged) water-cooled air conditioners in a school that pulled heat from the interior in cold weather and utilized it on the perimeter where heat is needed. Bridgers has shown that larger-size, heavy-duty package air conditioners up to 60 tons in refrigeration capacity may offer an attractive alternative to central chilled-water-plant systems. He has also done a number of buildings with large central-plant, internal-source heat pumps—giving special attention to some of the idiosyncracies of refrigeration-plant design that can cause operational difficulties—particularly with respect to the method of heat rejection from the chiller's condenser.

1954

In the Simms Building in Albuquerque, Bridgers designed an air-return system that captures some of the sun's heat and delivers it to a heat-pump system that redistributes the heat in winter to the cold side. Radiant heating-cooling panels, tied in with a solar compensator control, reduce air-conditioning air-supply requirements. The panels provide perimeter heat on the north side in winter, and on the south side when there is no sun. Well water is available as a standby if there is not enough solar energy or internal heat.

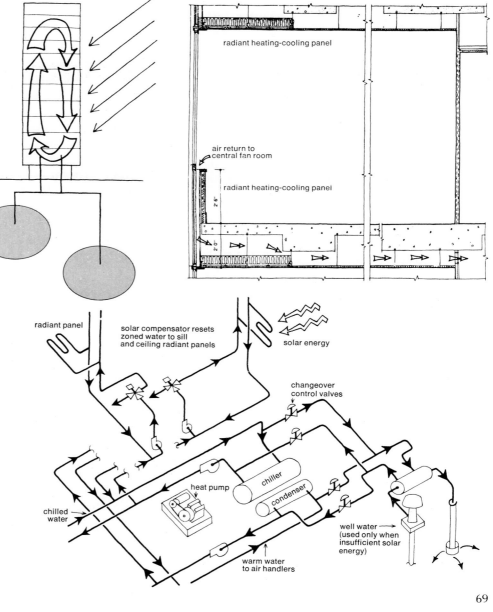

radiant heating-cooling panel

air return to central fan room

radiant heating-cooling panel

radiant panel

solar compensator resets zoned water to sill and ceiling radiant panels

solar energy

changeover control valves

heat pump

chiller

condenser

chilled water

warm water to air handlers

well water (used only when insufficient solar energy)

Benefits from solar energy are possible in both ordinary and special buildings

Frank Bridgers looks at the beneficial utilization of solar energy from two different standpoints: 1) use of solar collectors to pick up heat directly or indirectly from the sun's rays; and 2) controlling the sun's heat that manages to penetrate the building's glass. He was recently involved in the design of one of the largest solar-collecting systems for space heating application yet to be used—Denver Community College. One of the practical problems he had to deal with was how to prevent the freezing of the collectors at night. The solution was to provide an anti-freeze loop for the collector circuit only, with a heat exchanger to transfer heat to the solar storage tank. Although this solution reduces the efficiency of heat transfer to some extent, the operation and maintenance problem of venting air from a large amount of collection piping everyday

in winter would be a less practical solution. Bridgers points out that the technology of solar collection has changed little in 25 years; but, on the other hand, engineering data for design, the collectors themselves, and economic feasibility are changing.

Beneficial utilization of transmitted solar energy has been an integral part of the mechanical-system design of several office buildings Bridgers has been involved with. What has to be stressed in the future, he says, is a proper concern with building orientation, combined with carefully chosen (or designed) interior and exterior shading or sun control to make it possible not just to limit or reject solar radiation in summer, but also to "capture" it in wintertime.

The more dedicated engineers, such as Frank Bridgers, continually strive to improve upon their past designs, to broaden their background expertise, and to investigate new approaches involving a wider range of design

solutions. Furthermore, they put together highly-qualified engineering "teams" that get in-depth direction from a highly-qualified principal of the firm. Characteristically, the principals and chief associates of such firms have high educational qualifications—formal or otherwise—combined with broad practical design, installation, and field-testing expertise on a wide range of systems and equipment.

Bridgers has considered active technical and administrative participation in the American Society of Heating, Refrigeration and Air Conditioning Engineers—the consulting engineers' primary technical society—to be an important responsibility. Furthermore, his educational-engineering background has made him particularly aware of the value of basic fundamental data developed by ASHRAE. Designing a system that is *practical* is always uppermost in Frank Bridgers' approach, and some of the specific elements of that approach follow.

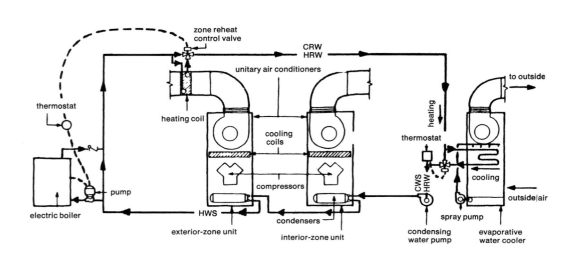

1968

Bridgers conceived the idea of using packaged unitary air conditioners for both heating and cooling in low-rise buildings with large interior areas. The interior units in cooling pick up heat and transfer it to exterior units. A boiler makes up any deficit in heat, and an evaporative water cooler rejects excess heat.
The approach is best for buildings with adequate space for low-pressure ductwork.

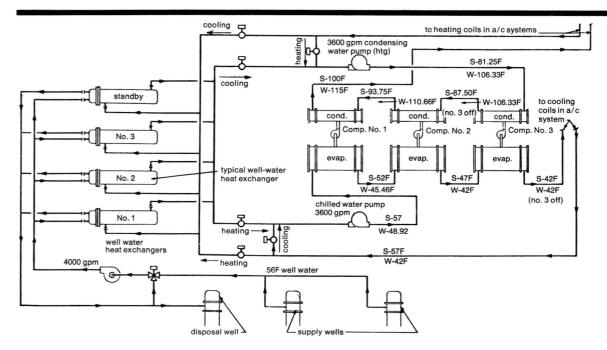

1972

This large (2500-ton) heat-pump system for the huge, high-rise LDS office tower in Salt Lake City uses well water as a source. At times internal heat will balance external load of the building. When more heat is required it can get it from the well water. If, on the other hand, there is excess heat, it is rejected to the well water. Use of separate heat exchangers avoids potential corrosion problems from well water.

Innovation can be made practical by using standard equipment packages

Bridgers' guideline to design for practical innovation include:

1) Use standard production-line equipment packages, combined with manufacturers' standard options—as proven by field experience. The component selection and arrangement and the piping design in a refrigeration system are critical. Use of other than standard "matched-performance-package" configurations can be troublesome and costly, and can limit bidding. This caution, to some extent, applies to centrifugal chiller heat pump systems employing double-bundle condensers because of the complexities in evaluations for stability of operation at the lower heating-load conditions they encounter;

2) Don't ask for custom features with which the manufacturer has not had experience. Rather, analyze the detailed performance of standard heating-cooling packages to see how they might be used in new and unique systems to improve over-all efficiencies;

3) When applying standard packages in new systems, think through the over-all system including: a) pipe and duct system dynamics, b) heat-exchange options and limiting factors, c) selection of control-system elements and their over-all coordination—perhaps the most essential element to ensure that the hvac system will perform as designed;

4) With unique systems, make sure the contractor is guided in terms of start-up, balancing, testing, and adjustment of the system. This means the consulting engineer must have experienced and knowledgeable engineers in these areas;

5) Optimize duct and piping system design and fan selection to achieve an optimum balance between first cost and operating cost of the heating and air conditioning system.

1978

Denver Community College has one of the largest solar heating systems in the country. The architects, ABR Partnership of Denver, favored the approach because it is pollution-free, would not be affected by the shortage or cost of natural gas, and because the climate of Denver is ideal for a solar system. There are 35,000 square feet of collector surface tilted at 53 degrees from the horizontal. Solar-heated water is stored in 200,000-gallon-capacity tanks underground. If the sun heats it to over 100 F it is used directly, if not, a heat pump system adds supplementary heat to raise it to 100 F.

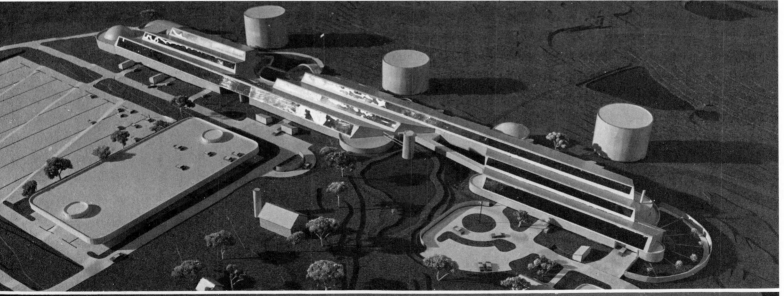

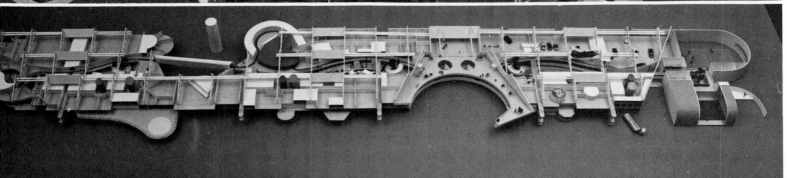

Frank Bridgers has been putting solar energy to good use, including the preparation of a design procedure for a solar-assisted heat pump systems for the National Science Foundation and ERDA. To validate the procedure, the solar system in the Bridgers and Paxton office building (below) was revamped and highly instrumented to get the kinds of data needed. The information was sent over leased wires to Penn State, where Professor Stanley Gilman plugged it into a computer model of the Bridgers and Paxton system. This article describes what Bridgers and Gilman are doing.

Frank Bridgers' comment that he has had more inquiries about solar heating in the last few years than in previous decades is hardly surprising. What is different about now and 30 years ago, when Bridgers and Paxton built their own solar building, is the escalated cost of energy, for one thing, and the considerable dollar backing for solar-energy research by the Federal government, for another. Of the 138 solar-heated buildings reported by William A. Shurcliff in his May 1975 survey,* nearly 100 of them were initiated after 1970. As might be expected, most of the buildings are houses, though several schools and office buildings are listed in this survey.

Solar-heated buildings that work well have been and are being constructed. Technology is not the basic question. The question, really, is how do the economics work out? Solar-heated buildings are capital-intensive because solar radiation is "low-level" energy. Large areas of collectors have to be provided to collect it, and some means has to be provided to store it to make up for nights and cold, cloudy daytime weather. Even so, solar-heated buildings are competitive now with conventionally heated ones at present energy costs when there is low-interest financing, as with

*Solar Heated Buildings, A Brief Survey, ninth edition, W. A. Shurcliff, Cambridge, Massachusetts.

Data from a weather station and from instrumented equipment in the Bridgers and Paxton building is acquired by computer and sent to Penn State for analysis.

public buildings. The really tough question is what is going to happen to the cost of electricity, gas and oil in the next 10 years. In 1973, engineer Bridgers estimated a 300 per cent increase in the cost of natural gas by 1990, and a 125 per cent increase in the cost of electricity. Now, he views these figures as very conservative.

Though the completeness and accuracy of weather data (solar and temperature) leaves a lot to be desired; though there is no commonly accepted design procedure (right now) for solar-heated buildings; and though, strictly speaking, the economics are far from simple, still a pretty good evaluation can be made of owning costs for solar-energy systems right now. The costs of owning a solar heating system include the amortization of the collector, the storage unit, the pumps and piping (or fans and ducting), and the cost of associated controls. Frank Bridgers reports that the increase in construction cost for buildings with solar-assisted heat pumps in the Mountain States is about 10 per cent for large commercial buildings, and about 20 per cent for small commercial buildings and for houses. A $60,000 house, then, would cost $72,000 with solar heating. Operating costs include the power for pumping fluid or moving air in the system, and maintenance of the system including any repairs to the collectors.

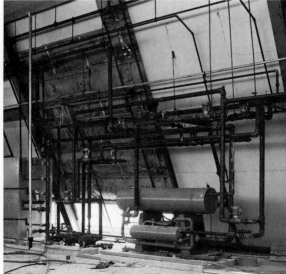

One of the major cost items for a solar-energy system is that of the collectors. Some published economic studies on houses have used collector costs under $10 per sq. ft. Yet, bids based upon a performance specification—received in 1975 by Bridgers and Paxton on Collectors for a 25,000-sq-ft building at New Mexico State University—ranged to $22 per sq ft. Though there are several well-known companies making collectors, most of the 60-some companies in the field are small—which means they have no mass-production capability. However, the market still has to justify mass production.

Bridgers feels that the only way there will be a serious market is if the government requires solar systems on their buildings wherever technically feasible. A market can then be developed on the basis of low-interest appropriated funds. If collector costs come down, then, he says, the private sector might get interested.

Automatic controls for the solar energy system are a significant premium cost over the controls required for conventional systems. The proper control system is very important, says engineer Bridgers, and he emphasizes that the consulting engineer must work with his peer at the controls company who will understand what the consultant is trying to accomplish.

In an energy-supply study for a major new town now under construction in South Carolina, consulting engineers Flack and Kurtz recommended that only heating of domestic hot water by solar collectors be investigated for direct use of solar energy. They also suggested that use of water-to-air heat pumps using sun-heated water from a pond through a secondary water piping system (serving fire protection, lawn sprinklering, etc.) might have economic merit.

Integration of solar systems and architecture is achievable

By now, most architects realize that a large area is required for the collector. Many recent designs and proposals exhibit skillful handling of this problem. In the hands of a good architect, the design can be both attractive and interesting.

An excellent example of a building in which the solar-collector system is well integrated into the building fabric is the design for the Shiprock Comprehen-

sive Health Facility in Shiprock, New Mexico (see page 77). The building is a major addition to an existing facility and was designed with a 150-bed inpatient capacity, expansible to 210 beds, and with complete outpatient facilities. The facility, designed by architects Flatow, Moore, Bryan, and Fairburn, is owned and operated by the Indian Health Service, a branch of HEW. Consulting mechanical engineer was Bridgers and Paxton.

A grant from ERDA (Energy Research and Development Administration) covers the additional cost of design, construction and installation of the solar energy plant, i.e., above the normal cost of a conventional heating plant. The IHS gets a heating system that will save energy and costs, and ERDA will be able to use the facility as a "test vehicle."

The original central plant did not have sufficient capacity for the addition, although there was enough steam available for sterilizing and for domestic hot water. Whenever the temperature of the solar storage tank drops below 60F, heat from the domestic water system is taken to elevate the temperature during nighttime only, when the requirement for domestic hot water is very low.

The various bed wings (surgical patients, children, postnatal, etc.) are square in shape and tipped on corners in relation to a long corridor. This corridor, which prevents congested and undesirable circulation through the wings, serves advantageously as a location for solar collectors.

Architects Burt, Hill & Associates suggest that if space heating

and domestic hot-water heating are the principal solar-system requirements, it is desirable to tilt collectors to favor the wintertime sun angles. This is done by adjusting the tilt from the horizontal to an angle from between 10 and 20 degrees added to the degrees of latitude. Thus in the Southwest, the collector tilt might be between 50 and 60 degrees.

If solar cooling is the primary consideration, then the latitude minus 10 to 20 degrees would tend to maximize collection during summer months. The firm notes that collector tilt is more sensitive in the higher latitudes, and that, in some instances, a vertical wall collector would not be out of the question.

Solar cooling takes more collector area and hotter water

When a building requires cooling,

the heat pump, of course, operates like a conventional air conditioner, rejecting its heat to an evaporative cooler or to a cooling tower. And running the compressor takes electrical energy. So for this reason, solar cooling with absorption refrigeration arouses interest.

Absorption refrigeration uses lithium bromide salt solution or aqueous ammonia solution to create an evaporative effect that results in cooling. As these solutions become more dilute in the receiver, they have to be reconcentrated in the generator by means of heat so that the process can continue. This usually is accomplished using steam or high-temperature water over 200F.

Some investigators have examined the potentialities of ab-

sorption refrigeration cooling in the heat generation range of 140F to 180F, considering the use of flatplate solar collectors. The coefficients of performance are reduced, and particularly, the capacities of available equipment are a great deal lower than when the heating source is 200F and higher. Capacity may be cut by 25 to 45 per cent of the rated capacity. If the temperatures are to be kept in the 200F plus range, then either a high-performance type collector is required, or an auxiliary energy source (a boiler) must be available to maintain the temperature.

Having to oversize an absorption refrigeration unit for a commercial or institutional building is not too important a factor, however, because refrigeration represents only about 10 per cent of the total hvac system cost. It would be more significant for a house, however, where the cooling unit would represent a higher fraction of the total.

The engineering analysis of a solar design for a 25,000-sq-ft building at New Mexico State University by Bridgers and Paxton showed that nearly three times as much solar collector area was needed for solar cooling as for heat-pump-assisted solar heating, and also a pressure-type water tank would be required for the higher-temperature water.

Frank Bridgers has said that solar cooling should be considered when the cooling load is predominant, as in Texas and Arizona and Southeastern states. Where the building is above 35 degrees latitude, and the heating load is significant, he feels that the heat-pump assisted solar system is the most economical.

Flat-plate solar collectors can produce summer water temperatures of 180F or so, but achieving 200F or more is difficult, unless high-performance types are used. A high-performance collector is one using two sheets of glass over a non-selective black surface, or one using one or two sheets of glass over a selective surface. (A selective surface is one that has a high efficiency in absorbing solar radiation, but a low efficiency in re-radiating heat to the sky; in technical terms, a high absorptivity for solar radiation, and a low emissivity for low-temperature—200F—radiation.)

Corning has developed a high-performance tubular solar collector that incorporates a selectively-coated flat absorber plate housed within a highly evacuated

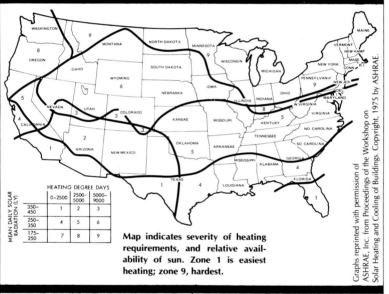

HEATING DEGREE DAYS

MEAN DAILY SOLAR RADIATION (LY)	0–2500	2500–5000	5000–9000
350–450	1	2	3
250–350	4	5	6
175–250	7	8	9

Map indicates severity of heating requirements, and relative availability of sun. Zone 1 is easiest heating; zone 9, hardest.

Graphs reprinted with permission of ASHRAE, Inc. from Proceedings of the Workshop on Solar Heating and Cooling of Buildings. Copyright, 1975 by ASHRAE.

glass tube. Corning says that working temperatures of 250F to 300F are possible with good efficiency. (With conventional flatplate collectors, heat losses increase greatly at higher temperatures because of edge and back losses.) The Corning collector is being produced in only limited quantities for experimental and demonstration purposes. Its cost now is about $20 per sq. ft.

Survey shows the public's interest is tempered with concern for cost
In their Phase O study for the RANN program of the National Science Foundation, the Special Systems division of Westinghouse Electric Corporation surveyed seven groups—architects, builders, labor, manufacturers, energy suppliers, financiers, and potential consumers—in regard to solar systems. Results indicated a broad spectrum of reaction, they say, ranging from interest and acceptance to skepticism. Following are some of their findings: Builder reaction ranged from skepticism to qualified acceptance. None is anxious to pioneer with an untried and unproven system.

Energy suppliers are the least enthusiastic. Their objections center on cost, complexity, and the constantly fluctuating demand on their services.

Manufacturers reacted quite favorably. Several said they were engaged in assessments of the feasibility of solar energy usage.

Consumers indicated a decreasing acceptability with increasing costs.

Architects favored considering all types of buildings in introducing solar heating and cooling.

Financiers believe that a solar supplement would have no direct or adverse effect on financing.

Environmentalists endorsed solar systems with some reservations concerning esthetics.

The Westinghouse group also noted that demonstration programs by the government can accelerate solar-system use, and they also can serve to help assess the extent that further government assistance will be necessary.

In its study for the same program, the TRW Systems Group suggested that a much more extensive effort is required to integrate the solar-system design with the building design in order to reduce the incremental capital costs.

TRW also states that the financial community must be educated to consider the operating savings associated with solar energy: "Unless the financial community recognizes the capital payback which results from lower operating costs, the market for solar energy will be restricted to the higher income segment of home buyers."

A new design procedure will be validated by data analysis
Because there are a number of uncertainties in the data available for the design of solar systems, engineers tend to be somewhat conservative in their approach. An example might be the provision of a larger water tank than experience might show to be necessary. In the past about the only measure of adequacy of a system was whether it met the load imposed upon it—or whether it didn't. Observations were made of storage water temperatures and the like, but instru-

mentation was meager, as was availability of correlated data.

For that reason, the National Science Foundation initiated a project (now being supported by ERDA) with The Pennsylvania State University, Bridgers and Paxton, consulting engineers, and the University of New Mexico for the development of a system design manual for solar-energy assisted heat pump systems that will be applicable to all geographical areas and all types of commercial and other non-residential buildings.

To do this, the Bridgers and Paxton office building in Albuquerque—the first commercial building to be solar heated (1956)—was taken as the test facility. The principal elements of the system for the 8,300-sq-ft building are: a 750-sq-ft solar col-

lector, a 6,000-gallon underground water storage tank, one 7½ ton water-to-water heat pump, and five small-tonnage water-to-air heat pumps. The collector has single glazing, is tilted 60 deg. from the horizontal and faces due south.

The original collector system was composed of tubular aluminum plates painted black. Plain water was used in the collectors, which were drained and vented from time to time in freezing weather. Shortly after the system was put in operation, leaks occurred due to corrosion of the aluminum panels. The problem was circumvented by soldering ½-in. copper tubes on 6-in. centers to the back of the plates. An epoxy cement was placed in the crevices between copper tubes and the plates with the hope of increasing heat transfer.

A secondary problem was the deterioration of the rubber hose connectors between the collectors and the steel piping collecting system. The hose connectors were replaced with copper.

During the first year of operation, Albuquerque had the cloudiest January in weather bureau history. Yet the building required only 8 per cent of the total yearly heating requirements in electrical energy (via the heat pump) for the entire heating season.

In 1962 the building was nearly doubled in size, and use of the solar system was terminated. Then in 1974 the system was reactivated. The collector fluid was changed to water and ethylene glycol (antifreeze). In order to minimize the amount of ethylene glycol required, a heat exchanger

was installed to transfer heat obtained from the collectors to the ordinary water in the 6,000-gallon storage tank.

(Engineers know now that precautions must be taken in the heat transfer fluid used with aluminum-tube collectors. Engineers Flack & Kurtz are using a special industrial heat transfer fluid—similar to a light oil—for the system they designed for the 10,000-sq-ft science facility for Madeira School outside Washington, D.C.).

The major steps involved in preparing the design manual are: 1) determine actual performance by analyzing collected field data; 2) correlate the results with computer-predicted performance; 3) develop and refine a computer model of the building and system; and 4) use the computer model to generate information for the system design manual. The computer model was programmed by Dr. Stanley F. Gilman and his associates at Penn State.

The Bridgers-Paxton system has several different operating modes. The solar collector circuit operates only when solar energy can be collected. The first mode is in operation when the storage water system can satisfy the space heating requirements. The air-handling unit is fed hot water directly from the storage tank, and the water-to-water heat pump is off. The second mode is in operation when storage water temperature cannot satisfy the heating requirement; then the heat pump operates with the storage water as the heat source, and delivers higher temperature water to the air-handling unit. The third mode is a cooling mode, when the occupied space requires cooling during the winter. Then the water-to-water heat pump shifts to cooling. The heat removed from the building is rejected to the storage tank as an additional heat source.

The "heart" of the data acquisition system is an IBM System 7 Computer. It measures some 70 points of data and sums or averages values over a basic six-minute cycle. Data collected include: 1) measurements from a "weather station" on the roof, 2) solar radiation on the plane of the collector, 3) indoor conditions, and 4) kwhr consumed by all electrical devices (compressors, pumps, lights, etc.). The frequency of measurement depends upon the variable involved: solar radiation is measured every half second; indoor dry-bulb temperature,

COOLING DEGREE DAYS			
MEAN DAYS SOLAR RADIATION (LY)	2000–4000	1000–2000	0–1000
500–650	1	2	3
450–500	4	5	6
450	7	8	9

Map indicates severity of cooling requirements, and is similar to the one across page. Effect of humidity is not considered.

which is nearly constant, is measured only every six minutes. The data is stored on a disc and, once a day, is sent over telephone lines to the Penn State computer facility where it is subjected to the analysis program. Results are computed on an hourly basis from the six-minute data. If closer scrutiny appears to be warranted, the six-minute data can be printed out or graphs generated (see page 76).

Data collection shows that the Bridgers system worked well
The data acquired over a 100-day period between December and March 1975 shows that the solar system, itself, was the primary source of heat on 51 days, and on the other 49 days there was heat-pump-assisted heating. Over the 100-day period, the over-all system coefficient of performance (COP), which is the total energy output divided by the electrical energy input, was about 7.0 with intermittent heat pump operation. This means that the heating was accomplished with only 14 percent of the electric power consumption that electric resistance heating would have required. The average COP during heat-pump operations was 4.0, including the power consumed by the water pumps.

Solar collection performance on a clear day (January 4, 1974) is shown in the graph on page 76. Collection efficiency is 44 per cent, which is only fair, indicating the possibility of some poor tube-to-plate bonds. Nonetheless, on a very cold January 4, when temperature dropped to 7F, 721,000 Btu were collected, which amounted to 73 per cent of the day's requirement.

In summer the system cooling energy is being measured and correlated with computer predictions. Infiltration, a significant cooling load, will be measured by a tracer-gas technique.

In 1975 the heating system was modified to take into account the water-to-air water-loop heat pumps that were added at the time of the building expansion. An additional storage tank was provided so that there is both a "hot" tank and a "cold" tank. The "hot" tank is used for direct heating with the water temperature being allowed to rise above 110F, which is too high for the water-to-air heat pumps to reject heat into. The "cold" tank then serves for heat rejection, and also as an additional heat source for the water-to-

air pumps. The over-all system efficiency is expected to improve markedly with the dual-tank system for storage.

The design procedure is tailored for use by typical design firms
The main objective of the design procedure developed by the Penn State group and by Frank Bridgers is to make it possible for a large number of engineers and architects to design solar-assisted heat pump systems with confidence and with a minimum of research effort. To accomplish this the procedure will: 1) incorporate design procedures familiar to hvac designers such as those in the ASHRAE handbooks; 2) use weather data that is available to all hvac designers; 3) provide a procedure for economic analysis and optimization of solar-collector area and storage that can be run on a small computer.

The critical design elements in the solar-assisted heat-pump system are the size of collector area needed and the capacity of the storage component. Amount of collector area, in turn, will depend upon the solar radiation available and the efficiency of the collector, and the heating load of the building.

The heating load of a building can be determined either manually using ASHRAE procedures or by one of the several computer programs available. The outdoor design temperature for calculating building heat loss will depend upon local experience. The total heating requirements for a given

period can then be approximated by using a modified degree-day method that considers internal energy from lights, people, equipment. The ASHRAE Handbook of Fundamentals lists average annual minimums, and temperatures that are not exceeded more than 1 per cent, or more than 2½ per cent, of the hours in December, January and February. But in some cases—and this is true of Albuquerque, for example—use of these values might lead to a considerably under-designed solar heating system. The 1 per cent temperature for Albuquerque is 14F. But the recognized *design temperature* is 0F. There have been periods, such as January 1971, when for a five-day period the minimum temperature was below 0F, reaching a low of −17F. Because a "pick-up" factor or other safety factors gener-

ally are not used in solar heating design, a conservative outdoor design temperature should be used.

The collector area depends upon the extent of solar contribution
The procedures listed below are tentative, "simplified" methods of obtaining the data necessary to design collector area and storage capacity of solar systems.

The type of weather data to be used for sizing collectors depends upon whether the system will consist of only solar energy plus a heat pump (called a "stand-alone" solar system), or whether there will be an auxiliary energy source. In many parts of the West, the days have 70 per cent or more

possible sunshine, and a stand-alone system will suffice. But in the Midwest and the East, 25 or even 50 per cent auxiliary heating may be necessary. In any event, the standby system for auxiliary heating will need to be designed for full heating requirements.

For this type of system, the weather data should be based upon an "average" year. (This data is available from the National Climatic Center in Asheville, North Carolina.) From this data, average daytime and average nighttime temperatures can be determined. Then with these values it is possible to calculate daytime monthly degree days and nighttime monthly degree days; and hence total heating requirements for a monthly period. For most parts of the country, the month of January should be used because it has the coldest average temperatures, and, in many cases, the least possible percentage of sunshine. The total heating load is the transmission load, plus the ventilation load, minus the internal heat.

Solar data for the auxiliary-type system: For determining collector area needed, it suffices to use sunshine data from the Climatic Atlas of the United States inasmuch as the solar contribution is not critical. Mean percentages of possible sunshine and mean daily solar radiation are given. With the charts, it is possible to interpolate values for any location in the 48 contiguous states.

Weather data for the stand-alone system. Because solar contribution is more critical, the weather data used to determine collector area and storage requirements should be that from the cloudiest period in the past 15 years coincidental with the maximum degree days, or the longest extended cold period. For example, for Denver, this period would be the winter of 1972-73. This is the combination of the cloudiest and coldest weather recorded by the Weather Bureau. Such a period can be called the "100-years' darkness" (comparable, in a way to the 100-year winds used for structural and curtain-wall design).

More accurate values for solar radiation than those from the Climatic Atlas can be obtained by using monthly summaries published by the Weather Bureau for 112 locations in the United States. These summaries give average per cent of solar radiation for the month. This percentage multiplied by the average clear-day radiation

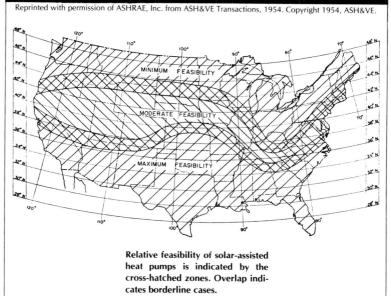

Relative feasibility of solar-assisted heat pumps is indicated by the cross-hatched zones. Overlap indicates borderline cases.

Data from an actual solar-heating system can be used to adjust and "tune" a computer program

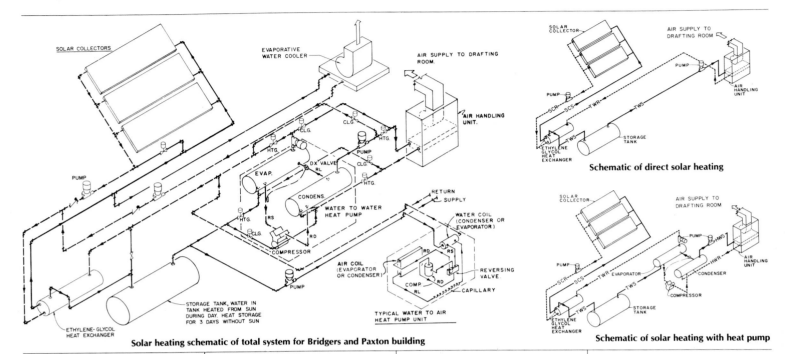

Solar heating schematic of total system for Bridgers and Paxton building

Schematic of direct solar heating

Schematic of solar heating with heat pump

(called insolation) gives the average direct solar radiation per day in Btu/day/sq ft. But, because the total radiation is made up of both direct radiation and diffuse radiation, it is necessary to also determine the diffuse component. Values for the average clear-day radiation and for the ratio of direct to diffuse radiation can be obtained from ASHRAE publications. Average clear-day radiation is given in the ASHRAE Transactions, 1974, in a paper by Morrison and Farber; and ratio of direct to diffuse is given in an ASHRAE bulletin on flat-plate collectors in a paper by Liu and Jordan.

(The mean solar daily radiation values published for U.S. cities may, in some cases, be inaccurate because of inaccuracies present in the solar measuring equipment.)

For the cities having no Weather Bureau, but with airports that record data, such information can be obtained from the National Climatic Center, though this data is not as precise.

Initial sizing of the collector area and storage capacity comes next

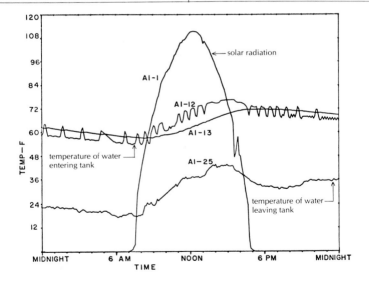

Computer-generated data from Bridgers and Paxton building

Collector efficiency is related primarily to the temperature of the fluid from the storage tank and to the outdoor air temperature: the larger the difference, the lower the efficiency. Efficiency also is related to the number of transparent covers over the collector. Up to about a 40F temperature difference, a collector with a single cover (e.g., glass) is efficient enough. With more than that, additional covers give higher efficiencies. Of course, the cost effectiveness of additional covers must be investigated in context with the total design.

The initial size of collector area can be determined by dividing the monthly heating required (January), in Btu's, by the average daily solar radiation multiplied by 30 days (one month) and by the collector efficiency.

A significant advantage of the solar-assisted heat pump system is that it is possible to use energy collected at very low differential temperatures between the collection fluid and the outdoor temperatures. Furthermore, solar energy can be collected at the highest efficiency when it is most needed, i.e., when the storage tank temperature is at the lowest level. In an area that has zero-degree temperatures, the average temperature of the tank fluid might be as low as 80F. Temperature of the

---

DAILY SUMMARY SOLAR HEATING STUDY

DAY	AVE. O.A. TEMP	TOTAL CLG.LOAD (TON-HR)	TOTAL HTG.LOAD (MBTU)	AVG.COLL. EFF.	PCT.POSS. SUNSHINE	INSOLATION BTU/SQ.FT.	TOTAL HEAT COLLECTED (MBTU)	HT.PUMP INPUT (KWH)	SUPPLEMENTAL HTG. STANDBY BOILER (MBTU)
1	26.8	27.	23391.	25.	53.	1105.	10639.	724.	0.
2	27.1	17.	23621.	0.	18.	437.	0.	1258.	0.
3	27.6	0.	32925.	0.	0.	94.	0.	1753.	12000.
4	28.3	0.	31657.	27.	32.	704.	7272.	1686.	24000.
5	31.7	341.	24244.	51.	46.	972.	18492.	1291.	12000.
6	32.2	276.	26864.	57.	92.	1849.	39362.	703.	0.
7	16.1	0.	32472.	31.	72.	1468.	17294.	1012.	0.
8	5.0	0.	42421.	45.	89.	1792.	30181.	2053.	0.
9	22.7	92.	28890.	0.	8.	247.	0.	1539.	0.
10	27.8	0.	30919.	54.	100.	2002.	40019.	935.	24000.
11	26.6	0.	32263.	48.	90.	1811.	32774.	686.	0.

Printout of system performance and solar data for modeled system of Denver Community College. (RECORD, mid-August, 1974)

**The architect
is concerned about
how the solar system
can be worked into
the building fabric**

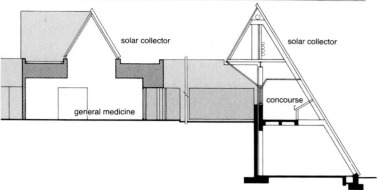

Layout of Shiprock Comprehensive Medical Facility was appropriate for the integration of solar collectors into the design. Drawing shows their location. Architects were Flatow, Moore, Bryan and Fairburn. Consulting engineers were Bridgers and Paxton.

water in the tank, which is "lifted" to utilization temperature by a water-source heat pump, cannot go below 50F if the system is to work properly.

A heat pump system is advantageous when a building needs both cooling and heating because most of the cost of the heat-pump unit can be charged to cooling requirements.

A solar-assisted heat pump system also makes sense from the standpoint of the auxiliary energy—in this case electricity. The utility will need to have the connected load for the heat pump operating as an air conditioner in the summer, so its use in the winter will probably be welcome either as a heat pump or an air conditioner. On the other hand, it is hard to imagine an energy company being happy about providing 100 per cent standby for a fully solar-heated building.

The critical design elements in the solar-assisted heat pump system are the size of collector area needed and the capacity of the storage component. Amount of collector area, in turn, will depend upon the solar radiation available, the efficiency of the collector, and the heating load of the building.

The calculations for amount of collector area required for the Bridgers and Paxton Solar Build-

ing indicated 793 sq ft of surface. The area of building heated is 5,000 sq ft. It has a limited number of windows and several skylights.

If the Bridgers and Paxton building were to have been designed for solar energy as the only source for heating, without the heat-pump booster, then the collector area would have had to have been three times larger and the storage tank two times larger than what was installed.

Tucson, Arizona, where the Copper Development Association has its solar house, has favorable climate for solar cooling. Architect: Arthur Kotch, AIA.

Size of the storage tank depends upon degree of solar contribution
Determination of storage tank size is based primarily on the percentage of the solar-energy contribution to the total. In Albuquerque, a three-day storage capacity based upon maximum heating requirements would be considered reasonable for a heat-pump-assisted solar system. The area of the solar collectors and the capacity of the solar system should be verified by computer. If, however, solar en-

ergy is only to supply a fraction of the total requirement, and a full-capacity standby system is provided, much less storage is needed. If the storage system is only to provide 70 per cent of the total, then it would be more economical to provide only a single day's storage capacity.

Economic optimization calls for computer analysis
Prior to economic optimization, it is possible to verify the preliminary calculation of collector area through computer analysis based upon 12-hour temperature readings for the entire heating season. A heat balance can be made on the storage water to determine when and how much supplementary energy is required. The amount of collector area and of storage can be verified, or an adjustment can be made to meet design objectives. A more accurate method of verifying the preliminary calculations would be to use 3-hour weather observations from the Weather Bureau Stations. And a still more accurate method would use 1-hr observations available from a very limited number of Weather Bureau Stations.

For economic optimization of collector area and storage-tank size, it is desirable to use a computer program that correlates the principal variables.

3

BUILDING UNDERGROUND TO CONSERVE ENERGY AND THE ENVIRONMENT

To different architects, building "underground" means different things. To some it is a solution of twentieth century pragmatism to twentieth century problems, of energy shortages, diminishing open space, and the need for shelter from different classes of disaster, both old and new. For others, underground space is an atavism—a romantic return to primal forms and a relationship symbolized by humanity's subordinateness to nature. And, for still others, the underground has yet to be shown as a field worthy of the practice of architecture.

There is little wonder that underground building has not received more attention from architects and clients in the past: cheap energy and cheap land encouraged consumption rather than conservation. Few problems were so pressing as to require a solution so radical as abandoning the earth's surface. Fears of leakage and the stigma of assumed windowlessness might be regarded as deterrents to underground development, yet it is more likely that the inertia of "surface thinking" itself has been so strong as to exclude even the consideration of other alternatives. The realization

that energy and land resources are finite—and that their limitation is expressed in cost—has initiated a new view toward opening the underground for development. With this new view has come a reappraisal of what an underground building is. Windowlessness, for example, is certainly not an inherent characteristic of underground architecture, as the following pages clearly show.

While the first generation of underground buildings designed for energy efficiency is just beginning to emerge, it is worth noting that the practice of underground construction has had an active and varied history, even though the progeny itself may be small. There have been, in fact, over the course of the past thirty years, not one but many underground "movements." All of these have had at their core more serious ideologies than most of the better publicized stylistic "isms" of the modern and "post-modern" period.

It is an interesting history, too, reflecting broad cultural values and popular concerns of the times. The use of underground space for shelter from nuclear fallout is a recurring theme which mirrors international politics. Shelters themselves may not be regarded as architecture in its higher forms, but the demand for fallout protection led to the subsurfacing of many neighborhood schools and even entire residences. Less familiar today than the shelter theme is the past promotion of "lithospheric" living areas (an early euphemism for improved basement-type space) throughout much of *House Beautiful's* 1949–1951 "Climate Control Project." This study, jointly sponsored by the AIA, advocated greater use of the space beneath the house in many regions of the United States. The emphasis in 1950 was on comfort and economy through natural means of climate control, clearly a modern forerunner of our present concern with energy efficient design.

The following decade witnessed a new concern with the quality of the environment. In the early 1960s, the visual landscape was much talked about, from "ticky-tacky" to billboards and other visual pollution. The sprawling suburb-building of the 1950s gave pause to many architects and planners; some advocated burying the offending elements, especially factories, warehouses, utilities, and transit facilities. The surface thereby liberated was usually envisioned for parks and residences of a conventional sort, although others sought to meld these as well into the topography. Still other designers celebrated "bulldozer architecture" as an art form in itself, land-shaping at a grand scale.

As the 1960s wore on, the mood shifted from concern with environmental *aesthetics* to environmental *ethics*. The underground alternative was now examined as an architecture of minimal impact, a means by which the apparent conflict between the ends of people and nature might be reconciled. The act of "submitting" to nature carried its own symbolic appeal, and by the early 1970s, the sentiment began to attract attention as a movement in its own right.

It has taken, finally, energy-induced economic incentives to attract attention to the underground in a major way. As of 1980, there are very few existing nonresidential underground buildings that have found their way below grade solely for reasons of energy conservation. The buildings presented in this chapter reflect this; for them, energy savings have been a happy windfall of other decisions and circumstances. Energy conservation, after all, is a fairly direct consequence of underground placement (the fine tuning of which is discussed in an essay included here) that applies as much to pre-energy crisis buildings as those of the present.

While building underground is a proven means of saving energy, there is not implicit in this move any dictates about how broader design questions are to be

restored. The two houses described here, for example, could scarcely be more different: Don Metz's Winston House was slipped into the brow of a New Hampshire hill in order to minimize its impact on the landscape. Elegant in its linear simplicity, its orientation maximizes winter solar gain (an early "passive solar" house), and uses conventional house building materials—a timber roof, block interior walls, and a reinforced concrete retaining wall—to demonstrate the immediacy of underground construction using existing technology. William Morgan's Dune Houses, at the opposite end of the East Coast, exhibit a playful exercise in form and a novel structure "tuned" to the loading of earth pressure. The sod cover and the recessed, scooped openings, much like the pair of sunglasses they suggest, shield the interior from the tropical sun. The egg shape, the single window portal to each unit, and the intimacy of size create a den-like split level volume completely unlike the Winston House. Even the motivations may be said to differ: While Metz wished to preserve the nature of the landscape, Morgan has long explored an interest in using earth actively as a formal element in design.

The other buildings exemplify both unique and recurrent themes of underground building. The Pusey Library preserves a hallowed, campus site while at the same time making rigorous use of it. The architects of the Pacific Northwest Bell office have taken a facility that all too often is a blank, massive presence, and made a public amenity of it. The Baily Library—altogether different from the Pusey Library—provides a new central focus for the campus with its recessed amphitheater-like plaza, while the bermed forms that embrace the library establish a visual note that is echoed elsewhere on campus. Philip Johnson's own art gallery illustrates architecture at one with landscape—a building, however unusual in plan, that is scarcely discernible from the rolling topography in which it is situated. And the remarkable differences between the houses designed by Don Metz and William Morgan testify to the wide-ranging diversity in interpretation possible within a single building type.

Underground architecture does mean different things to different architects. Although the potential of underground construction for energy savings is universal to all, it may very well be that the variety of ideas about building underground is its own greatest virtue. The contents of this chapter exhibit the strength of this diversity, and reveal how underground design can be a vital and successful alternative to the architecture we routinely see about us.

On the next pages...

BUILDING UNDERGROUND:
A TEMPERED CLIMATE, EARTH AS INSULATION, AND THE SURFACE-UNDERSURFACE INTERFACE

BUILDING UNDERGROUND: A TEMPERED CLIMATE, EARTH AS INSULATION, AND THE SURFACE-UNDERSURFACE INTERFACE

by Kenneth Labs

Major energy-conserving advantages of underground architecture result directly from locating the building in a more favorable climate than that of the surface. The ground is a great equalizer of climatic events: Summer is averaged with winter over time and with depth so that ground temperature eventually becomes constant throughout the year. This radical change in thermal environment significantly reduces both peak and average rates at which a building exchanges heat with its surroundings. The diminished rates of energy transfer yield not only reductions in heating and cooling loads, but the more constant rate of heat exchange offers important opportunities for greater efficiency in mechanical systems operation as well.

The actual process of heat exchange between underground buildings and the soil is not readily predictable, but the thermal advantages of underground placement can be explained by considering individually the *climate of undisturbed ground*, and the means by which the *earth isolates underground spaces from the surface* under an assumed condition of steady-state heat transfer. Both soil climate and the soil insulating effect have direct thermal (external) advantages as well as specific implications for the design of (internal) mechanical systems. These are discussed in the following sections.

A TEMPERED CLIMATE

Although temperature fluctuations at the ground surface generally approximate those of the air, these variations are rapidly reduced with depth and are eventually damped out altogether. Daily temperature variations effectively disappear at a depth of less than two feet, meaning that no earth-protected portion of a structure will see significant if any daily temperature changes. Annual temperature variations in undisturbed soil penetrate to depths of 16 to 32 feet, depending on soil type and the magnitude of the surface variation, for a ± 1°F subsurface fluctuation. Below a depth of about 20 feet, therefore, ground temperature may be regarded as stable for building engineering purposes. For most parts of the country, these stable ground temperatures exceed the mean annual air temperature by 2° or 3°F. In areas of heavy, continuous snow cover, steady-state ground temperature may exceed the mean annual air temperature by more than

5°F, thereby lending particular advantage to underground building in northern zones. An estimate of the distribution of steady-state ground temperatures is given in Figure 1.

In addition to the attenuation of temperature fluctuation with depth, there is a second advantage of ground climate: The temperature wave in the soil lags behind the surface temperature wave in linear relation to depth. This lag amounts to about one week per foot for typical soils, so that when it is December at the surface, it is "September" at a depth of 12 or 13 feet. The maximum heating loads contributed by conduction to the ground and by the heating of intake (ventilation) air are therefore separated in time. The shift in the peaks of these loads out of coincidence with one another reduces overall peak heating—and cooling—loads normally created by their superimposition.

Degree Day Reductions

The average temperature of an undisturbed vertical soil profile over any selected range of depths can be modeled reasonably accurately by a sinusoidal mathematical function.[1] Substitution of appropriate values into the model reveals that the overall range of temperatures experienced by a soil profile extending from 2 to 26 feet (corresponding to the wall of a two story underground building) varies only about 8°F over the course of a year. For a 2 to 12 foot profile (corresponding to a typical single-story underground building), the range is about 18°F, still no more than a 9°F change over the course of a three-month season.

Summation of the number of degrees bounded by the average profile temperature and a selected temperature index provides a method of determining "underground degree days" for different depth ranges and different

[1]Mathematical representation of soil temperature, parameters governing it, and the degree day calculation technique used here are discussed in detail in Kenneth Labs, "The Underground Advantage: Climate of Soils," plenary session *Proceedings*, 4th National Passive Solar Conference, October 1979, Kansas City, Missouri.

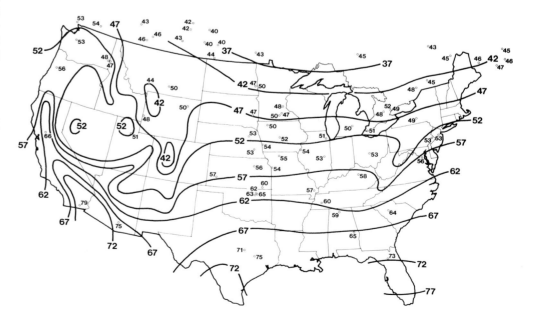

Figure 1. The isothermal lines shown here represent well-water temperatures estimated by W. D. Collins from air temperature data in the 1925 U.S. Geological Survey *Water Supply Paper 520-F*. Observed mean annual ground temperatures have been superimposed on the Collins map by the author. Note that Collins' estimates in the northern states are low, probably due to insufficient allowance for the insulating effect of snow.

geographical areas. The shaded areas in Figures 2(*a*) and 2(*b*) graphically represent annual underground heating degree day (UGHDD) values for typical conditions at Minneapolis, Minnesota, and Temple, Texas, utilizing a 65°F reference index. The underground degree day value for a 2 to 12 foot profile in Minneapolis is computed to be 6205, as compared to a normal surface value of 8382, yielding a 26% reduction. An identical reduction is obtained for a 2 to 26 foot profile. For both profiles, cooling degree days (base 65°F) are eliminated. In the Temple example, heating degree days for the 2 to 26 foot profile are eliminated, and the base 65°F cooling degree day index is reduced by 21%. Heating degree days for the shallower 2 to 12 foot profile are reduced by 91%, and cooling degree days are reduced 15%, as compared to the surface values of 2039 HDD and 2769 CDD.

These degree day evaluations are abstractions, and cannot be used to predict energy consumption in their present form. Every building has its own balance point as a result of its design; "free" heating contributions from solar energy, occupants, lighting, and other internal operations may eliminate space heating requirements even for external temperatures well below 50°F. The conventional 65°F degree day index itself is somewhat arbitrary in that it already assumes some free heating to make up the difference between it and the lower limit of the comfort zone (68° to 72°F, depending on clothing and other factors). The fact that the underground degree day calculation technique presented here is based on undisturbed ground temperature means that the method does not account for warming of the soil by heat losses from the building, a phenomenon which in itself retards the rate of further losses. Because the ground stores heat lost from underground structures (whereas the atmosphere does not) the ground is less effective as a heat sink than even mildly "stirred" air.[2] This consideration suggests that heating and cooling degree day values obtained through the undisturbed ground temperature analysis technique are very conservative indicators of the reductions in actual heating and cooling loads effected by underground placement.

Regional Considerations

In most parts of the continental United States, deep ground temperatures fall below the lower limits of the comfort zone. In areas where steady-state ground temperatures approach 70°F, late summer profile temperatures (especially for shallow, one story depths) may exceed the upper limits of the comfort zone (78ET[2]). While underground placement can help reduce the cooling load of buildings in southern zones, it often will not in itself be a sufficient means of satisfying cooling requirements. This will be especially true in buildings

[2]One index of a material's effectiveness as a heat sink is its *conductive capacity*, the square root of the product of conductivity and heat capacity. The conductive capacity of a "neutral stirred air" is about two and one-half times greater than that of an average soil, and that of a "very unstable" stirred air is as much as twenty-five times greater. See C.H.B. Priestly, *Turbulent Transfer in the Lower Atmosphere*, University of Chicago Press, Chicago, 1959.

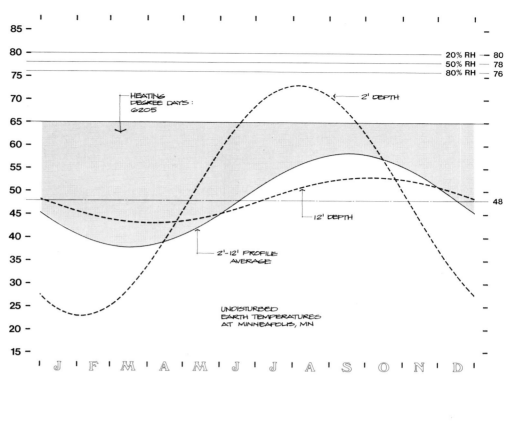

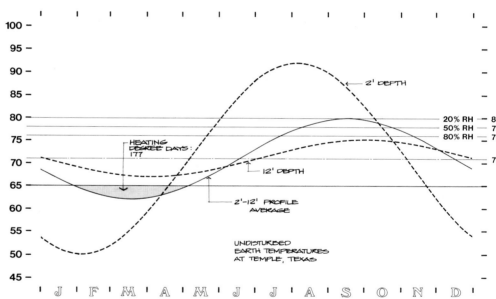

Figures 2(*a*) and 2(*b*). Degree day values can be computed for various soil profiles by summing the area between a temperature index (here 65°F) and the average temperature of the soil profile. The shaded area in Figure 2(*a*) represents underground heating degree days at Minneapolis, Minnesota, and in Figure 2(*b*) at Temple, Texas. Note that the 2 – 12 foot profile temperature at Temple exceeds comfort zone limits in September, when mean monthly humidity level is approximately 70%.

having large internal heat gains. In southern regions where natural ventilation is an important passive cooling strategy, care must be taken to ensure that ventilating effectiveness is not compromised by underground placement. Some discussion of integrating above-surface passive design strategies with underground design is presented in the concluding section of this article.

As a climate-tempering technique, underground construction offers advantages in all climates characterized by significant heating or cooling demand, and in regions characterized by wide-ranging seasonal extremes in temperature. Underground building offers particular advantage in areas that have both large heating or cooling demands *and* great annual temperature ranges. Examples include the northern Midwest and parts of the arid Southwest. Since ground temperatures are significantly elevated above the mean annual air temperature in areas of continuous snow cover, the climate of the northern Midwest is especially able to benefit from underground development.

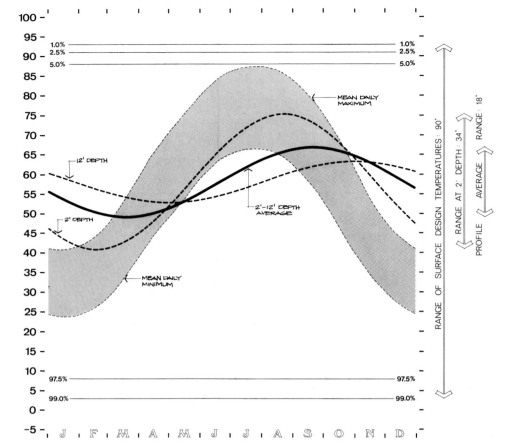

Figure 3. The average temperature of a 2–12 foot profile at Lexington, Kentucky is compared here to temperatures at 2 and 12 foot depths, the range of mean daily temperatures (shaded), and summer and winter design temperatures. This clearly illustrates that mechanical systems for underground spaces need be designed to deal with only a fraction of the temperature range confronting the systems of above-surface buildings.

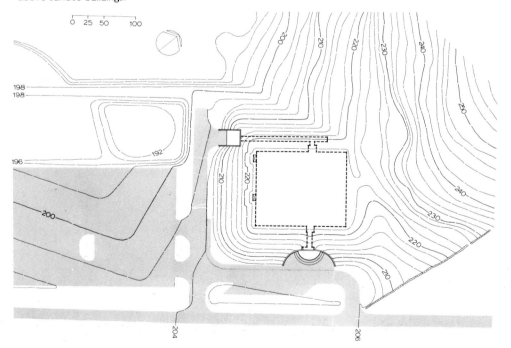

Figure 4a. The fully underground Federal Emergency Management Center, located outside of Boston, has passed through more than ten winters on the "waste" heat produced by lighting and other electrical equipment. Since the building is windowless, no solar gain is contributed to the heat production. Mechanical engineers for the facility were Metcalf and Eddy.

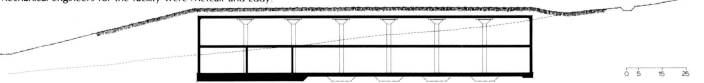

Figure 4b. The structure is positioned within the toe of a long slope. Excavated earth was used for bermed backfill and as fill over low areas for leveling of the parking lot. The blast resistant roof is designed to sustain a 2160 psf load, and is blanketed with a nearly uniform soil cover 3 feet in depth.

Implications for HVAC Systems

The major differences between the above-surface climate and the ground climate are illustrated in Figure 3.

Mechanical systems are ordinarily designed to produce comfort conditions within all but the most extreme 1% or 2% of the hours of the summer and winter seasons. These design temperatures greatly exceed even the lowest mean daily minimum and the greatest mean daily maximum for the year, and they typically define a range of more than 90°F to 100°F within which the mechanical system is required to perform. This broad spectrum of load conditions means that the HVAC system can spend relatively little time operating within its own level of greatest efficiency. A typical 2 to 12 foot soil profile, on the other hand, sees an annual temperature range of only 18°F, or about one-fifth of the design air temperature range. An HVAC system designed to serve this smaller range of temperatures is certain to operate at much greater efficiency, at lower capital and energy cost.

An even more immediate benefit of the smaller design range of temperatures encountered underground is the reduced need in equipment size and capacity. Smaller equipment means smaller capital cost, a welcome addition to the anticipated greater operating efficiency and the reduced annual loads indicated by the foregoing degree day analysis.

A further implication of reductions in equipment capacity is the suitability of a variety of relatively low energy sources that would not be able to meet extreme above-surface load demands. The relatively constant nature of heat exchange underground calls for a similarly continuous system of heat supply or removal, free from the inherent discomfort and inefficiency of off-on cycles. Prime among the possibilities is solar energy, although, in areas where appropriate, wind-driven heat generation systems may also be satisfactory.

One ubiquitous source of low-level heat supply that in many areas may nearly satisfy winter heating demands is the sum of ordinary internal heat gains. Chief among these is the heat-of-lighting, although the heat generated by occupants and activities, including machinery and industrial processes, may often be of far greater significance.[3] The underground Regional Office of the Federal Emergency Management Agency Center in Maynard, Massachusetts, for example, has wintered through more than a decade almost exclusively on the heat-of-lighting and occupancy [see Figures 4(a), 4(b), and 4(c)]. The 33,600 square

[3]Electric lights typically produce 3.41 BTU per hour per watt; the body produces between 400 and 500 BTU per hour (about one-half latent, and one-half sensible heat) when seated at light-activity levels.

foot facility does not have a conventional heating system, except for a few supplementary electrical strip heaters. The building is designed to accomodate an emergency staff of 300, yet with an active regular staff of 50, the building's heating needs are satisfied by 24-hour continuous lighting and the heat generated by the occupants and electrical gear. Under normal conditions, 80% of indoor air is recirculated. Return air is drawn through inlets in the fluorescent lighting fixtures into the ceiling plenum, where it is induced into the supply air stream for redistribution. During unoccupied periods, no outdoor air is admitted and all building air is continuously recirculated. In rare instances the strip heaters are used, and these only in areas of low occupancy.

EARTH AS INSULATION

While the average profile temperature provides a rough indication of the severity of ground climate, most heat transferred from shallow underground walls will occur between the wall and the surface, rather than horizontally to the subsoil. ASHRAE's 1977 *Fundamentals Handbook* suggests a procedure for estimating heat loss from subgrade walls via a radial heat flow path; it assumes a steady-state exchange of heat from the wall to a constant (winter) surface temperature. Since the temperature of the surface fluctuates over the course of a year, the condition is not truly steady state, and the procedure cannot be used for simulating annual energy fluxes. As a technique for predicting maximum rates of heat loss, however, it has been shown to be adequate, at least for portions of subgrade walls near the surface.

The effect of the earth as insulation can be readily explained by this supposed radial heat flow phenomena, even if it is not fully accurate. It should first be noted that soil itself is not a good insulating material: a typical soil *in-situ* has a conductivity not much less than concrete, about $0.7 - 0.9$ BTU/hr(ft²)°F/ft, or R1.3 per foot.

The range of soil conductivities varies from about 0.2 BTU/hr (ft²)°F/ft for light dry soil to 1.4 BTU/hr(ft²)°F/ft for a wet soil (see Table 1). This means that 5½ feet of earth is required to equal the resistance of 2 inches of beadboard. The cost of carrying this load on a roof is hardly practical, but as the heat flows in an arc-shaped path from the buried wall, the resistance there is quickly compounded. In the language of heat conduction engineering, the magnitude of the produced effect is described as a *shape factor*. From the designer's point of view, it is more easily understood as an "effective" R value. An example will best illustrate this phenomenon.

In the radial path calculation method, the variables consist of the resistivity of the soil, the depth of the wall, and the slope of the surface. For any single given depth x, the Effective R is given by

$$ER_x = 2\pi(x) (R_{soil}) \frac{90 - m}{360}$$

where m is the slope of the surface in degrees, R_{soil} is the unit resistance of the soil, and ER_x is the effective resistance at depth x (see Figure 5). As an example, the Effective R for a depth of 8 feet under a horizontal surface is given by

substituting $x = 8$ and $m = 0$, so that

$$ER_8 = \frac{2\pi(8)}{4}R_{soil} = 12.6 \ R_{soil}$$

The geometrical component of the heat flow is independent of the soil's thermal properties. For a typical *in-situ* soil, unit resistance may be assumed to be about R 1.25/ft. Substituting 1.25 for R_{soil} yields a product of ER 15.75. A horizontal strip of wall at 8 feet below grade, therefore, can be regarded as having inherent resistance of R16, without benefit of any insulating materials (a concrete wall having virtually the same unit resistance value as soil is assumed).

The same technique can be modified to determine the *average* resistance provided by the earth for the wall profile. This average wall R value will be denoted $\overline{ER}_{(x-y)}$, referring to a profile of depths ranging from x to y. The formula for this resistance is given

$$\overline{ER}_{(x-y)} = \pi R_{soil} \left(\frac{x^2 - y^2}{x-y}\right) \left(\frac{90 - m}{360}\right)$$

For a basement wall extending from a horizontal grade to a depth of 6 feet, the Average Effective R of the wall profile is

$$\overline{ER}_{(0-6)} = (3.14) R_{soil} \left(\frac{0 - 6^2}{0 - 6}\right) \left(\frac{90}{360}\right) = 4.7 \ R_{soil}$$

For a fully subgrade wall extending from a

depth of 2 feet to 12 feet, the profile's Average Effective R computes to $14(R_{soil})$, or $\overline{ER}$ 17.5 for $R_{soil} = 1.25$.

Berming

The radial analysis procedure also allows the effectiveness of berming to be tested against recessed placement. For example, if instead of a 6-foot deep basement, a wall bermed to a height of 6 feet at a slope of 30° is considered, $\overline{ER}$ works out to 3.4 R, instead of 4.7 R. This occurs because the slope factor is reduced from $\pi/4$ for horizontal grade to $\pi/6$. Although heat loss cannot be expected to precisely follow these fine differences, the principle clearly indicates that berming is not as effective as recessing below a horizontal grade. Where site conditions make berming otherwise the more appropriate alternative, a compromise may be struck by carrying the grade away from the building horizontally as far as possible before pitching the surface downward.

Supplementary Insulation

One need not go through the calculations at various individual depths to surmise that the greatest heat flow will pass through the roof

TABLE 1: THERMAL PROPERTIES OF SOILS, ROCKS, AND CONCRETE*

Material Description	Density (lb/ft³)	Thermal Conductivity, k (BTU/h.ft.F)	Unit Resistance, R (1/k) (1' thickness)
Dense rock	200	2	.5
Wet soil†	117		
Average rock	175	1.4	.7
Dense concrete	150	1.0	1.0
Solid masonry	143		
Heavy soil, damp‡	131	.75	1.33
Heavy soil, dry	125		
Light soil, damp	100	.50	2.0
Light soil, dry	90	.20	5.0

*Reprinted with pemission from the 1978 *Applications* volume, ASHRAE Handbook and Product Directory.
†A characterization appearing in the 1974 *Applications* volume.
‡A typical condition of soils *in-situ*.

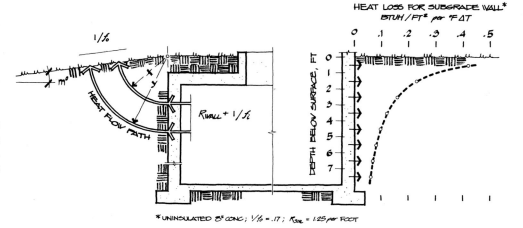

HEAT LOSS FOR SUBGRADE WALL*
BTUH/FT² per °F ΔT

*UNINSULATED 8" CONC; 1/fo = .17 ; R_{soil} = 1.25 per FOOT

Figure 5. The calculation of heat loss from underground spaces as recommended by ASHRAE assumes steady-state heat flow, following an arc-shaped path to the surface. Plotting predicted heat flux by this method for an uninsulated wall indicates that the rate of tranfer rapidly diminishes with depth. This points out the special need for insulation at the upper perimeter of the wall.

and the upper part of the undersurface walls. This is evident in Figure 5; these flowpaths are the shortest, and therefore offer the least resistance. Acknowledging the low unit resistance of soil as a material, it should be clear that earth is no substitute for judicious use of manufactured insulation materials at the roof and the upper portions of the wall. Researchers at the University of Minnesota have emphasized the critical need for roof insulation, stating that losses through the roof may exceed 50% of the total transmission losses.[4] Since the inherent Effective R increases with depth, it can be reasoned that the most efficient use of wall insulation requires specification of the greatest thicknesses near the surface, decreasing with depth as the soil ER appreciates.

The pattern of radial heat flow near the surface means that insulation may be placed either vertically against the wall or horizontally, parallel to the surface (or in between, as long as the plane of insulation is perpendicular to the heat flow). Simulations conducted at the University of Minnesota's Department of Mechanical Engineering indicate that horizontal installations are superior for northern zones, reducing winter heat loss by 20% as compared to vertical placement. Summer heat loss—a desirable cooling effect—is improved by 17% in the horizontal versus vertical installation. The horizontal insulation layer better buffers the subsoil from surface temperature events, and thus extends the effective thermal massiveness of the walls. This same idea has been suggested by Robinsky and Bespflug[5] as a means of reducing frost depth, for the purpose of promoting construction of shallower foundations in northern zones.

While these radial flow exercises serve to explain the insulating value of shallow underground construction, it must be remembered that they are based upon less than fully valid assumptions of steady-state transfer. In the upper several feet of the soil—where the greatest heat exchange occurs—the procedure is most acceptable. It is not sufficiently accurate to represent conditions below the upper soil horizon. Fortunately, it isn't necessary to depend upon imprecise theory and unverifiable assumptions to establish the insulative and isolating benefits of underground placement. Studies have been conducted by the University of Minnesota at Williamson Hall, the University's bookstore and admissions building, to document observed heat flow from underground walls. The record indicates that the rate of winter heat loss diminishes with depth, averaging $7-8$ W/m^2 [$2.2 - 2.5$ BTU/(ft²) hr] over the profile from 4 to 12 feet, 1-2 W/m^2 [.32 - .64 BTU/(ft²) hr] from 12 to 24 feet, and 1 W/m^2 [.32 BTU/(ft²) hr] from 24 to 34 feet. Only the uppermost 4 feet of wall is insulated (with 1½ inches of rigid foam), and over this

area the average rate of heat loss has been observed as 4 W/m^2 [1.3 BTU/(ft²) hr]. During the period from January to April, heat loss over the entire wall profile averaged 4.5 W/m^2 [1.4 BTU/ft(²) hr]; this compares to an R38 to R40 above-grade wall in Minneapolis's average

[6]Heat loss data provided through the courtesy of the Underground Space Center, University of Minnesota.

January temperature of 12°F. The overall insulative performance is so satisfactory that, when occupied, the building has not drawn steam for space heating (prior to installation of the building's solar heating system) until an outdoor temperature of 10°F is reached [see Figures 6(a), 6(b), and 6(c)]. Architects of Williamson Hall are Myers and Bennett of BRW, Inc.

Figure 6(a). Williamson Hall, which houses the bookstore and admissions offices of the University of Minnesota, has been the subject of extensive underground heat transfer studies by the University's Mechanical Engineering Department. Monitoring has shown that the average January heat loss rate for one of the buried walls is 4.62 W/m^2, or 1.5 BTU/(ft²)hr.

Figures 6(b) and 6(c). The diagonal pedestrian route which crosses the roof of Williamson Hall is repeated in the corridor beneath it [Figure 6(a)]. The corridor and the spaces below are flooded with natural light from an upper clerestory on one side, and a sunken light well that is suspended above the bottom floor on the other, Figure 6(b). Architects Myers and Bennett have made horizontal planter boxes containing Engelmann Ivy an integral part of the building's sun shading design.

[4]T.P. Bligh, P. Shipp, and G. Meixel, "Where to Insulate Earth Protected Buildings and Existing Basements," Appendix IV of Earth Covered Buildings: Technical Notes, Volume I of the proceedings of the conference, "Alternatives in Habitat: The Use of Earth Covered Settlements," Frank Moreland, editor, 1978 (distributed by NTIS, Springfield, VA).

[5]E.I. Robinsky and K.E. Bespflug, "Design of Insulated Foundations," Journal of the Soil Mechanics and Foundations Division, ASCE, vol. 99, no. SM9, September 1973.

Underground HVAC Implications

The temperateness of the ground climate and the great effective resistance provided by the earth to heat exchange with the surface combine to produce very small perimeter loads within heated (or refrigerated) underground buildings. The near elimination of perimeter loads effectively creates all "interior" space, which may be dealt with in much the same way as most of the floor area of large office buildings. The overall ramification to the mechanical engineer is to simplify the problem: A single all-air ventilation system with heating and cooling ability should be satisfactory to service most underground buildings. Perimeter baseboard systems will not be necessary, except in those areas where there is an interface with the above-ground (at large glazing areas, for example).

A heretofore undiscussed attribute of subsurface placement is the elimination of most heat exchange by means of infiltration. Infiltration varies widely from one building to the next, so it is difficult to quantify the effect of its impact on mechanical equipment capacity without comparing specific building designs and use patterns. In most underground structures, however, it can be assumed that air leakage losses will be insignificant, and the resultant savings will be appreciable.

Because of the low rate of perimeter losses and the high thermal mass usually associated with the underground structure itself, the potential for maintaining comfort below ground is very high. The system, however, must be matched to the very stable conditions, so that off-on cycles themselves don't create discomforting artificially imposed swings in interior temperature. The temperature of delivery air, therefore, needs to be carefully controllable within a fairly narrow range bounding the desirable space temperature. This again suggests the overall applicability of relatively low temperature heat sources such as flat-plate collectors and the heat-of-lighting. The same principle applies to the cooling source, where a number of alternatives—including well water, ice-maker heat pumps, evaporative cooling (in arid climates) and outside air—are possibilities. Underground spaces do not necessarily require novel systems, but the shift from above to below ground may make feasible systems not ordinarily considered. This requires a fresh outlook and a familiarity with a broad range of system alternatives.

Figure 7(a). This heat wheel—similar to those utilized in Gerogetown University's underground student athletic center—transfers heat from exhaust to intake ducts (or vice versa, depending on operation), reclaiming up to 85% of what otherwise would be wasted energy. Photo courtesy of Wing Industries, Inc., manufacturers of the equipment used in the Georgetown facility.

If large occupied spaces are to be located underground—particularly if without a view to the outside—the psychological sense of estrangement from the out-of-doors may heighten one's sensitivity to physical comfort. Complaints of stuffiness may be more readily made by occupants of underground spaces than by their above-surface neighbors. Similarly, draftiness may be more quickly felt in the absence of a compensating view. Environmental stimulation and environmental boredom are intriguing subjects that merit special considera-tion when building below ground, in the acoustical and visual environment as well as in the thermal. In relation to these considerations, the details of the comfort control system itself are likely to be of special importance, particularly whether or not variable controls are accessible to individual zones or work stations.

Two other points may be made about the nature of underground HVAC systems. First, the simplification of the system to predominantly all-air distribution will reduce initial costs. Secondly, the smaller rate of heat exchange through the shell means that a greater proportion of energy will enter or leave the building with intake and exhaust air. Much of this heat energy can be recovered by rather simple devices. Heat reclamation, therefore, should receive high priority among efforts to enhance the energy efficiency of underground buildings.

The new student recreation facility designed by Daniel Tully Associates for Georgetown University in Washington, D.C., provides an excellent example of heat recovery at work, as shown in Figure 7(a). Four mechanical *heat wheels* are interposed between the intake and exhaust ducts. In operation, the rotating finned wheels absorb heat carried by warm air passing through one duct (exhaust, in winter), and discharge it into the airstream flowing in the opposite direction in the other duct [Figures 7(b) and 7(c)]. This system reclaims up to 85% of heat energy that would otherwise be wasted to the outside. The combination of underground location and the heat wheel system is calculated to cut operating costs to one-third that of a comparable above-ground structure without heat recovery equipment. In the Georgetown installation, the cost of the basic mechanical system was less than would be required above-ground, but the addition of the specialty heat recovery devices increased the total cost to approximately 5% in excess of the conventional structure. This small investment will quickly be returned in the system's reduced operating costs. The heat wheels are active in both summer and winter operation.

Figure 7(b). More than 3 acres of recreational facilities are housed beneath football and playing fields supported by hyperbolic paraboloid structural system, patented by the building's architect, Daniel F. Tully. Underground facilities include two 1-acre fields with a 200-meter track, twelve muliuse courts, four handball courts, four squash courts, a ¼-acre dance floor, lockers for 2,000, and a swimming pool with a separate diving well.

Figure 7(c). Georgetown University's student recreation center was built on the site of the school's football field. The field has subsequently been re-established atop a 3½-inch composite concrete roof diaphragm supported on light steel columns spaced 7 to 8 feet apart, which in turn bear on the hypar shells.

Given that the effect of placing the building underground is to create the equivalent of all interior space, then it may be reasoned that small structures (of high surface-to-volume ratio) will benefit the most from underground placement. With the diminished perimeter exchange that is characteristic of underground architecture, it is also true that the overall compactness of form and configuration of the exterior itself will be less critical. This means that a "sprawling" underground building will be less energy wasteful than its sprawling surface counterpart.

THE SURFACE—UNDERSURFACE INTERFACE

There are, of course, many building types that do not require windows, and others in which fenestration may be considered a liability. Auditoria, for instance, often require the exclusion of daylight, rather than its use. In the underground lecture hall designed by Herbert Hewman Associates for Yale University (page 96), no sacrifice was made in eliminating windows. In a facility like this, which is used largely for slide lectures and screening films, openings to the outside are more often a problem than an amenity.

Buildings used for the storage and display of books, works of art, and other precious artifacts commonly are constructed with few or no windows in order to minimize damage from ultraviolet light. Moreover, the elimination of fenestration allows more precise temperature and humidity control, as well as limiting vulnerability to theft and vandalism. All of these are important programmatic considerations in the design of libraries and museums. It should not be surprising, then, that numerous examples of these and other building types that are essentially windowless by nature have found their way underground. What is of greatest interest about these is how and where daylight is introduced to the interior.

The design by Hugh Stubbins and Associates for the Nathan Marsh Pusey Library at Harvard University makes use of a bermed and recessed moat to open large expanses of glass serving offices and reading areas to the outside (page 98). The invaluable collection of rare books itself is well isolated from daylight, while a two-story deep sunken courtyard illuminates private study carrels without disrupting the continuity of the hallowed green above. Philip Johnson opted for total windowlessness— except for the entryway—in the Bailey Library at Hendrix College in Arkansas (page 108), as he did in the design of his own "art bunker" in New Canaan, Connecticut (page 110). Windows were eliminated also for reasons of security and environmental control in Zimmer Gunsul Frasca's design for the Pacific Northwest Bell office and data processing center in Portland, Oregon (page 104).

While many building types are able to take uncompromised advantage of total isolation from the surface, it must be recognized that valuable energy resources exist above ground as well. These can be grouped into categories of daylighting, solar gain, and natural ventilation. It is the design of this interface—the synthesis of surface and subsurface benefits— that offers the greatest challenge to the design-

88

A TAXONOMY OF UNDERGROUND BUILDING FORMS

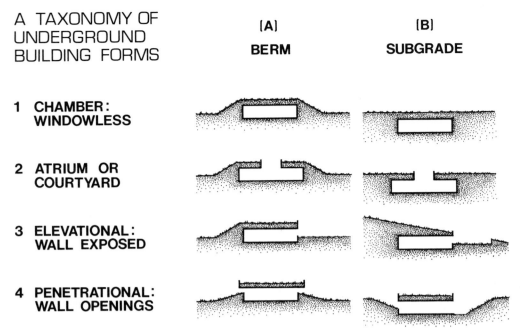

	[A] BERM	[B] SUBGRADE
1 CHAMBER: WINDOWLESS		
2 ATRIUM OR COURTYARD		
3 ELEVATIONAL: WALL EXPOSED		
4 PENETRATIONAL: WALL OPENINGS		

Figure 8. The principal relationships between the surface and the subsurface are described in this taxonomy of underground building forms (K. Labs, *The Architecture of Underground Space*, master's thesis, Washington University, St. Louis, Missouri, 1975).

er. It is also the resolution of this bridge between worlds that will most often determine the overall success of the building as architecture, from both within and without. The full energy-conserving potential may also be realized or lost in the design of the interface, since the temperateness of the undersurface climate often may make above-surface "passive" strategies sufficient in themselves to maintain building comfort.

Daylighting

Most underground buildings have been designed with some window exposure to the surface. As shown in many of the examples illustrated elsewhere in this chapter, the most intensely occupied spaces are usually organized around these carefully located apertures, while low-use areas remain windowless. Ordinarily, the ways in which daylight is admitted to interior spaces can be described as one or a combination of the fundamental relationships defined graphically in Figure 8.

Daylighting is a subject that is likely to receive renewed attention as the demand for conservation measures increase. How this is achieved—whether through skylights, clerestories, or windows with a view—may take on great psychological significance to inhabitants of underground spaces. In most underground structures, architects have been unwilling to compromise the space-expanding sense of view windows for overhead natural lighting. Even when the windows are gathered around a sunken courtyard with little view other than within itself, care is usually taken to provide some visual focus within the space. This may be done through landscaping, as in the case of the specimen tree selected for the recessed Blodgett Court of the Pusey Library (page 98), or by making the courtyard itself accessible as an activity area. The problem with daylighting is that window light doesn't normally penetrate very far into the interior, and skylights are

thermally vulnerable interruptions in the least protected portion of the building, the roof. Effective daylighting, therefore, necessitates either providing many breaks in the earth sheltering blanket, or very careful organization of the interior to make most effective use of the least window area. William Morgan's Dune Houses (see page 91), exemplify how the entire structure can be used to guide the eye to a single, all important view, in this case, the Atlantic Ocean.

Passive Design

It is shortsighted to regard windows in general as an energy sink, since these can be oriented and detailed to capture and control solar gain as desired. In northern climates, the south slope "dugout" house has become a kind of stereotype of passive solar, earth-integrated design. Don Metz's elegant New Hampshire Winston House (see page 94), was perhaps the first of these, and it remains almost uncontested in its deft handling of interior spacial organization.

Fortunately for the designer, summer breezes throughout much of the United States come from southerly directions, so that operable south-facing glazing usually provides positive cooling as well as heating advantages. A space can't be ventilated unless it has openings at the leeward as well as on its windward side, so outlet openings are essential. Metz's design suggests a possibility here as well—the open-ended corridor and roof monitor offer excellent exhaust portals for both pressure- and chimney-effect overheat relief.

Climates in which overheating is more of a concern than underheating require a somewhat different approach. For a reverse osmosis (water purifying) plant in Death Valley, California, a team of National Park Service architects and engineers completely buried the facility, and used the recessed delivery truck ramp as a light well for a wall of clerestory north windows (see

Figure 9). Although this facility itself is not occupied, the sensitivity of the system components to excessive heat necessitated air conditioning of the interior. The two-story deep design relieves the mechanical system of dealing with the severe temperature extremes of the surface climate, offering in its place a fairly constant "outside" temperature of 75°F. Aesthetic programmatic criteria also favored a "non-building" (it's near a restored frontier town), but the practical benefit is thermal, and measurable in cost reductions for cooling the plant.

Other common passive design strategies are also adaptable to, and even enhanced by, underground placement. Atrium houses, for instance, are the norm in many arid zones of the world, largely because of the ability of the enclosed courtyard to collect and contain a pool of dense, cool nighttime air. The wall surrounding the courtyard shades the space, preventing it from heating, while evaporative devices such as fountains or "desert coolers" (wetted porous screens or mats, through which air is driven) continue to cool the air in the courtyard space. The dense air collected within

the atrium will displace warmer indoor air, so it may assist in driving a convective cycle through the interior. Building the atrium house underground can enhance this cool pooling effect through contact with the more stable underground climate. The Texas house designed by architects Coffee and Crier of Austin (Figure 10) possesses these elements, and so combines and transplants some ancient ideas in a contemporary setting.

A recessed courtyard is an effective space planning device for introducing daylight into the interior of a building, and in southern arid

Figure 9. This water treatment plant in Death Valley, California, was buried by National Park Service architects, largely to reduce air-conditioning loads. The fact that the facility is near a restored frontier town makes the inconspicuous design an especially appropriate solution. Note that the fenestration here faces north.

Figure 10. Traditional arid-zone features of a courtyard and a pool of water are incorporated into this modern underground dwelling near Austin, Texas. The house was designed by Coffee and Crier, Architects.

zones these possess excellent climate control features. However, courtyards will not offer the same climatic advantages in northern zones. Winter sun angles are so low for the upper latitudes that excessively large, shallow courtyards are required to permit any sunlight penetration of their enclosing walls, and the courtyard floor itself is likely to receive little, if any, sunlight. Visions of "sunny, secluded spaces" must be checked on paper with seasonal solar angles (see Figure 11) to insure that a preconceived effect is in fact possible in the given latitude.

Summary and Conclusion

The ground offers a building climate that is free of much of the thermal stress and the peaks in heating and cooling load that make comfort control too often an inefficient, energy-intensive task. Its thermal stabilizing effect leads directly to opportunities for first-cost savings in reduced and simplified HVAC design, as well as smaller envelope loads that mean accrued operating savings. Diminished peripheral loads also alter the focus of mechanical conservation design strategies to leave different forms of heat recovery and energy reclamation free for examination. The change in context from the surface to the subsurface calls for a change in viewpoint of comfort-control system design; if handled with some sensitivity, it should result in considerable savings in both systems and operating costs.

While the overall nature of subsurface

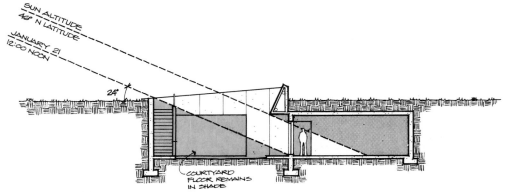

Figure 11. While underground construction offers great heat conservation advantages in northern zones, recessed courtyard designs may limit valuable solar gain. Even when a glazed facade is fully exposed to noonday sun in the middle of winter, the floors of sunken courtyards are likely to be shadowed and cold, a place where snow is slow to melt.

placement may seem to allow simplified engineering design, relocating the building below ground demands greater attention in subtleties of space planning, daylighting, "ambience," and the probable attitudes of occupants toward their environment. Underground spaces can be lively, dramatic, and even cheerful, as well as energy efficient. The several buildings presented within this chapter testify to this, as well as to the range of potential applications and architectural expression available in subsurface design.

The fact that underground climate varies geographically suggests the desirability of regional approaches to underground design. The windowless, buried box is no more univer-

sally appropriate than the ubiquitous glass tower. Individual sites, varying living programs, and requirements for image or for invisibility all combine to produce a myriad of possibilities, a vast majority of which are unexplored. Despite the superficial simplicity, there is as much challenge as there is benefit in building underground; and accompanying this challenge is a rich palette of harmonies and contrasts with which the surface—subsurface interface may be drawn. Some of the most successful compositions of recent years are included in this chapter. The fine precedent established by these buildings presents us with a high standard with which to evaluate the work that will surely follow.

Dune House, Atlantic Beach, Florida

Looking rather like a pair of picture-box Easter eggs, these grass-covered concrete shells in fact represent an extension of architect William Morgan's continuing fascination with "earth architecture." Impelled primarily by a wish to avoid obtruding on neighbors' views of the ocean, the architect/owner buried his buildings in a dune formed by erosion in a '60s hurricane. The structure evolved both from the shape of the dune and from the need to build compactly in order to fit two one-bedroom apartments on a small 50-ft lot.

The apartments occupy a pair of thin (4-in.) concrete domes acting in compression to resist earth load—Morgan's analogy is a submarine hull. The lower part of the structure was built much like a swimming pool—a 4-in. slab bounded by a vertical wall constructed of pneumatically applied concrete on metal lath. In plan this wall curves to resist bending forces, and in elevation it slopes from 2 ft at the oculus to 8 ft at the entrance.

The lower wall also carries long No. 3 reinforcing bars which become basic members of the dome form. Protruding upward, these bars were bent across a "keel" running down the center of each shell. The plywood keel served both to guide the lateral members in their proper curvature and to maintain the curve under uneven loading as concrete was applied. Curvature along the outside edges was maintained by a series of wood templates.

Since the completed structure, after backfilling, works in compression, the bars were not needed as concrete reinforcement but merely as support for the birdcage form, which was built up of metal lath and a few diagonal bars to lend stiffening. The cage was then sprayed with an exceedingly thin layer of concrete to thicken and rigidify the form and to serve as a base for the sprayed concrete of the structural shell.

At the oculus, especially heavy reinforcement *was* required, and a transverse template was employed both to control the changing curvature at this point and to form a groove for the sliding-door frame.

The interior of the shell is also untreated sprayed concrete, though the architect confesses a certain "impurity" of design here: in some areas, notably at the tight overhead curves around the entrance, concrete was troweled.

Morgan is quick to raise, and himself answer, some questions about underground concrete buildings with continuous curved interior surfaces. Humidity: the architect reports that the installed dehumidification equipment proved needlessly elaborate, as dampness was for the most part spontaneously dispelled when the house was occupied. Acoustics: the reverberation evident in the empty shells is controlled by carpeting and by the casework around stairs, kitchen and bedroom loft. (At the same time, the curving walls nicely reinforce stereophonic speakers.) Temperature: inside temperature, thanks to the insulating earth, is a constant 70F, though some heat gain is observed in the morning when sunlight comes through the oculus, which faces east; this light, as well as ocean glare, is controlled with reflective blinds.

DUNE HOUSE, Atlantic Beach, Florida. Owner: *William Morgan.* Architect: *William Morgan Architects.* Engineer: *Geiger Berger Associates—Horst Berger, partner-in-charge*

Alexandre Georges photos

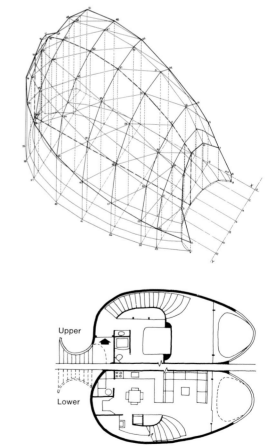

Upper

Lower

To enter the beach house, visitors descend through a low tunnel (bottom right) and thence down a spiral staircase into the main living area. At the other end of each egg, an oculus opens onto a sheltered beachfront terrace (top left). After curing, the structure was backfilled and turfed.

Winston House, Lyme, New Hampshire

On property he already owned in Lyme, New Hampshire, designer Don Metz built this sod-roofed house for sale. "I was bothered," says Metz, who holds a Masters degree in architecture from Yale, "by the prospect of anything other than the low-profile, 'anti-building' solution I knew the site demanded, so I borrowed and built on spec. The present owners—Mr. and Mrs. Oliver Winston were interested before it was completed, made a few minor changes, and that was that."

The finished house is built into a mountainside and embraces a panoramic, 50-mile view to the south. Metz has drawn the earth back down over the roof to a depth of 16 inches. Wildflowers and grasses

have already taken root and a stand of nearby maples is slowly spreading to the rooftop. Its designer hopes the house will gradually disappear among the things that grow around it.

Metz reports that in winter solar gain is sufficient on sunny days to keep the temperatures in the house up to 70°F while outside temperatures are as low as zero. In summer, when the thermal process is reversed, the insulating mantle of earth keeps the house pleasantly cool.

The projections through the sod roof are functional and, though some readers may feel that they compromise the purity of the design parti, it is hard to see how to do without light scoops or roof vents in a plan

with such a long "blind" perimeter. As constructed, the dining area (photo upper right) is suffused with natural light and free of unwelcome glare. The living room opens south across a terrace and small pool to a broad vista of mountain and valley.

Exterior walls are concrete block spanned on 18-inch centers by 6- by 10-in. pine beams. Floors are oak strips nailed over sleepers. The roof is built-up (see detail, opposite page) and finished with a parapet of vertical boards.

WINSTON HOUSE, Lyme, New Hampshire, Designer and contractor: *Don Metz.* Structural engineers: *Spiegel & Zamecnik, Inc.* Landscape architect: *Dan Kiley.* Built-ins: *William Porter, Inc.*

Robert Perron photos

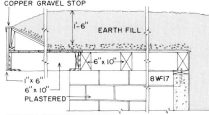

COPPER GRAVEL STOP

EARTH FILL

1'-6"

6" x 10"

1" x 6"

6" x 10"

8 WF17

PLASTERED

SECTION THROUGH GARAGE

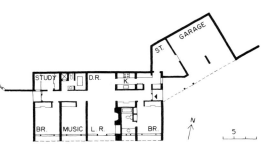

GARAGE

ST.

STUDY

D.R.

K

BR.

MUSIC

L.R.

BR.

N

5

Center for American Arts
Yale University
New Haven, Connecticut

Yale needed a new lecture hall with an up-to-date audio-visual installation, and new and remodeled gallery space for American art and ancient art. Architect Herbert S. Newman decided to place the new auditorium under Weir Court, a unique and once almost secret enclave on the Yale campus. Long considered beautiful for its shape, sense of enclosure and intimacy, it is graced by three ancient elms. Since the giant elms contribute so much to the beauty of the Court as seen from the adjoining Art Gallery building designed by Louis Kahn, Newman devised a scheme which preserves the trees and retains the level, materials and textures of the Court. This effort shaped the auditorium as can be seen in the isometric (opposite page top).

The scheme opens Weir Court to public use. Auditorium entrances and exits are related to the old circulation system of winding stone stairs and passageways which connect the Court to the street. This circulation network permits the new auditorium to be used at night when the Art Gallery building is closed. It is entered by means of the winding stair.

The new auditorium takes over the functions of Yale's famous Room 100, a reverberant and uncomfortable two-story hall where generations of students attended lectures on the history of art and architecture. Vincent Scully, under protest, has been relocated to the luxurious and efficient podium below. His former domain is now a two-story art gallery as can be seen in the section (opposite page bottom). The new auditorium also serves as Yale's principal motion picture theater.

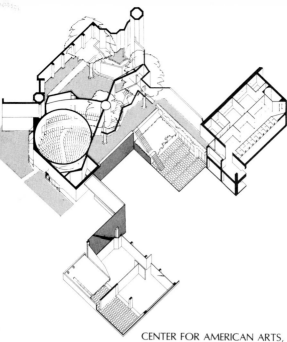

CENTER FOR AMERICAN ARTS, Yale University, New Haven, Connecticut. Architects: *Herbert S. Newman Associates—partner-in-charge of design: Herbert S. Newman; project architects: Glenn H. Gregg (partner), William Newhall and Joseph Schiffer (associates); assistants: Peter Clegg and Tom Hopper. Consultants: Spiegel & Zamecnik, Inc. (structural); Van Zelm, Heywood & Shadford (mechanical); Sylvan R. Shemitz (electrical/lighting); Bolt Beranek & Newman (acoustics); George Fuller Co. (costs).* General contractor: *W. J. Megin, Inc.*

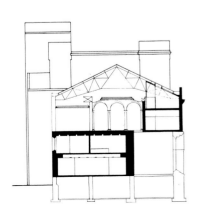

Edward Jacoby

**Nathan Marsh Pusey Library
Harvard Yard
Cambridge, Massachusetts**

By partially burying this three-level library underground and covering its roof with grass, planting, and paths which reinforce the existing circulation patterns of Harvard Yard, architects Hugh Stubbins and Associates have added an essential structure while preserving open space. Glass windows, concealed by sloping berms along two sides of the exterior and a central light court introduce natural lighting to staff and reader areas. Shown above is the principal entrance. The mobile in black steel is Alexander Calder's "The Onion."

All the interiors and custom-built fixtures were designed by the architects. Nylon carpeting is used throughout except in bookstack areas. Most of the furniture is of oak, as is the trim. Walls are covered with a textured vinyl fabric with a flat off-white, non-reflective surface. The acoustic ceilings are also off-white. Chairs are upholstered in either muted tweeds or brown leather. The daylight is softened by window hangings of natural hemp in an open-weave geometric pattern. All metal, from the window mullions to the smallest door hinge, is of bronze or bronze-finished aluminum. Accent lighting is either incandescent, or fluorescent warmed by gold reflectors within the light fixtures.

The photo (top) is of the reading room for the theater collection. The principal corridor (middle) is an exhibition gallery. It contains four large oak framed, acrylic-fronted exhibition cases for changing exhibitions. The gallery opens into the lounge (left) with a long display case beneath the window overlooking the moat. The lounge is a hub that provides access to the theater collection and archives, as well as to the central circulation desk just visible at the edge of the picture.

The most recent addition to Harvard Yard is a courteous and restrained new library. It is a background building constructed for the most part below grade on a site that was too constricted for a building above ground. Harvard Yard, of course, is a place of great historic interest, a museum of native American architecture of every period and an environment revered by generations of Harvard students, Cambridge citizens, and lovers of campus architecture.

Before being asked to design the Pusey Library, Hugh Stubbins Associates had been engaged to survey the entire twenty two-acre Yard with the object of improving access and services.

After careful observation of the patterns of activity and circulation within the Yard, the architects proposed that it be completely closed to automobiles and parking except for service and emergency access. This was implemented by the university.

Originally it had been thought that the proposed library should be completely subterranean, but new concepts of landscaping led to the idea that the building could emerge at least slightly above ground. The architects foresaw an opportunity they have since effectively capitalized upon—that of designing the library in a way that would open up new vistas within the Yard as seen from the inside of the new structure, or from its landscaped roof. Just as importantly, allowing the building to surface brings daylight into the interiors.

From the beginning, the Pusey Library was seen as an interconnecting link among three existing libraries — Widener, Houghton and Lamont (see site plan right), and an extension of each. Its roof has become a link as well, its paths and landscaping reinforcing the existing circulation network in the Yard. Inside the library, the principal circulation corridor is directly beneath the main diagonal path on the roof. The three major entrances to the new library are at important campus nodes. The principal entrance is directly to the east of the grand staircase of the Widener Library; the second is at the corner formed by Houghton and Lamont; the third is adjacent to 17 Quincy, the former official residence of the president of the university, now used for miscellaneous functions.

The new structure, which has been so precisely and definitively attached to its neighboring build-

The view across the landscaped roof of the new library (right) is as seen from the front of the Widener Library. The steps lead to the principal diagonal path, which connects with the circulation system of the Yard. The main entrance of Pusey is below grade at the foot of a staircase to the right of this stair. The stairway (below) also leads to the landscaped roof of Pusey. It is located between Houghton Library and Lamont Library.

© Steve Rosenthal

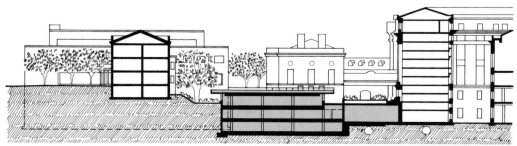

SECTION A-A

100

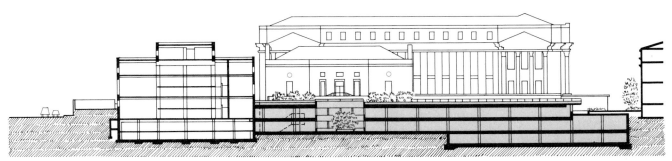

SECTION B-B

ings and to the campus infrastructure, adds 87,000 square feet to the buildings that comprise the Harvard College Library, which is a subdivision of the Harvard University Library, the largest university library in the world. Of the eight libraries within the College Library, three required their own reading rooms and better conservation of their priceless collections. These are the Harvard Theatre Collection, the Harvard University Archives and the Harvard Map Collection. The memorabilia of President Theodore Roosevelt needed adequate storage and display. Since, with the passage of time, books once regarded as commonplace have become rare, space had to be created that would allow such books to be kept at a temperature and humidity protective of their paper and bindings. Finally, as in all college libraries, the variety of services had increased and the collections were growing at rapidly accelerating rates. The new library accommodates the expanding general collections of Widener Library and the manuscript collections of Houghton.

In visible exterior form, the Pusey Library is a slanting grass-covered embankment as can be seen in the photos at right. Its roof is a stone-rimmed platform of earth containing a lawn, trees and shrubs, diagonally bisected by paths and stairs. On axis with the Neo-Georgian bow-front of Houghton is a square sunken courtyard (opposite page bottom right), which admits light to major interior spaces.

The portion of the building that appears above the surface is surrounded by a broad band of brick paving, which forms a moat between the berm and the window wall. At the top of the berm is a deep concrete trough planted with shrubs and vines.

Construction began on the Pusey Library in 1973 and was completed in 1976 at a cost of $5,653,000.

NATHAN MARSH PUSEY LIBRARY, Harvard Yard, Cambridge, Massachusetts. Owner: *President and Fellows of Harvard College.* Architects: *Hugh Stubbins and Associates, Inc.—design: Hugh Stubbins, Peter Woytuk; project architect: Merle T. Westlake; project manager: Howard Goldstein; landscape: Robert Fager; interior design: Tetsuo Takayanagi.* Engineers: *LeMessurier Associates/SCI (structural); Haley and Aldrich (foundations); van Zelm, Heywood and Shadford (mechanical/electrical).* General contractor: *The Volpe Construction Co., Inc.*

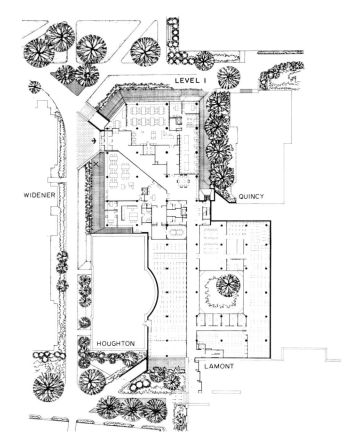

LEVEL 1

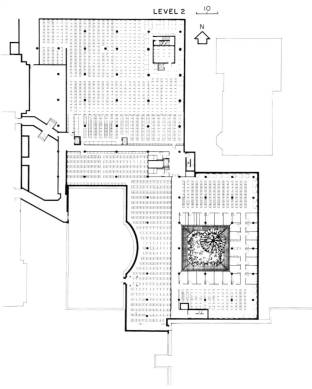

LEVEL 2

LEVEL 3

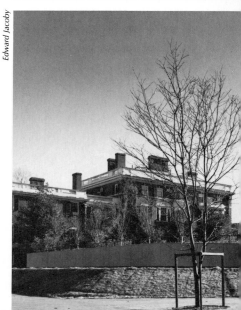

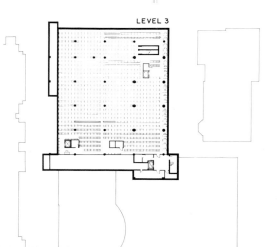

As the main level plan (opposite page top) indicates, the library has been organized to provide good visual control from the circulation desk located just beyond the lounge adjacent to the exhibition gallery. The photograph (top) shows the degree to which the apparent bulk of the library has been minimized by the slanting berm. To the left of the photo is the corner of Emerson Hall and 17 Quincy. To the rear are Lamont and Houghton and to the right is Widener. The courtyard (right) is two levels deep. It is faced with panels of shipsaw granite alternating with bands of glass. The court is a small garden with a brick surround.

Larry Mills photos except as noted

PNB Fourth Avenue Office Complex, Portland, Oregon

Architects Zimmer Gunsul Frasca were faced with a program that might have required a three-story windowless and accordingly "faceless" building next to one of Portland, Oregon's most popular pedestrian-scaled amenities, Lawrence Halprin's Lovejoy Fountain. The program was for 80,000 square feet of space on a site that was only slightly larger. The space was to be protected from natural light and vandalism for data processing equipment for the telephone company. Also included was twice that area for parking spaces. In the proposed location, a three-story building of such character not only might have intruded on the lively nature of the Fountain, but would have cut off pedestrian access from one side as well.

Instead, the architects have produced what appears to the public as a landscaped lawn containing an airy polished-aluminum and glass pavilion, which forms a pleasant and

reflective screen in front of the blank wall on an older telephone-company facility. The new building space is underground. And the "pavilion" is the entrance and employees' cafeteria, where workers can come up for views of the lawn and fountain from their closed environment below.

PNB FOURTH AVENUE OFFICE COMPLEX, Portland, Oregon. Owner: *Pacific Northwest Bell Telephone Company.* Architects: *Zimmer Gunsul Frasca Partnership—partner-in-charge: Brooks Gunsul; design team: Raymond Boucher, Robert Frasca, Michele Lewis, Jack Walling; project architect: Brainard Gannett.* Engineers: *Rose', Breedlove & Mc Connell, Inc. (structural); Shannon & Wilson, Inc. (foundation and soils); C.W. Timmer Associates, Inc. (mechanical); Langton, Mehlig & Associates, Inc. (electrical).* Landscape architects: *SWA Group.* General contractor: *Todd Building Company.*

Ed Hershberger

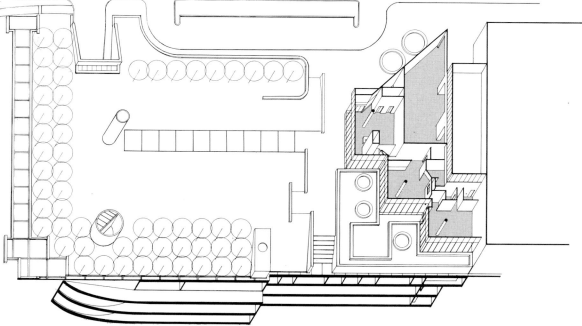

The underground location of Pacific Northwest Bell's $7.3-million facility provides an obvious suggestion for other types of utilitarian structures in urban areas. In the case of PNWB, the owners not only received a great public relations benefit from their gesture to the City, but they answered their program of sealed and secure spaces in a most effective way. They have significant energy conservation savings (as much as thirty per cent over an ongrade structure) to help their life-cost calculations.

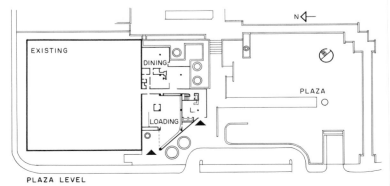

PLAZA LEVEL

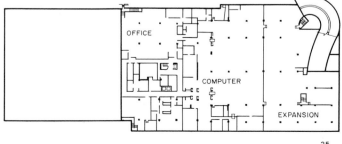

LOWER LEVEL

25

Bailey Library, Hendrix College, Conway, Arkansas

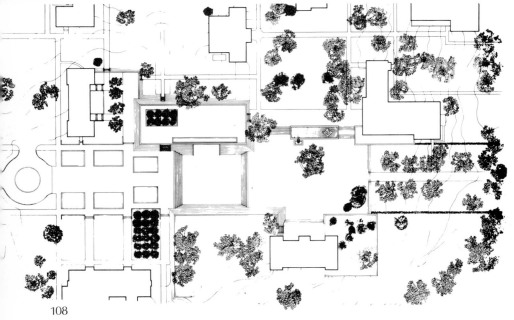

AN UNDERGROUND LIBRARY solved an interesting planning problem for this college in Arkansas. It was strongly desired that the library be centrally located on the campus for maximum convenience and usage, but there was not land available in such a spot without sacrificing open spaces also considered indispensable. The result solves both with a two-story concrete building burrowed within earth sculpture, landscaping and plazas on a series of interrelated horizontal planes. In addition to library facilities, the college has a vital new focal point. The sunken plaza doubles as an effective space for ceremonial outdoor functions.

BAILEY LIBRARY, Hendrix College, Conway, Arkansas. Architects: *Philip Johnson* and *Wittenberg, Delony & Davidson, Inc.*; engineers: *W. H. Goodman, Jr.* (mechanical); *Charles E. Dietz* (electrical); *Engineering Consultants* (structural). Landscape consultant: *Joe Lambert*; graphics: *Walter Kacik Design Associates.*

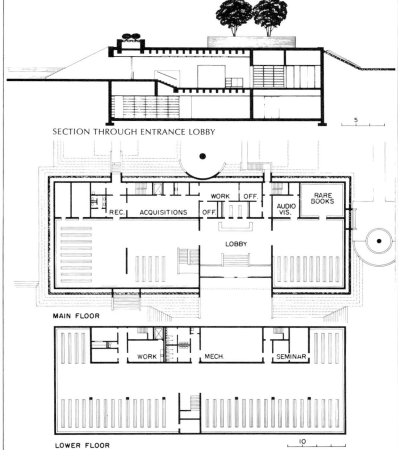

SECTION THROUGH ENTRANCE LOBBY

5

MAIN FLOOR

| REC. | ACQUISITIONS | WORK | OFF. | AUDIO VIS. | RARE BOOKS |
| | | OFF. | | | |

LOBBY

LOWER FLOOR

| WORK | MECH. | SEMINAR |

10

The architects realized a number of advantages with an underground library: maximum utilization of available land; diversion of funds from finishing the exterior to landscaping needs; reduction in the amount of traffic congestion; better control of light, dust and humidity; and earth insulation to minimize heat loss in winter. The earth removed for the building and the big sunken court was used to form the surrounding berms.

Philip Johnson Gallery
New Canaan, Connecticut

Reminiscent of an old-fashioned root cellar, architect Philip Johnson's art gallery is seemingly burrowed into a grassy slope, although in reality it is built upon a hillside shelf and buried by berms. This came about because Johnson is interested in the esthetics of earth mounds, because he did not want any outside distractions to interfere with the study of his collection, and because it is easy to maintain optimum temperature and humidity control in an underground space. Furthermore, the architect did not want another building within the carefully studied outdoor space of his New Canaan estate, the gallery's location. The interior space comprises three tangential circular areas, each containing a set of swinging panels for the display and storage of paintings. Sculpture and furniture are on casters, so the arrangement can readily be changed.

- -
PHILIP JOHNSON GALLERY, New Canaan, Connecticut. Architect: *Philip Johnson;* structural engineers: *Lev Zetlin & Associates;* mechanical engineers: *Jaros, Baum & Bolles;* general contractor: *E. W. Howell Company.*

Ezra Stoller photos

Philip Johnson explains that this gallery was constructed as a demonstration of one way in which the very real problem of storage and viewing space for art can be handled. Many large museums can show only 10 per cent of their permanent collections, and store the remainder in racks difficult of access. Johnson is glad his gallery makes it possible to show educators and collectors a new way in which paintings can be studied and enjoyed.

4

ENERGY CONSERVING TECHNIQUES IN HEATING AND AIR CONDITIONING, IN LIGHTING, AND (MOST EFFECTIVE OF ALL) IN BUILDING OPERATION

T he need to conserve energy in buildings has proved a new challenge and opportunity not just to architects—but to the engineers who work with them in the design of heating, ventilating and air-conditioning systems, the design of lighting, and the design of the "nerve system" of a building—its controls.

Like architects, engineers are finding it useful and necessary not just to set off in search of new techniques, but to "rediscover" some of the basics of building engineering that they learned back in school—but had ignored during the years when power was cheap. "Muscling" comfort conditions was the cheapest (at least cheapest first-cost) way to provide services.

This chapter explores some of these techniques:

• Beginning overleaf is an article describing a major heat-pump installation in Florida;

• On pages 118, a description of two special hvac systems involving provisions for projected changes in processes for two electronic plants;

• On page 121, a description of a system that minimizes energy waste despite the need for high-volume air changes, and an outline of an automated control system for a major university;

• On page 122, a system which uses air three times is described;

• On page 124, a unique system of hvac pods atop stair towers is detailed;

• On page 126, an experimental heat pump/ice storage system for heating and cooling is outlined;

• A system for thermal storage permitting use of 100 per cent off-peak power is described on page 129.

• And two buildings which explore a wide variety of energy-conserving systems—the Federal Home Loan Bank Board Building in Washington and the equally inventive Government of Canada Building in Toronto—are described on p. 130 to 137.

Lighting is perhaps the most obvious user of energy—for the simple reason that it is . . . well . . . so *visible*. Our standards of lighting (remember when the utilities were pushing for more and more footcandles and the manufacturers were promoting 'luminous' ceilings?) have come under careful study—and this book's first chapter on standards has outlined progress there.

But equally important are the physical techniques of getting maximum lighting for minimum power usage, and beginning on page KK are outlined some of the most innovative techniques, including the much-talked-about task-ambient lighting systems—in which the emphasis is put on lighting not the building, but the work.

Finally, this chapter offers some thought-provoking ideas on saving energy through more effective operation of the building. As engineer Larry Spielvogel says in the introduction to his article on page 168: "The one factor that, more than any other, determines energy consumption of a building is how it is used. 'How it is used' has more impact than the type of hvac system, or the boilers, or the chillers, or the energy source. More than how much glass, or installation, or lighting a building has. It is the people who occupy a building that place the demands on systems and use energy. It is the hours of operation of systems and components that are the major determinants of energy consumption . . . ." Engineer Spielvogel outlines some of the ways to control building operation . . . and two final articles in this chapter describe progress toward automating this all-important factor in energy consumption and conservation.

EXAMPLES OF INNOVATIONS IN HEATING, AIR HANDLING, AND AIR CONDITIONING

Winewood Office Park, Tallahassee, Florida

The first eight buildings of an office-park rental complex in Tallahassee, Florida are being heated and cooled with 151 split-system heat pumps with a total cooling capacity of nearly 1500 tons. The 388,000-square-foot complex includes seven two-, three- and four-story buildings, a separate auditorium and banquet hall for 150 people, and a cafeteria for 150 people. The eighth building, a three-story office structure, is scheduled for completion in December.

The split system heat pumps range in capacity from 5 to 20 tons. Almost half of the units are either 7½, 10, 15 or 20 tons. The advantage of the split-system arrangement is that the fan-coil section can be located close to the zone served, minimizing the amount of ductwork necessary.

The outdoor units on the roofs of the buildings contain the compressor, outdoor coil and fan. The indoor air handlers contain a coil and blower. The sectional drawing on the next page indicates that only a small amount of space is required for running the refrigerant piping from the outdoor units to the air handlers. The ductwork consists, then, only of horizontal runs in the suspended ceiling space.

The heat pumps, of course, can either heat or cool, and this is advantageous in climates where there are wide swings in daily temperatures during some seasons of the year. And because the heat pumps operate on electricity, they avoid the problems posed by local fuel shortages and, as in Tallahassee, a recent moratorium on new natural gas customers. Still another advantage of these unitary systems is that they can be operated individually, and a shutdown of one unit does not knock out the entire system. Obviously, too, the initial cost of this unitary equipment is attractive to office-building developers.

According to the owner, the energy consumption for the complex is below the amount that had been programed. Furthermore, with so little space taken up with the mechanical system, more rentable area is available.

WINEWOOD OFFICE PARK, Tallahassee, Florida. Architect: *Joseph N. Clemons.*

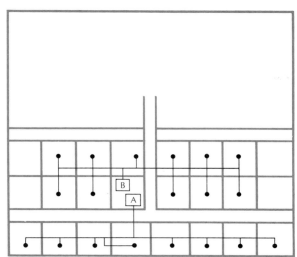

PLAN

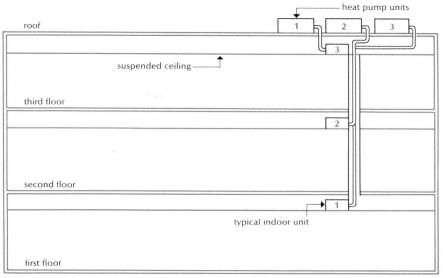

SECTION

The $15 million office park has 2-, 3- and 4-story buildings. Because it is feasible to run refrigerant piping at least four stories, the use of split system heat pumps meant that there was no need for vertical duct shafts. Condensing sections were located on the roofs of the buildings, and indoor units with blowers and coils on the floors of the zones they serve. Spaces could be zoned along the lines of the diagram above. The heat pumps ranged in capacity from 5 to 20 tons, at least half of them being 7½, 10, 15 and 20 tons. Altogether there are 151 separate heat pump systems totaling 1,494 tons. The drawing, above right, shows diagramatically how refrigerant piping runs from rooftop units to indoor sections.

Tektronix Mechanical Products Building and Electronic Devices Building Oregon

Art Hupy

Interstitial spaces make it easy to modify mechanicals to suit production changes.

Tektronix, Incorporated, an Oregon manufacturer of cathode-ray-oscilloscopes, needed people-oriented flexibility for its new Electronic Devices Building, and machine-oriented flexibility for its new Mechanical Products Building. In response, the architects, Wolff Zimmer Gunsul Frasca, and their engineers, Nortec, Inc., took two different approaches to the design of the mechanical systems and of the structures.

For the Electronic Devices Building, in which large numbers of people work in a highly controlled environment on the construction of integrated circuits, two interstitial floors were provided for three working floors. Because constant change and modification in this facility was anticipated, the supporting systems had to be dynamic as well. To facilitate easy removal and installation of large instruments and equipment on the working levels, the architects designed the continuous glazing at the working levels for easy removal of the glazed framed units. Likewise, for access to the mechanical levels, the exterior metal panels also are removable. And the overhangs serve as convenient working platforms.

The Mechanical Products Building, with activities ranging from clean-laboratory space to very heavy metal- and plastic-forming processes, required flexibility of a different sort. The architects' charge was to provide a space that would accommodate completely unknown processes in the future without incurring premature or excessive capital costs. The issues that required resolution were: 1) The building had to provide for heavy equipment such as punch presses which implied on-grade bearing. On the other hand, there were certain wet processes that required low-slab drainage. The location of these operations and processes could not be established prior to construction;

Ed & Carol Hershberger photos

Flexibility for people was required here.

Ed & Carol Hershberger

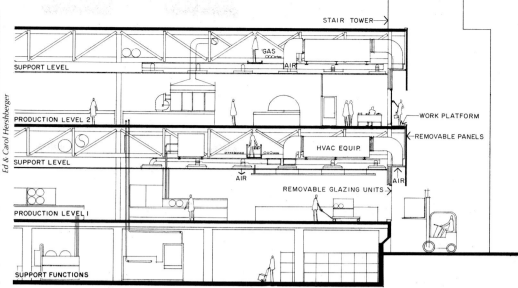

Removable glazing and exterior panels allow new production or mechanical equipment to be easily brought in.

2) future offices and laboratories requiring air conditioning and exhaust had to be anticipated; 3) no determination could be made as to what extent processes might be automated in the future.

The design solution was a light-steel-frame, high-bay industrial building, uncommon in the electronics field. The unrestricted height made it possible to preserve a layer of space below the ceiling plane for future conveyor systems or other forms of automated production.

The mechanical solution consisted of a series of large air-handling units located in a monitor above the ceiling plane. This system provides thermal conditioning for the entire facility, and is sized to accommodate anticipated exhaust systems. If the capabilities of this system are exceeded in the future, the only addition needed will be that of make-up air for exhaust. If closed spaces such as offices or laboratories are added, fan equipment is provided for ventilation only which relies on the in-building air system for supply air rather than on ductwork connections to the main systems in the monitor.

Flexibility for machines was required here.

High-bay building has a materials-handling "layer" for easy changes. Mechanical equipment is on the roof.

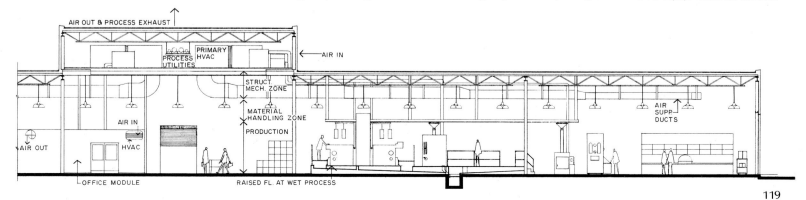

Aircraft Accessories
Overhaul Shop
North Island Naval Air Station
San Diego, California

A large portion of the Navy's Aircraft Accessories Overhaul Shop is devoted to metal finishing operations that require effective removal of noxious fumes. Both the process engineering and the building design were performed by Daniel, Mann, Johnson & Mendenhall, making it possible for the firm to integrate the process fume control system into the design in an effective and architecturally pleasing manner.

The processes, which included chemical cleaning, anodizing, electroplating, painting and plasma spraying, dictated air supply rates as high as 62 cfm per sq ft (in comparison, normal air conditioning uses only 1 to 2 cfm per sq ft). To avoid drafts, a suspended perforated metal ceiling was used to form an air supply plenum and serve as an air diffuser covering the entire ceiling. Air handlers on the roof deliver tempered air to the plenum. With this design large and expensive ductwork was eliminated, and, further, a finished ceiling was provided.

The processing tanks require many utility and piping services, and to provide space for these, the tanks were placed in a pit, but extending above the operating floor. Utilities and fume collector exhaust ducts were arranged for clear access for maintenance. The main exhaust ducts were actually tunnels crossing aisles below the pit floor and running to the outside of the building, then rising into the bottom of scrubbers prior to discharging the fumes to the atmosphere.

Because the building is in a prominent location, special enclosures made of fiberglass-bonded resin, with an integral orange pigment, were fabricated for the exhaust-air scrubbers to give them a neat appearance. Vertical air scrubbers were located over the tunnel risers, with in-line centrifugal fans on top of the risers, and stacks extending above the roof.

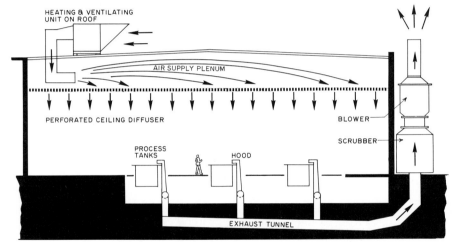

The entire ceiling is a diffuser to avoid drafts.

The scrubbers were set inside specially-fabricated plastic enclosures to organize the equipment neatly.

Console controls and monitors 65 buildings.

Honeywell photos

Automation control center in the Health Sciences building now handles a 10-building complex.

University of Minnesota
Minneapolis, Minnesota

An automated control network at the University of Minnesota, monitoring some 2000 check-points in 65 buildings, is estimated by its physical plant director to be saving a half-million dollars a year in operating costs, not to say the energy to heat and light a small city.

By employing digital pulse transmission, only a pair of leased telephone lines is required for the automation control console to check, correlate and control systems in buildings as near as 200 ft apart and as far as 200 miles away.

The University had installed a hard-wired automation system a decade earlier in its 10-building medical complex, and five years ago, a desk-sized console in the Shops building. But because of the involved and expensive station-to-station wiring, this latter hook-up was limited to 16 buildings on the Minneapolis campus. Both of these systems will be gradually phased into the over-all master system. A third automation system, started in 1965, that handles four buildings on the University's west bank, also will be absorbed into the master system.

The automation system includes an "electronic calender" that automatically starts up systems in each building at a preset time and shuts them down later, reflecting actual building use. Even on below-zero days, heating in many buildings can be turned off at 1 P.M. not to be started again until 4 A.M.

In monitoring the thousands of check-points, the automation console flashes an immediate warning if any of them go off-normal. An alarm printer gives a permanent record of all off-normal conditions. A second printer provides a summary of all critical points on all campuses, enabling the operator to pinpoint problems before they become serious. Further, efficiencies of equipment can be checked, and maintenance conducted more effectively.

Pasteurizer is monitored by the console 10 miles away.

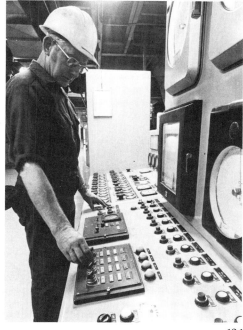

Steam plant is just a half-mile away.

County of Santa Clara Service Center, San Jose, California

Maximum benefit is wrung from conditioned air at the $12.5-million Service Center for the County of Santa Clara located in San Jose, California. Return air from the middle of the three buildings that compose the center is first used to condition the skylight-covered central court of this four-story building. But exhaust air from the court is not dumped to the outdoors; rather the engineers use it still another time for the warehouse portion of Building 1 and for the shops in Building 3.

The buildings are interconnected by an underground utility/access tunnel that also serves as a duct for the air supplied to the warehouse and to the shops.

The system works this way: Conditioned air is supplied to the office spaces through 4- by 4-ft air-handling luminaires. Air is returned through the lamp compartment of the luminaires and flows into the plenum above the ceiling. From the plenum, the air is pulled out into the court through slots in the concrete fascia beam surrounding the court on each floor. Air in the court is drawn down into the exhaust/return fan through wood grilles around the perimeter of the court planting areas. Pres-

sure from the exhaust/return fan forces air through the utility tunnels.

Air supplied to Building 1 provides general ventilation for the warehouse area, as well as for some shops and specialty-type storage areas. Air supplied to Building 3 provides ventilation for the general shop areas, as well as make-up air for the wood shop exhaust system and for the paint booth exhaust system.

The main fan room below Building 2 is used as a discharge plenum for the exhaust/return fan. Automatically controlled dampers determine how much air is directed to the supply fan systems of Building 2, how much to the utility tunnels, and how much to the exhaust. When outdoor temperature allows the system to supply in excess of 50 per cent outdoor air, automatic dampers located at the roof in two exhaust duct risers start to open; at 100 per cent outdoor air they are fully open. These dampers are controlled by pressure sensing devices that maintain pressures in the fan room high enough to force the excess return air through the utility tunnels.

Building 2 has vertical utility shafts to get conditioned air to the office floors. They each

house a cold-duct riser; an exhaust-duct riser; plumbing risers; sprinkler-pipe risers; steam, hot-water and chilled-water risers. The shafts also act as warm-air plenums.

By not using a ducted return-air system, the engineers, Westcon Associates, estimate that approximately 460 square feet of building floor area was saved for other uses.

The court was designed to be colder than the enclosed office spaces in winter and warmer in summer. The balconies around the court serve as circulation between offices and from offices to exits. The engineers explain that these temperature differentials help make the court seem like an outdoor area, yet not so warm or cold as to cause discomfort.

A central heating and cooling plant for all three buildings is located adjacent to Building 2. Buildings 1 and 3 have their own mechanical rooms with hvac equipment to condition the air for their office areas.

COUNTY OF SANTA CLARA SERVICE CENTER, California. Architects: *Hawley & Peterson*. Engineers: *T. T. Seibert* (structural); *Westcon Associates* (mechanical/electrical). Mechanical contractor: *O. C. McDonald*.

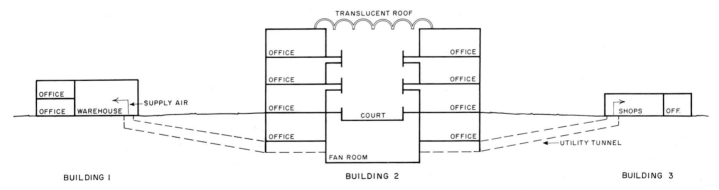

Return air from office spaces is drawn by a large exhaust/return-air fan from ceiling plenums into the central court, through grade-level return grilles, and into the main fan room of Building 2. Pressure from this fan pushes air through utility tunnels connecting Building 2 with Buildings 1 and 3, where this air is used to ventilate warehouse and shop areas. Vertical utility shafts in Building 2 are used to supply cold and warm air to offices and to contain plumbing and sprinkler piping. The shaft itself serves as a warm-air plenum. Exhaust air is ducted to the roof. Automatic dampers regulate how much air is exhausted, depending upon the amount of outdoor air introduced, but sufficient pressure is always maintained to force air returned from the court through the tunnels to Buildings 1 and 3.

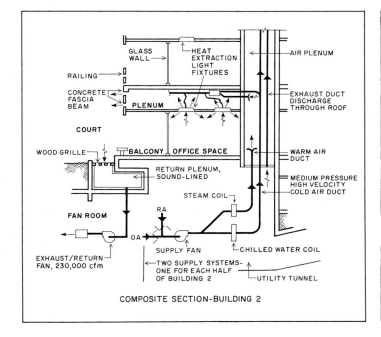

COMPOSITE SECTION-BUILDING 2

Julius Shulman photos

Offices for Fluor Engineers & Constructors
Irvine, California

An effective, uncomplicated, energy-conscious design for Fluor Corporation's new office building in Southern California is a result of the total integration of engineering and architectural concerns that also achieve a showcase for the client. A consolidation of seven offices in the area, the building provides 1.3 million square feet for nearly 4,400 persons—expandable to 7,000—wrapped in silver reflective glass and punctuated by three visually prominent mechanical towers.

Because of the mild climate, there is no central heating plant or boiler. Rather, a combination of electric radiant heating panels, fluorescent lighting and body heat provide heat for the entire building. The mirror glass (⅜-in. thick and single-glazed because of warm winters) obviously is a key factor in maintaining a comfortable atmosphere.

A total of 1,300 radiant heating panels is located either above a narrow perimeter corridor (not used for circulation) or in the relatively few private offices. They are activated only on the rare cold days. Fluorescent lighting provides 110 footcandles fully illuminating the open-plan work areas.

Placing the fan rooms atop the freestanding stair towers, and using them as visual elements, accomplished several objectives. The separation permits an esthetically-pleasing roof line and isolates noise and vibrations. Furthermore, this allows flexibility in future building expansion, as each tower at maximum capacity can serve two sections (called "pods" by the architects). Presently, only one tower is used this way and it incorporates two supply and two return variable-pitch, axial-flow fans. The remaining towers have only one supply and one return.

Air returns to the towers from the work areas through slots in the recessed light fixtures. These systems are controlled by a central computer which "reads" outside temperature and humidity before the workday begins and determines when to turn on the lights and radiant heating panels and to start the fans.

OFFICES FOR FLUOR ENGINEERS & CONSTRUCTORS, Southern California Division, Irvine, California. Architects: *Welton Becket Associates—Alan Rosen, director of Los Angeles office and project director; John Parr, assistant project director; Karl Schwerdtfeger, project designer.* Engineers: *Brandow & Johnston Associates (structural); Leroy Crandell (soils); James A. Knowles & Associates, Inc. (mechanical); Brad Karr of Welton Becket Associates (electrical); Shuirman Rogoway & Associates (civil).* Landscape architects: *Fong Jung Nakaba Associates.* General contractor: *C. L. Peck Contractors.*

Three identical 93-feet-high mechanical towers house variable volume fans and cooling equipment to serve two building sections. Their shape directly reflects their function, and they have become an important over-all visual element and also separate vibrations and noise from the building.

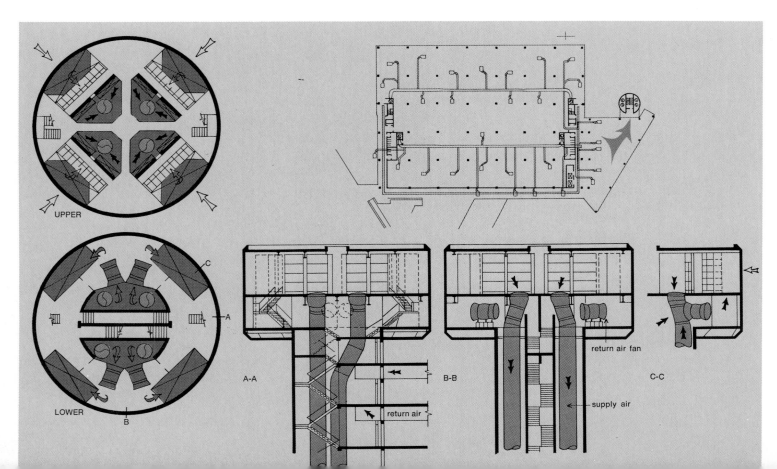

UPPER

LOWER

A-A return air

B-B return air fan

C-C supply air

Annual Cycle Energy System Demonstration Residence Knoxville, Tennessee

A new strategy for reducing energy costs in the heating and cooling of residential, institutional and commercial buildings that has recently emerged from ERDA's Oak Ridge National Laboratory utilizes ice-making to get Btu's for heating in the winter and "free" cooling in the summer. The approach, called Annual Cycle Energy System (ACES), takes advantage of the physical fact that 144 Btu's of heat must be extracted from a pound of 32 F water to convert it to ice, and the same amount of heat must be applied to melt the ice. A crude parallel is old-timers' use of winter-frozen ice to preserve fresh foods in the summer.

At the heart of the system is a heat pump that extracts heat from the outdoor air during the heating season until the air's temperature drops to around 40 F. When the outdoor air is colder than this it "frosts up" the outdoor coils of the heat pump with a resulting drop in the efficiency. But what if the heat pump were to make ice in a large tank when outdoor air temperatures are at freezing or below? Not only would the efficiency of the heating cycle be improved, but the ice could be built up in the tank to be melted in warm weather.

This basic idea of making ice to heat a house was suggested by engineers over 40 years ago. Credit for reviving it belongs to engineer Harry C. Fischer who, as a heat-pump engineer in the '50s, tried to interest the industry in a heat pump that made ice for heating and kept the ice accumulated for space cooling. As Fischer notes, the idea didn't "fly" because of the cost of storage for the ice and the low cost of energy. But eight months after the Arab oil embargo, Harry Fischer, then in retirement, presented his ice-storage idea to the Energy Division at Oak Ridge National Laboratory (ORNL), which had been looking for conservation approaches for building thermal envelopes, water heaters and heat pumps. ORNL, operated by Union Carbide Corporation, liked the idea and hired him as a staff consultant to pursue development. In December 1974 HUD awarded Fischer's group a $100,000 grant for the ACES project, and by February, the first test ACES system was built and operating. A month later Westinghouse Electric Corporation, which had been urged by Fischer to build an ACES system, had one installed in their domestic engineering center near Pittsburgh. Now an ACES demonstration residence (shown right) has been built in Knoxville, Tennessee as one of several houses in the Tennessee Energy Conservation in Housing program sponsored by

This ACES (Annual Cycle Energy System) house at the University of Tennessee will have its operation compared with a solar house and a conventional house. The system comprises a heat pump on the second level behind the outdoor radiant/convector coil and a 16- by 21- by 8-ft ice bin. System makes ice in winter to get heat and melts it in the summer to get cooling. To make more ice in summer, refrigerant is rejected to the outdoor coil.

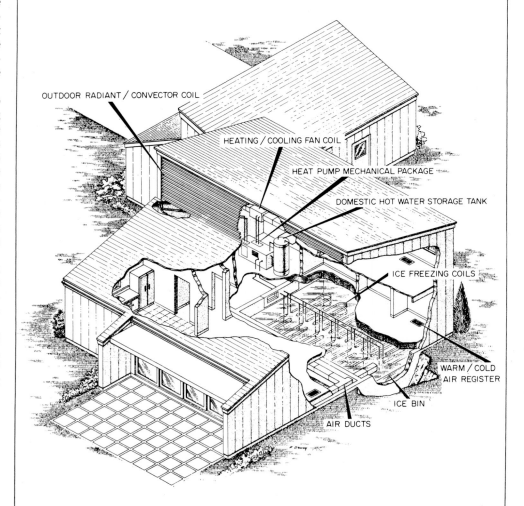

OUTDOOR RADIANT / CONVECTOR COIL

HEATING / COOLING FAN COIL

HEAT PUMP MECHANICAL PACKAGE

DOMESTIC HOT WATER STORAGE TANK

ICE FREEZING COILS

WARM / COLD AIR REGISTER

ICE BIN

AIR DUCTS

The ice bin has 1300 ft of aluminum finned tubing for its cooling coils. The ½-in. tubing and 3-in. fins are extruded as one section. Same material is used for the outdoor coil. In Knoxville, the ice bin has enough capacity to keep adding ice for the entire heating season, so there is no need for heat input from the outdoor coil. Ice made in winter will last most of the summer for cooling. When the ice has melted, the compressor will run at night to chill the tank's water.

ORNL, the University of Tennessee, and the Tennessee Valley Authority.

Cost of an ACES system for an 1800-sq-ft house has been estimated to be $5,000-6,000 for Washington, D.C. and Philadelphia, compared with $1500 for electric heating and air conditioning (figures from 1977). Even so, engineers say, this is less than the cost for a

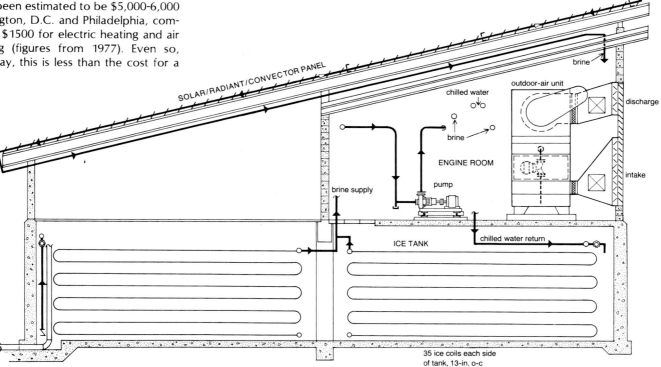

35 ice coils each side of tank, 13-in. o-c

completely solar heating-and-cooling system. And Oak Ridge engineers have been talking to manufacturers about application of ice-makers normally used for food preservation to reduce ice-tank costs: an ice-maker installed over a bin could merely slough off ice into the bin, eliminating pipe coils in the bin, itself. But until this is tried out in practice, some engineers will have questions about the efficacy of heat transfer from ice to water.

Because of the higher capital costs for ACES, its advocates are looking for applications in building types where owners are receptive to life-cycle costing. For this reason, they are eyeing a research installation by the Veterans Administration in a 60-bed nursing home at Wilmington, Delaware (illustrations this page). Though the nursing home had been designed when VA mechanical engineers heard about ACES, in their effort to promote energy savings they decided to have the project bid both conventionally and ACES, and brought in consulting engineer Robert G. Werden, a consultant to Oak Ridge on commercial development of ACES, to design the system. Werden—who has a long-time background in the development and application of heat pumps in commercial, industrial, school and apartment construction—has designed an "energy bank" that will provide 75 tons of cooling and 800,000 Btu of heating. Because of the storage capability of the system, not only are operating-cost economics of the heat pump improved, but electric demand can be reduced greatly by making ice at nights during the summer. A special computer monitoring the system will decide which of eight modes of operation (shown next page) will satisfy space-conditioning demands, will control storage according to season, and will choose the most economical mode as governed by both weather and season.

Because the 60-bed VA nursing home in Wilmington had been designed before VA engineers decided to use the Annual Cycle Energy System, consulting engineer Robert Werden put his "energy bank" in a separate structure. It incorporates refrigeration (heat pump) equipment, a 40- by 50- by 10-ft ice tank, a solar/radiant/convector panel, and a computer system to monitor and control the operation. During the heating season, the outdoor air unit extracts heat from the air until it drops into the 40's. At lower air temperatures, refrigerant circulates through the brine (methanol) cooler so it can make ice. The roof panel absorbs solar energy to melt excess ice in winter, and rejects heat to outdoor air and the night sky in summer.

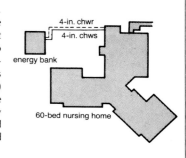

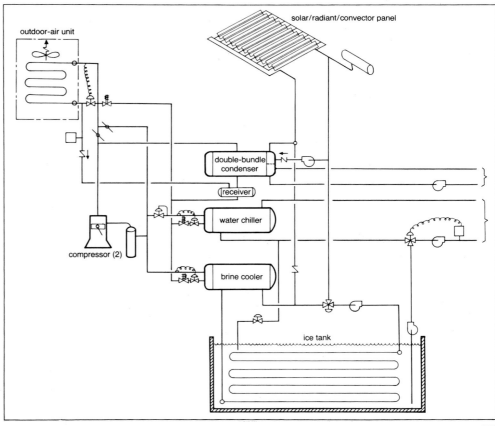

During the heating season, the outdoor unit extracts heat from outdoor air until the weather is in the 40's (Mode 1). In its least efficient operation, this cycle has a coefficient of performance (COP) of 4.6. Cold refrigerant circulates through the outdoor unit picking up heat, and the heat of compression from the two 37.5-ton reciprocating compressors (800,000 Btu/hr max.) is rejected to the double-bundle condenser for space heating.

When outdoor air is too cold for efficient operation of the outdoor unit, the system makes ice (Mode 2). Refrigerant chills the brine (methanol solution) to water-freezing temperatures, and the heat of compression, again, is used for space heating. Ice can build up on the coils to a 6-in.-dia. "doughnut," and, in this least-efficient condition, the COP is 3.38.

When there is useful solar heat and the system is calling for heating (Mode 3), brine is circulated through the solar panel and then through the tank to melt ice. Heat from this process is added to the heat of compression of the refrigerant.

If there is more heat available from the outdoor unit than is needed for space heating by itself (Mode 4) the excess can be used to melt ice in the tank, in preparation for more freezing later.

When outdoor temperature is mild during the heating season, and the building is not calling for heat (Mode 5), solar heat can be used to melt ice in the tank, in preparation for more freezing.

At the beginning of the cooling season (Mode 6), enough ice has been allowed to build up on the coils to provide cooling for the building without any need for running the compressor.

During the warmest weather when the ice has run out (Mode 7), the cooling effect can be produced by discharging the heat of compression to the outdoor unit, and also to the radiant/convector panel if the temperature of the brine in the panel is less than that of the refrigerant in the condenser.

When nights are cool in summer (Mode 8), the system can make ice off-peak for cooling during the warm day, saving energy and taking demand off the utility.

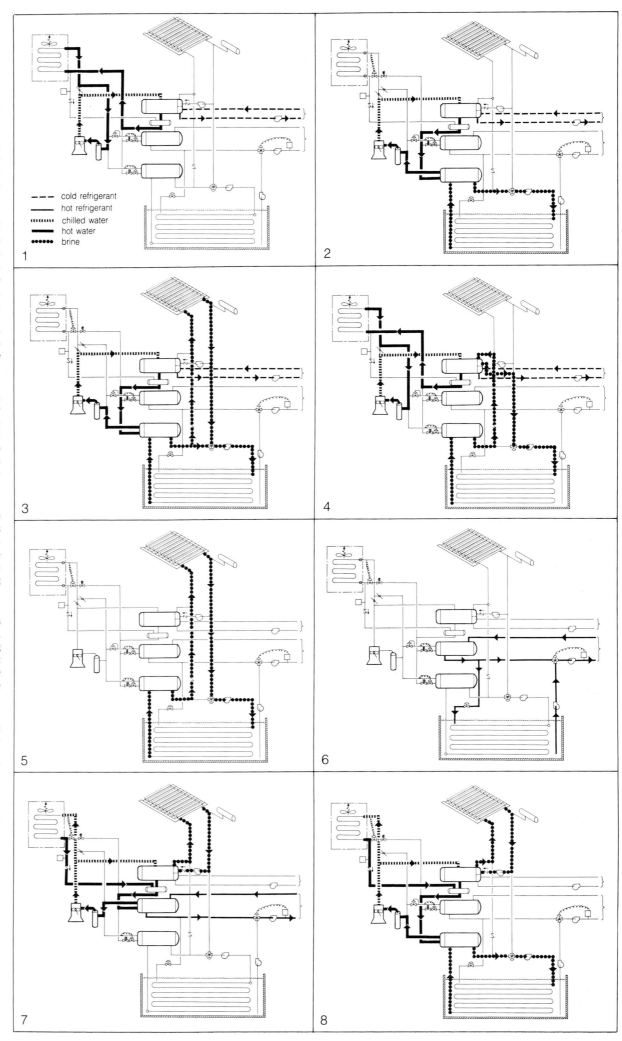

Legend:
- – – – cold refrigerant
- ——— hot refrigerant
- ·········· chilled water
- ━━━━ hot water
- ●●●●●● brine

Catholic Medical Center
Manchester, New Hampshire

Catholic Medical Center in Manchester, New Hampshire, a 250,000-sq-ft hospital formed by the merger of two existing institutions, will have all of its heating requirements supplied by a thermal storage system that heats water by electricity during off-peak hours from 8 p.m. to 7 a.m. The heating system will serve 70,000 sq ft of an existing building and a new 181,000-sq-ft building designed by architects Huygens and Tappé Inc. Consulting mechanical and electrical engineers are Cosentini and Associates. Associate architects are Isaak and Isaak, and structural engineers are Weidlinger Associates.

Because Public Service Company of New Hampshire is a winter-peaking utility, the company is encouraging off-peak consumption during the winter to help bring its load into better balance. Similar, but smaller, installations are in use in 15 other buildings in the state. The inducement is that, effectively, there is no demand charge for the off-peak usage. Also the electric rate is lower.

The storage system comprises eleven 11,-000-gallon tanks—eight for space heating, two for domestic hot water, and one for spare capacity. The tanks are filled with water, to a predetermined level, and this water, which remains in the tanks, becomes the heating source. Electric immersion elements heat this water to from 160 F to 280 F. Water for space heating, or for domestic hot water, is circulated through a heat exchanger to extract heat from

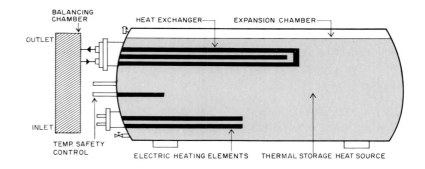

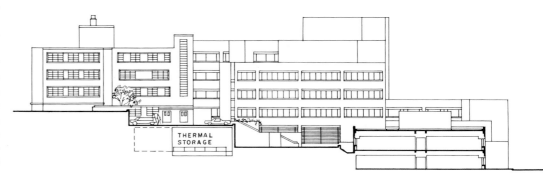

the water stored in the tank. In the system, developed by Megatherm of East Providence, Rhode Island, the water to be heated first passes through a tempering condenser. Control of tank temperature, or capacity, is achieved by pressure controllers.

Only in severe cold weather will all units need to be in operation at the start of the off-peak period. Furthermore, a sensing system

has been included to allow part of the heating tanks to come on during peak hours when the demand by the hospital for other purposes is below peak.

For steam, electric steam generators have been provided. Make-up water for these generators is supplied from the thermal storage system; thus, the cost of steam is reduced by using water preheated at off-peak rates.

Federal Home Loan Bank Board Building
Washington, D.C.

In its design of the facade of the new Federal Home Loan Bank Board Building, Max Urbahn's office has been properly deferential toward the Executive Office Building across the street, which a Washington architecture critic has said is "treasured for its robust immodesty." In the facade design the architect also has been mindful of GSA's energy-use guidelines, inasmuch as GSA is the client of record for the building.

The walls comprise bays of glass outlined by exposed concrete ledges and limestone-faced fins, and punctuated by exposed concrete columns—the glass bays being interrupted by sections of limestone-veneered masonry.

Masonry walls are insulated to achieve a U value of 0.07. The double-glazed clear glass occupies roughly only 35 per cent of the wall. To help building energy usage approach GSA's guideline of 55,000 Btu/equivalent gross sq ft/yr, the remaining glass is backed by panels of rigid insulation and gypsum board. On the exposed elevations, Venetian blinds will block unwanted sun. Sliding doors at balconies (identified by the double-thick ledges) are more deeply recessed, and are shielded by the ledges.

The mechanical engineers, using the AXCESS computer energy-use-simulation program, estimate annual energy consumption at about 77,700 Btu/EGSF/yr. If kitchen usage, 13-hr operation, and commercial lighting (the ground floor will be leased to stores) are accounted for, this figure would drop to 57,000.

The architect and consulting engineer Syska & Hennessy collaborated closely in developing systems and architectural elements for delivering air, light and power to the open-plan floor areas as inconspicuously and as efficiently as possible. For example, three air systems are used rather than the usual two; lighting (2¼W/sq ft) is entirely from the office work stations (task/ambient); and power and communications wiring is run below the 4-in.-high access/raised flooring that is used for all office floors.

Other energy-saving steps by the engineers were: 1) use of vari- able ventilation and unheated air for garage areas, and 2) supply of only 105 F water to lavatories by a single pipe instead of both cold and 120 F water. Also the building includes a building automation/fire/security system for hvac monitoring and control, fire and sprinkler alarm, automatic smoke purging and security.

The choice site of the building was not easy to acquire. In fact, one of the client's obligations was to rehabilitate the adjacent Winder Building—a five-story cast-iron office structure built in 1842. The plaza between the two buildings has an ice-skating rink that, in summer, is turned into a reflecting pool bridged by duckboards for umbrella-shaded tables. And Sasaki Associates has designed a two-story glass pavilion to abut the Winder building.

Because of two levels of underground parking plus a basement, Lev Zetlin Associates, the structural engineer, had to be careful in their foundation design to minimize underpinning of the Winder Building. Superstructure of the FHLBBB is waffle slab.

FEDERAL HOME LOAN BANK BOARD BUILDING, Washington, D.C. Client: *General Services Administration*. Architects: *Max O. Urbahn Associates, Inc.* Engineers: *Lev Zetlin Associates (structural); Syska & Hennessy, Inc. (mechanical/electrical).* Sitework: *Sasaki Associates.* Interiors: *Max O. Urbahn Associates, Inc.* Contractor: Turner Construction Co.

FEDERAL HOME LOAN BANK BOARD BUILDING

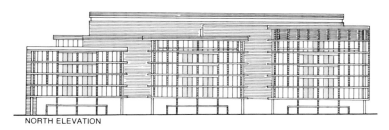

NORTH ELEVATION

Design for modest energy use

Energy consumption is reduced mainly via the wall design, the types of air-handling systems and air distribution systems (right), and task/ambient lighting. Offices in the spine will have full-height partitions (see plan), but with continuous clear-glass transoms to preserve an open feeling. The masonry wall has a 0.07 U value; windows are double-glazed, and those shown with a gray tone in the elevation have insulated panels in back.

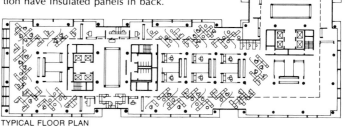

TYPICAL FLOOR PLAN

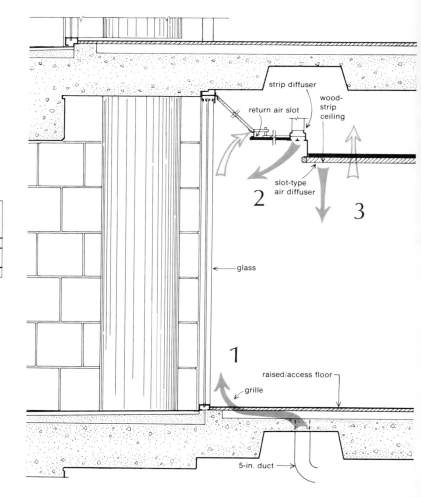

strip diffuser
return air slot
wood-strip ceiling
slot-type air diffuser
glass
grille
raised/access floor
5-in. duct

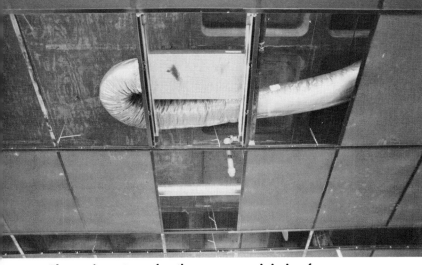

Three air systems for three zones minimize fan energy use

The engineers divided air distribution into three separate systems, each with its own characteristics for doing its job efficiently. The three are illustrated in the section across page, and in the photographs across the top. At the exterior wall, the engineers have used a constant-volume reheat system (reheat coil at air handlers) to produce a curtain of air in front of the glass and walls to neutralize conducted heat or cold, to afford comfort near them. This system need not operate when the outdoor temperature is from 60 to 80 F. Air-return ducting for this system is shown at right. For the second zone, the perimeter (exterior wall to 12-15 ft

inside), the engineers chose a variable-air-volume system that neutralizes the loads of lights, people, and direct solar gain when it occurs. (The linear supply grille for this system is shown across page.) For the third zone, the interior, the engineers decided to use air-powered, above-ceiling induction boxes. When the load drops (fewer lights or people), the system reduces primary air supplied, and thus fan energy. This air is supplied from slot-type diffusers (see above), and is returned through slots between the ceiling wood strips to the plenum. Black-painted acoustical panels over the wood strips close off the plenum.

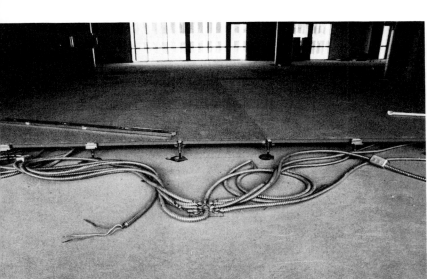

Electrified floor panels allow task lighting to be anywhere

Floors are blanketed with 4-in.-high access flooring that gives complete flexibility for lighting, 120-v power and telephone wires. (Carpet squares were factory applied.) Every 30- by 30-ft area has a junction box buried in the slab. Each of these has the capacity for 10 lengths of flexible metal conduit, though the client is installing only six at this time in most areas. Generally, an electrified access panel will be used every 150 sq ft.

The wood-strip ceiling defines the spine of the building; white acoustical tile, the perimeter. Though the wood

reflectance diminishes potential ambient light, the effect is even, not harsh. The 4-ft "sausage" fixture has two HO-fluorescent lamps for uplight and one HO-lamp for downlight. A refractive-grid, low-brightness lens is on top (the consultant thought occupants should be aware of the source), and a twin-beam lens is on the bottom. The utility module at the corner has deluxe-white-mercury uplight. A flexible-arm incandescent fixture will replace the extendable mock-up fluorescent unit. Lighting by Design Decisions of Syska & Hennessy.

Government of Canada Building
Toronto, Ontario

A whole series of energy-reducing steps in design, including two strikingly new departures—one in ceiling lighting, another in thermal storage—held consumption in this Canadian federal office building in Toronto to 66,600 Btu/sq ft/yr without sacrificing the quality of working space.

Indeed, few buildings whose office floors cost only $33/sq ft, as did these, offer such amenities as provided by architect Macy Dubois. The zigzagged facade of this building, for example, provides more perimeter wall than a square building twice its height, and thus opens pleasant vistas for office workers. In addition, three atriums offer interior views. The main atrium, shown across page and in plan, is five stories high, and is entered from grade. Reason for the opaque wall was anticipated construction of a parking garage adjacent. Columns support the sloping roof and skylight structure, and were braced for lateral stability. Another large atrium (see top photo) will have a louvered exterior wall to exclude direct sunlight.

Undoubtedly the most dramatic advance in the design of the building is the ceiling task lighting, which requires only 2W/sq ft to provide 100 footcandles (required by union contract) on desktops. This feat is accomplished by movable, plug-in, two-lamp luminaires that can be dropped randomly into an exposed 5- by 5-ft raceway grid.

The exposed 2½- by 6-in. raceway is multifunctional: 1) it carries 347-v power (Canada) for the plug-in lighting, 120-v power for convenience outlets, and telephone wires; 2) it supports luminaires and acoustical panels; 3) it accepts linear diffusers, designed to issue up to 265 cfm per 5-ft length; 4) it accepts sprinkler heads, partition anchorages and service poles.

A large percentage of the energy savings in the 825,000 sq ft building is attributable to the design of the hvac system, which allows very large reductions in fan energy as compared with conventional installations. Moreover, a considerable amount of heat is recovered from lights, people and machines, and stored in four 75,000-gallon concrete tanks in the basement.

Reductions in fan energy are effected by 1) variable air volume distribution, 2) the use of low-temperature salvage heat in under-window radiation heaters, rather than air at the perimeter, and 3) the substitution of small air-handling units (two per floor, 26 altogether) for larger stations, substantially lessening total friction loss.

According to mechanical engineer Robert Tamblyn, the storage of salvage heat yields energy savings comparable in magnitude to the air side of the hvac system. Indications are that thermal storage will reduce heating costs by as much as 60 per cent. On the cooling side, furthermore, thermal storage makes it possible to reduce the size of the chillers by 30 per cent, and to save 20 per cent on cooling costs by cutting electric demand 30 per cent by running chillers during off-peak periods. Chilled water will be stored year-round.

GOVERNMENT OF CANADA BUILDING, Toronto. Architects: *DuBois-Strong-Bindhardt and Shore Tilbe Henschel Irwin, associated architects and planners.* Engineers: *R. Halsall & Associates Ltd.* (structural); *Engineering Interface Limited* (mechanical); *Jack Chisvin & Associates Ltd.* (electrical). Project manager: *Public Works Canada, Ontario Region.* Construction management: *E.G.M. Cape & Co. Ltd.*

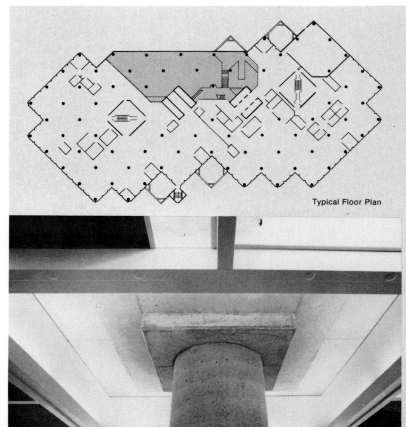

Typical Floor Plan

Ceiling task lighting providing 100 fc at desks is by two-lamp, plug-in luminaires, dropped into the ceiling grid over the desks. Uplight at columns is for accent and nighttime lighting.

sprinkler

thermostat pole

service pole

luminaire

Robert E. Fischer photos

GOVERNMENT OF CANADA BUILDING

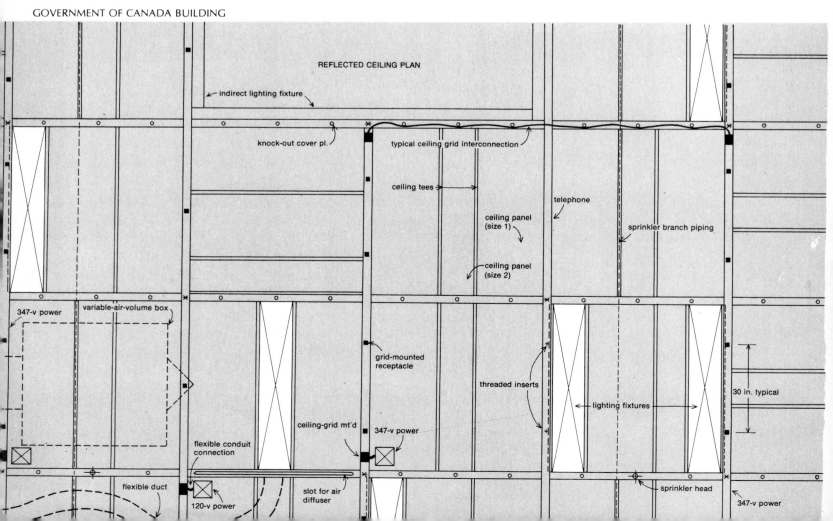

REFLECTED CEILING PLAN

← indirect lighting fixture

knock-out cover pl.

typical ceiling grid interconnection

ceiling tees

telephone

ceiling panel (size 1)

sprinkler branch piping

ceiling panel (size 2)

347-v power

variable-air-volume box

grid-mounted receptacle

threaded inserts

30 in. typical

lighting fixtures

flexible conduit connection

ceiling-grid mt'd

347-v power

flexible duct

120-v power

slot for air diffuser

sprinkler head

347-v power

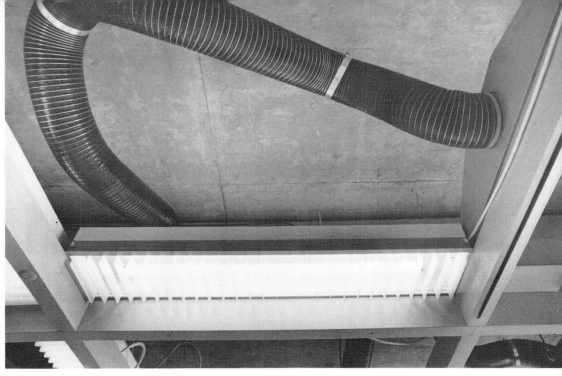

The ceiling grid performs multiple architectural and engineering functions

The first purpose of the grid system is to support luminaires for task lighting—and to allow variation in their placement according to the location of work stations. The grid further incorporates raceways to power the luminaires, which are plugged into twist-lock receptacles via power cords. Though luminaires are arranged in a more or less random pattern, the regular spacing of the 6-in. deep grid helps organize the ceiling visually. Orange-colored acoustical panels, matching the grid, come in two standard sizes to fill the 5-ft module whether one, two or no luminaires are inserted.

Every other raceway carries 347-v wiring for lights; they alternate with raceways for 120-v receptacle power and raceways for telephone wires. The 347-v raceways are on 10-ft centers because power cords for luminaires are limited by code to 6-ft lengths. Cords for 120-v power to service poles can be 12 ft, however. Telephone wires and 120-v cords to service poles are enclosed in the dummy grid members running perpendicular to the raceways. The raceway spacings thus give complete flexibility in the location of work stations.

Grid members running perpendicular to the raceways provide for a number of functions: slots for linear air diffusers, button-type knockouts for the installation of spring-loaded service poles, and round holes for sprinkler heads. The raceway grid has threaded inserts for partitions.

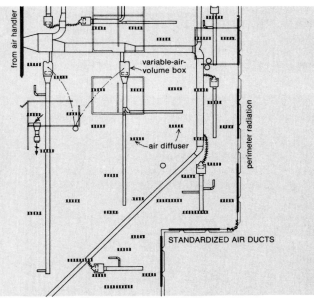

from air handler

variable-air-volume box

air diffuser

perimeter radiation

STANDARDIZED AIR DUCTS

The hvac system combines energy savings with a low first-cost

Four 75,000-gallon concrete tanks like the one at left will store "waste" heat recouped from lights, equipment and people. During cold seasons, this stored heat will provide 100F water for finned radiation at the perimeter. Chillers will run in offpeak periods to reduce demand charges, and cooled water will be stored in the tanks. A problem in storing chilled water is that supply and return water may not mix, or else the supply water will not be cool enough for dehumidification.

Engineer Robert Tamblyn's ingenious solution to this dilemma was to provide a plastic baffle in the shape of a huge square bag, which moves back and forth as relative volumes of supply and return water vary at night and during the day. The storage tanks cost $175,000, but saved $75,000 in chiller costs and promise to save $10,000 a year in demand charges. Six standard sections of ducts rather than many different sizes cut hvac costs. The total system bid cost under $3.40/sq ft.

IBM Regional Office
Southfield, Michigan

Presented on the following pages is one of Gunnar Birkerts' recent works, a regional office building for IBM in the Detroit suburb of Southfield. The building is a captivating essay about the role of intuition in design, and about the sources of energy—physical and spiritual—that Gunnar Birkets has so efficiently and elegantly packed together in the course of his own development.

Near the intersection of too many expressways, in the Detroit suburb of Southfield, is a distinguished business machine.

It is the 14-story steel-framed regional office building for IBM, designed by Gunnar Birkerts and Associates—a compact proposition about architecture's role in saving energy. Which is precisely what IBM wanted to do, having long-term economy in mind, and also wanting to set an example for others. What IBM has gotten is, more than an example, an inspiration of enormous technical refinement and symbolic power.

Energy conservation in buildings is not just a function of high-tech tomfoolery, wonderfully efficient new gadgets, or convening a lot of solar panels; it is fundamentally a matter of basic design character: orientation to the site and the natural elements, fenestration, the choice of materials, coloration. Every architect knows about these "passive" factors, or should—yet the simplest ways of saving energy have not been given their esthetic due in proportion to their great practical potential. Birkerts' building is a pause for reflection on this score.

The key element was the skin of the building, and when it comes to basic design character, the skin here is fundamentally new in both its formal composition, technical make-up, and visual effect. So fundamentally new, in fact, that the skin has been copyrighted. Here is how this taut metallic sheathing works, with its glistening glass ribbons:

First of all, the glass area of the facades is only 20 per cent of their total wall area. Far from being a "come down" for glass, Birkerts has made the two-foot-high horizontal ribbons of it all the more expressive in a perfect balancing out of utility and beauty. Because of the inward slope of the glass, it is shielded by the exterior wall for most of the working day, and yet (this is an eye-opener) the sense of the surroundings, looking out these "windows", is if anything larger, easily as luminous, as what we used to get looking out through ye larger lites of yore.

Daylight is introduced (and pleasingly diffused) inside by way of a curved matte-finished reflector of stainless steel (a most spiffy kind of sill) that runs along the lower edge of the ribbons of glass. This "sill" bounces the light onto a curved panel *inside*, an eggshell-colored reflector of prefinished aluminum runs along the upper edge of the ribbons. The light is thus bounced deep into the floors, from the inside reflector, up onto the ceilings, and back down into the spaces; moreover, the placement of the inside reflector and the play of softened light occasioned by it seems to open up the view toward the outside, in effect making the glass ribbons seem much bigger than they actually are.

Now around the perimeter of the ceilings, where they intersect with the upper edges of the interior reflectors, there is a continuous fluorescent lighting strip, and at night, or on dark days, this arrangement reverses the direction of the light. For example, on dark winter days, it illuminates the

Gunnar Birkerts' office building for IBM combines sleek metallic surfaces and an extremely elegant and innovative window system to produce a poetic image for an energy-saving epoch

A bright, natural aluminum clads the IBM building on its south and west elevations, reflecting the heat and light, whereas a charcoal gray color is used on the north and east elevations for absorption. Although this contrast of color does not greatly affect the level of energy-usage in this energy-saving structure, the contrast does send out signals as to the over-all purpose and character of the architecture. Where the same finishes meet, an elegant rounded corner detail is used; where they contrast, a crisp notched-out corner appears. The main entry (above), embellished with orange and red, has an oblong vestibule, shooting the red theme inside to denote all circulation (right) from corridors to elevators.

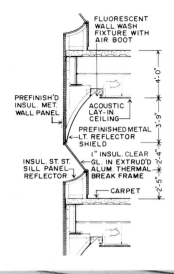

FLUORESCENT
WALL WASH
FIXTURE WITH
AIR BOOT

PREFINISH'D
INSUL. MET.
WALL PANEL

ACOUSTIC
LAY-IN
CEILING

PREFINISHED METAL
←LT. REFLECTOR
SHIELD

1" INSUL. CLEAR
←GL. IN EXTRUD'D
ALUM. THERMAL
BREAK FRAME

INSUL. ST. ST.
SILL PANEL
REFLECTOR

CARPET

4'-0" 3'-9" 2'-4" 2'-5"

Only 20 per cent of the exterior wall area of the IBM building is glass. Horizontal ribbons of it (see section, left) slope inward, picking up light from a curved reflecting surface running along the bottom and throwing the light upward onto a curved interior reflector where it is diffused and thrown deep into the office spaces. In plan (opposite) the building is a straightforward square with an elevator core; the no-nonsense activity to be found in such a business machine is efficiently arrayed around the core. Economical but elegant surfaces are used throughout the building, set off by flourishes of color. Great energy savings are a direct result of basic design character.

interior reflector, supplementing what daylight is coming in, and because this reflector is the wall surface above the window, the comparatively small area given to glass is made to appear more generous—this in contrast to the normally dark wall surfaces that would surround window openings in more conventional installations. The fluorescent fixture is housed in an aluminum cove that is contoured, in turn, to the larger reflector below. A marked reduction, or absence, of natural light coming in activates photocells, activating the fixtures; the technology— reaching fulfillment— disappears.

The energy efficiency of this solution is enhanced by the thickness of the wall, the inward curves of the two reflectors requiring an over-all thickness of 24 inches. Although this extra thickness had some effect on the ratio of net to gross square footage, it was determined that this "premium" would be repaid in under eight years by the energy savings—and indeed, the savings in peak solar load is about 40 per cent, taking into account the fact that some heat is transmitted by the reflector through the glass. Inside, the levels of artificial light have been kept to 50 footcandles, using two watts per square foot of electricity, this being supplied with prismatic acrylic lenses. Taken with the unique character of the outer wall and window treatment, reliance on electric light is minimized. All told, these design measures have achieved a usage level of 54,000 Btus per square foot, and that meets the norms that have been proposed by the Federal government—a great buy, and without one corner cut as to design quality or conceptual conviction.

In metaphorical terms, Birkerts' solution also conveys what the building is mainly meant to accomplish; for example, its exterior is a two-tone job. A metallic silver, on the southerly and westerly elevations, reflects the light and heat; a charcoal black, on the northerly and easterly elevations, absorbs them. Not that this color contrast affects energy savings all that dramatically. What it does do is symbolize the importance of careful orientation (a consideration that our "endless" supplies of energy almost squelched, along with our glib assumptions about the ability of technology to overcome the "inconvenient" unevenness of nature). As such, the IBM building is a signal that such traditional considerations in architecture as orientation, the ways our buildings latch onto the movement of the sun and the lay of the land, are more eternal than our piteously short-lived infatuation with our supremacy over them. Even with the familiar square-plan structure, even with all four sides gotten up according to the same methods and with the same materials, that color contrast—simple as it may seem— is the metaphorical tie that binds this building and its innovations together and makes them live and read as a unified message.

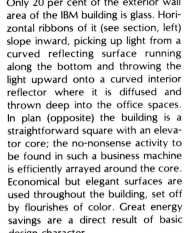

The dining area of the IBM building (left), directly accessible from the lobby (previous page), shows off the building's skillful balance of natural and artifical lighting with especial drama. Although there is comparatively little dependence on artificial lighting, the fixtures are cleanly designed. The exterior ribbons of glass, sloping up to meet the curving interior reflector, are a model of immaculate detailing and the suave joining of surfaces and fittings.

EXAMPLES OF INNOVATIVE LIGHTING

Conserving energy in lighting:
proposals emerge from both the design professionals and industry

Buildings, altogether, take a large portion of the energy consumed by this country. And, because lighting load—compared to the total—is large in itself, and, in turn, affects the amount of air conditioning required, it has become the focus of much controversy in the current era of energy shortages. The need for conservation of energy with lighting systems is not only being argued for by architects, engineers, and lighting consultants, but it is acknowledged, as well, by the lighting industry itself.

As might be expected, suggestions of what to do about it run the gamut of reasonableness and practicability. With respect to the energy demand of lighting, some say footcandle levels, as commonly used, ought to be arbitrarily reduced. Others say that too much emphasis is laid on footcandle levels *per se;* that from an energy standpoint, lighting should be given a budget, and that the building designer should then utilize this budget to obtain the best type of lighting appropriate to the various building spaces. The Illuminating Engineering Society says that their recommended lighting levels provide for a range of values in buildings such as office buildings and schools, depending upon the degree of difficulty of the tasks involved. One of 12 recommendations made by IES in 1972 for conserving lighting energy was that higher levels of light be provided for seeing tasks as compared with non-working areas—corridors, file space, etc. Obviously such an approach requires a lot more design talent and time than is commonly employed in office buildings today, where an entire floor is a uniform geometric pattern to suit a particular office planning module, ceiling-grid module, and/or a particular budget constraint. While it is obvious that the concept of completely flexible modular space is not consistent with efficient energy utilization—with a lighting fixture being provided in each module so that partitioned offices can be located at will—the "put the light where it is needed" approach may not be so easy. It may require the client to make up his mind sooner how floor areas are going to be used. The owner has to have the right talent available when changes are made in the future. The lighting design in the beginning is likely to take a higher level of expertise (both lighting design and architectural design) than is normally brought to bear on the problem to achieve results that are both functionally effective

Higher intensities of lighting for difficult tasks can be provided locally. With the desk lamp off, illumination is 100 fc; with it on, it is 200 fc. Brightness ratios in the viewing area are well within the comfort range. Of course the lamp has to be positioned to avoid reflected glare.

and esthetically satisfying. It is liikely to be more expensive initially than the ubiquitous 2-by 4-ft recessed troffer in a lay-in ceiling.

But even with the "blanket" approach to lighting, savings could be made in energy usage—if not demand—by local switching to turn off lights in unoccupied spaces, or switching off part of the lights when the building is being cleaned in the evening. Local switching has not been done much recently in office buildings because it increases initial cost. And the question is who wants to pay for it now? Dimming of banks of fluorescent lamps on a programed basis or in response to the availability of daylight is technically feasible using solid-state dimmers, but the energy savings vs. higher initial cost picture needs to be fully examined.

Another approach is to provide a level of general illumination, somewhat less than is required for critical seeing tasks, to give certain degree of brightness to room surfaces and some on the tasks, and to add the balance required with local luminaires. Carrels in schools and libraries are an example. And, more recently, a system has been developed for office buildings in which indirect general lighting and local lighting have been built directly into office-

landscaping-type furniture wherever needed.

Greater utilization of daylight would require more care in designing for proper brightness relationships within rooms, in evaluating the impact on air conditioning, and in planning spatial arrangements (deep interior spaces cannot benefit except by skylighting).

I.E.S. lighting levels stem from value judgments based upon data from Blackwell

Lighting levels have increased over the years as the state of the art has advanced in efficiency of lamps, efficiency of luminaires, and in the control of glare and heat from lamps. For example, before fluorescent lamps were introduced, the radiant and convected heat from incandescent lamps put a virtual ceiling on footcandle levels. Energy costs have not been an appreciable deterrent because they have been, particularly in recent years, small in comparison to the other owning costs of buildings such as taxes and maintenance.

A new set of recommended illumination levels was announced by the Illuminating Engineering Society in 1958. It was based upon 56 "practical tasks"—many of them, industrial —submitted by IES application committees to

People experience a wide variety of lighting levels during a day: from 10 footcandles on a subway platform, to the 20-50 fc range in an airlines ticket office to the 50-70 fc at seats in a commuter train. Toronto's SEP systems schools provide 70 fc for only 2 watts per square foot.

Dr. H. Richard Blackwell who ran tests to determine the illumination needed on these tasks to permit maximum practical accuracy of seeing (99 per cent at a normal rate of eye movement.) The tests were conducted using college students with normal vision, and the illumination in the tests was essentially diffuse. There were a few over a dozen tasks that related to office or school work. And among them Blackwell found that: a typed original with good ribbon required about 1 footcandle (fc), as did 8-point text type; ink writing of one sixth-grade student, 1.4 fc; no. 2 pencil writing on white matte paper of sixth-grade students, 63 fc; shorthand copy with no. 3 pencil, 76.5; typed carbon, fifth copy, 133 fc. Keep in mind that these values represent diffuse illumination (absence of reflected glare, also known as veiling reflections). Additional factors that need to be accounted for include disability glare (reduced eye sensitivity resulting from extraneous sources of light such as luminaires); transitional adaptation (eye moving from task to other objects in the room and back); and age.

Of all these factors, except for age, the one having the greatest effect on the seeing activity is Contrast Rendition Factor (CRF), which is a measure of how well a particular lighting system produces contrast between a task (typed or written character) and its background (paper, chalkboard, etc.), as compared with the illumination from a uniformly lighted hemisphere (diffuse lighting; close to minimum reflected glare). The quantitative measure in footcandles of how well a particular lighting system fares with respect to "glare-free" illumination is called Equivalent Sphere Illumination (ESI)

There are many different Contrast Rendition Factors in a room depending upon where a person sits with respect to the luminaires, which direction he faces, and what angle his lines of sight make with the task. Because of reflected glare, a lighting system at one particular location might the only 25 per cent effective as compared with diffuse (hemispherical) illumination, while at still another

location it might be 100 per cent effective.

All other things being equal, potential efficiency of seeing increases with improvement in contrast and added illumination, though a very small increase in contrast is equivalent to a very large increase in illumination. The only way that Contrast Rendition Factors can be determined accurately is through actual measurements in rooms; or they can be predicted when sufficient photometric data are available through a computer program (Hyde & Bobbio, Detroit consulting engineers, have one.)

As might be expected lighting systems that produce a lot of diffuse illumination (indirect systems, luminous ceilings, etc.) fare quite well in contrast-producing illumination (these systems come as close to hemispherical illumination as can be achieved in practice); so do systems that send out light at low angles with respect to the task (perimeter systems); twin-beam luminaires are helpful (more so in a direction parallel with the luminaires); and vertically plane-polarized light enhances contrast (more so at the larger viewing angles because of the physics involved).

What really counts, however, from an energy utilization standpoint are the systems that produce the most contrast rendition on visual tasks for the fewest watts. A particular luminaire might have high contrast-producing capability, but low efficiency in terms of light output (luminaire with a low-light-transmission diffuser, for example). The opposite also

can be true.

Critics of the I.E.S. recommended illumination values ask the question whether 99 per cent accuracy is really needed. But more to the point is their contention that comprehensive investigations have not been made into who performs which task, where, and how often. Though I.E.S. in its school lighting standard says that in one study, 62 per cent of the total time was spent with visual tasks, and of this percentage 64 per cent was spent on such tasks as reading, writing with pencil, working with duplicated materials. "This indicates that the greater part of a student's visual time was spent on tasks requiring 60 to 100 footcandles."

Does the secretary need 99 per cent "seeing" accuracy for filing correspondence? Does she take stenography with no. 3 pencil, ballpoint pen, or felt-tip pen? Many questions such as the above undoubtedly will remain unanswered on any sort of human-engineering-study basis. In practice up to now, illumination levels often have been selected with one eye on recommended values, and the other on economics—what seems reasonable in context of total building economics. Further there is the question of what kinds of lighting systems are appropriate to the type of building and its activities.

I.E.S. is quick to point out that they do not have one single value for office spaces and one single value for school classrooms. For example I.E.S. recommends the following for offices: 150 fc for reading poor reproduction and for business machine operation; 100 fc for reading handwriting in hard pencil on poor paper, reading fair reproductions, active filing, etc.; 70 fc for reading handwriting in ink or medium pencil on good quality paper, etc.; 30 fc for reading high contrast or well-printed materials (private office). It should be noted that all these values that appear in the most recent recommendations (1972) are Equivalent Sphere Illumination footcandles (i.e., hemispherical). Actual "raw" footcandle in most cases would be higher to make up for loss of contrast.

Hollis Middle School, Hollis, New Hampshire

After several previous middle-school designs had exceeded the client's budget, the Hollis, New Hampshire school board hired architect Michael B. Ingram and asked him to try a new approach, within a budget limit of $20 a square foot. Ingram switched the site from an appendage to the existing elementary school to a sloping site nearby—the reason for the stepped profile of the building. The new site avoided a septic tank field of the previous one, and proved more economical over-all.

The raked ceiling did not lend itself to traditional forms of lighting, however. At first, Ingram considered attaching bare fluorescent strips to the bottom flanges of the open-web joists. But electrical engineer Robert Fairbanks, of Kaufmann Associates in Boston, suggested outdoor-type mercury floodlights for indirect illumination. This approach appealed to Ingram because it took the fixtures away from the ceiling plane—avoiding the image of bare-lamp supermarket-type lighting. The indirect approach helped him realize his concept of a large space all under one lid.

The indirect lighting system, using phosphor-coated, 1000-watt metal-halide lamps, provides an illumination level of 50 foot-candles at desk height for an energy expenditure of only 1.5 watts per square foot.

In the classroom areas, one luminaire is used for every 26- by 28-ft classroom unit. Lamps of 400-, 750-, and 1000-watt sizes, operating at 277 volts, were considered. The 400-watt size would have required twice as many luminaires; the 1000-watt size meant heavier mountings at the wall, but yielded obvious savings over-all. Theoretically in favor of

146

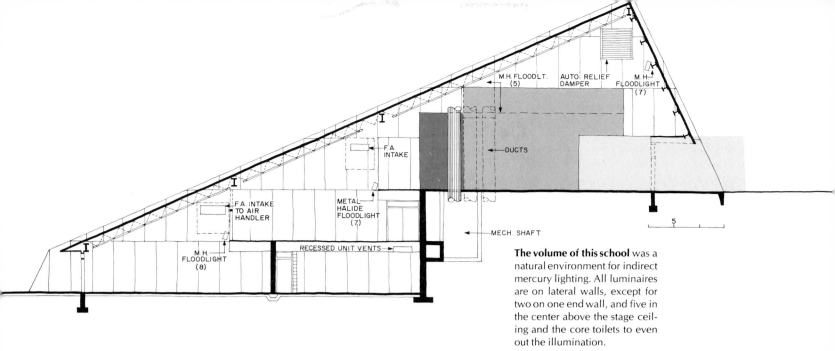

The volume of this school was a natural environment for indirect mercury lighting. All luminaires are on lateral walls, except for two on one end wall, and five in the center above the stage ceiling and the core toilets to even out the illumination.

The lighting situations at the upper level, lower level, and the west side wall are shown above and on the next page. The concrete block structure at left is the resource center office, and over it is part of the faculty lounge area. Luminaire shields in the classroom areas are only partial on the sides. The lighting level is 50 footcandles at 1.5 watts per sq. ft.

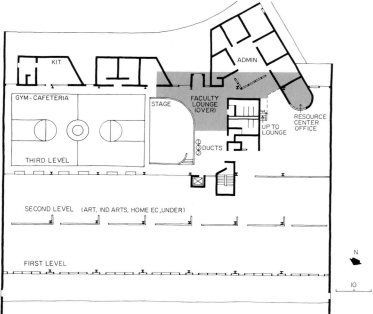

the larger number of luminaires was the possibility of a more even band of brightness on the ceiling. With the 1000-watt lamps, the luminaires needed to be located as far down the balcony faces as possible to even out the brightness.

Scoop-type shields around luminaires shut out the glare of the 1000-watt lamps from side angles, but the bright lamps can be seen when luminaires are viewed from across the room.

The school is heated and ventilated by means of air-handling units using electric heating.

In the main classroom areas on first and second levels, one air handler on each side of the building, connected to a fresh-air intake in the outside wall, serves half the area. Interior classrooms on the first level have ceiling-recessed unit ventilators. The third level and the teachers' lounge are served by air handlers above the stage area and above the core toilet rooms. Fresh air for all interior rooms comes from a tunnel under the middle of the building. The administrative offices have packaged terminal air conditioners.

The building has a minimum area of glass in front and back, and the roof uses urethane-insulated cement-fiber plank having a 0.08 U-factor.

The steel-framed building cost $730,000 or about $22 for 34,000 sq. ft. The school was designed for 415 pupils. The hvac contract was $80,000, and the electrical contract, $75,000.

HOLLIS MIDDLE SCHOOL. Owner: *Hollis School District.* Architect: *Michael B. Ingram.* Engineers: *Albert Goldberg Associates* (structural); *Kaufmann Associates* (mechanical/electrical). Contractors: *Norsa Corporation; Seppala & Aho.*

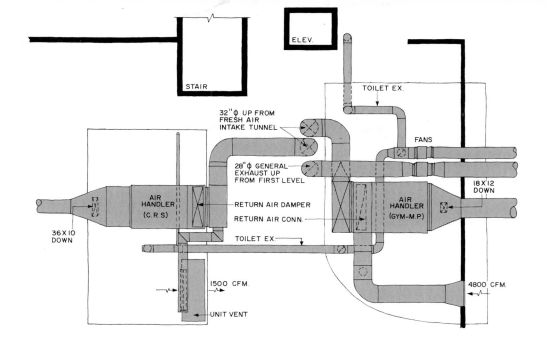

Air-handling units for heating and ventilating the upper level of the school and the gymnasium are shown in the plan. Fresh-air risers for these air handlers and an exhaust riser for the interior classrooms emerge at the third level, and are made a colorful feature. The faculty lounge area is conditioned by a 1500-cfm unit ventilator. The pneumatic controls can be seen in the photo bottom, left. All ductwork is left exposed, except where there is none in the interior classroom spaces at the first level. These have positive exhaust by means of in-duct exhausters. Main classroom areas, on the other hand, have automatically-controlled relief dampers set high in the end walls to allow vitiated air out.

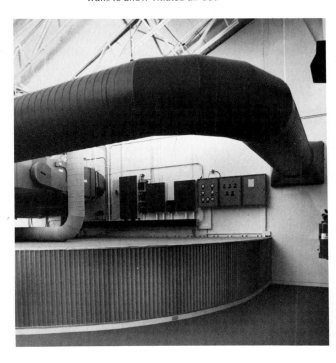

Aid Association for Lutherans Headquarters
Appleton, Wisconsin

Robert E. Fischer photos

Architects, it seems, are beginning to rediscover the wonderful qualities of daylight, though with more impressive results, as here, when inventive designers develop new concepts through modern materials and technologies.

John Carl Warneke's office (William Pedersen, designer) created this remarkable daylighted space that has the relaxing ambience of an art museum, yet the greater interest of outdoors because of the modulating effects of its ceiling design elements.

No museum this, however, but rather a 525,000-sq-ft office building (expansible to 1-million) for the Aid Association for Lutherans, the world's largest fraternal insurance organization. The new headquarters sits in the open countryside, amidst farm fields, a few miles from Appleton, Wisconsin, within commuting distance of Oshkosh and Green Bay.

Outwardly, the dramatic ceiling forms on the upper floor of the two-story structure are devices for controlling and suffusing daylight, or supplemental electric light during dark periods from tubular luminaires directly under the reflective-glass skylights.

Because of the balanced brightnesses within the spaces (one never sees the skylights without looking nearly straight up), an observer can hardly believe that lighting levels at midday in
150

summer are about 200 fc.

The ceiling elements do much more than might be guessed, however. The unique cylindrical shapes in the ceiling, called "socks" by the architect—and now, too, by the building's tour guides—house all the mechanical paraphernalia for delivering and controlling conditioned air, sprinkler piping, roof drainage, and even speakers that create masking sound.

The ceiling also traps sound and absorbs it by means of the "socks" which have fiberglass cores behind the white fabric, stretched in a smooth, taut double-curvature between hoops. The panels are clamped by a special plastic molding.

Because AAL continues to grow, and because support services, such as electronic communications, are changing so rapidly, AAL decided to have a complete access/raised floor for all office areas—nearly 218,000 sq ft.

Mechanical systems and components were selected always with energy savings in mind. Air-handling equipment is in four long, extendable penthouses, running perpendicular to the skylights. Altogether there are 28 air-conditioning systems using packaged air handlers and return-air fans with controllable-pitch blades that are efficient even at low-capacity air delivery.

On the upper level, which has much wider swings in air-conditioning load because of the skylights, three different types of air-handling systems are provided: 1) an interior-zone, variable-air-volume cooling system; 2) a single-zone system for perimeter areas (all glass is double glazed); and 3) a multizone system for areas with large, variable loads.

On the ground floor, perimeter zones are handled similarly to those on the upper floor. Interior zones, however, use air-powered induction boxes, because cooling load stays fairly constant.

Electric heaters are used under the skylights to keep air temperature near them in winter at 72 F to prevent downdrafts. Electric draft-barrier heaters also are provided at all perimeter glass, which turn on at 25 F, and step up to 100 per cent capacity at −20 F.

The all-electric building has three chillers, one of them operat-

ing as an internal-source heat pump. Two 25,000-gal tanks store hot water when it is efficient to do so. The heat pump can be supplemented by two electric boilers.

To implement energy conservation, and also for security and life-safety, the building has a computer-type building automation fire/security system.

The tubular, lensed, twin-lamp luminaires under the skylights can have either half or all lamps switched off as daylight varies. While the control center can provide automatic switching, the owner is doing this manually to learn what is really needed.

AID ASSOCIATION FOR LUTHERANS HEADQUARTERS, Appleton, Wisconsin. Architect: *John Carl Warneke & Associates, Architects and planners.* Engineers: *Paul Weidlinger Associates (structural); Joseph R. Loring & Associates, Inc. (mechanical and electrical).* General contractor: *Oscar J. Boldt Construction Co.*

Two different areas of the AAL building demonstrate the soft, modulated ambience created by the cylindrically-shaped "socks" and deep, sheathed girders that control and disperse daylight from skylights (and supplemental fluorescent fixtures) overhead. The area at top is directly behind a two-story skylit passage on the north side. The area at left is between this passage and an interior garden to the south.

151

AID ASSOCIATION FOR LUTHERANS

In addition to their light-control function, the fabric-covered ceiling "socks" neatly conceal supply-air ducts and their associated volume-control boxes, and sprinkler piping. Further, they integrate linear diffusers for supply and return air. The "sock" itself serves as the plenum for returning air to fan rooms. A row of fluorescent fixtures used at night or during marginal daylight conditions can be seen above, right. The one luminaire that is lit is on the emergency circuit. The deep rectangular members are sheathed, long-span girders that span as much as 88 ft, and the cross members are roof purlins. While the sky-lighted office space is only on the upper floor, the ground floor, lighted by low-brightness fixtures, shares the two-story-high skylighted passages and interior gardens.

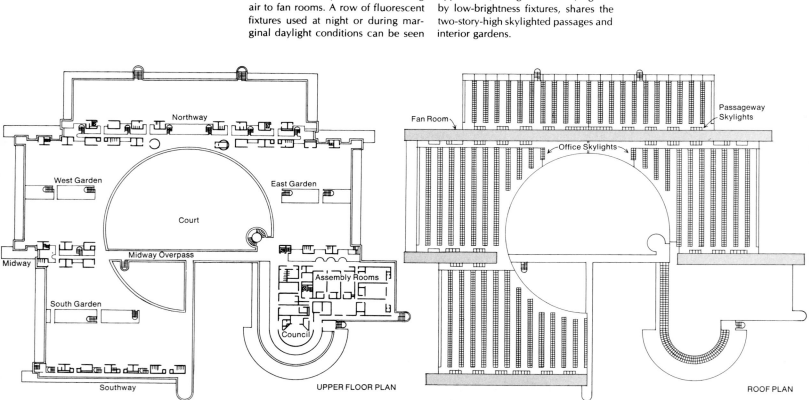

UPPER FLOOR PLAN

ROOF PLAN

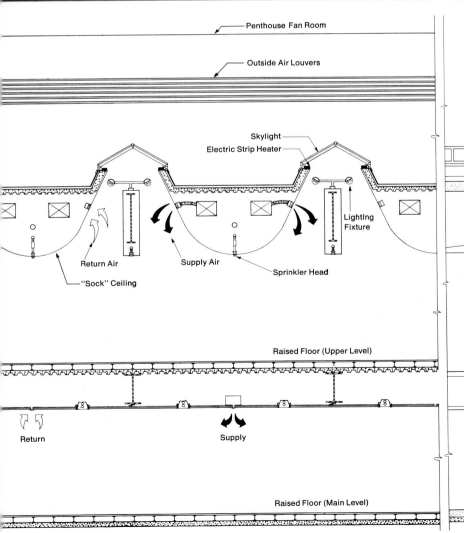

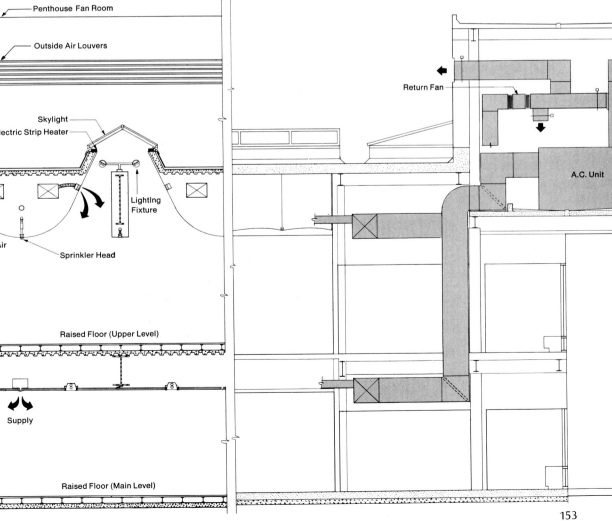

Penthouse Fan Room

Outside Air Louvers

Skylight

Electric Strip Heater

Lighting Fixture

Return Air

Supply Air

Sprinkler Head

"Sock" Ceiling

Raised Floor (Upper Level)

Return

Supply

Raised Floor (Main Level)

Return Fan

A.C. Unit

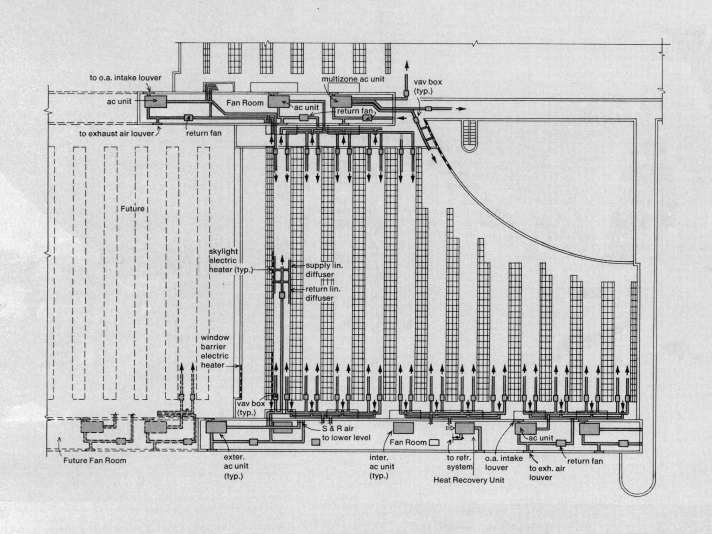

to o.a. intake louver

ac unit

Fan Room

multizone ac unit

vav box (typ.)

ac unit

return fan

to exhaust air louver

return fan

Future

skylight electric heater (typ.)

supply lin. diffuser

return lin. diffuser

window barrier electric heater

vav box (typ.)

S & R air to lower level

Fan Room

Future Fan Room

exter. ac unit (typ.)

inter. ac unit (typ.)

Heat Recovery Unit

to refr. system

o.a. intake louver

ac unit

return fan

to exh. air louver

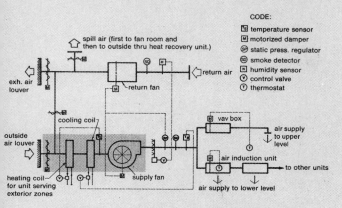

spill air (first to fan room and then to outside thru heat recovery unit.)

exh. air louver

return fan

return air

cooling coil

outside air louver

vav box

air supply to upper level

air induction unit

to other units

heating coil for unit serving exterior zones

supply fan

air supply to lower level

CONTROL DIAGRAM—SINGLE ZONE AC SYSTEM, INTERIOR AND EXTERIOR

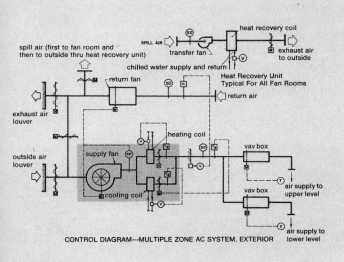

spill air (first to fan room and then to outside thru heat recovery unit)

SPILL AIR

transfer fan

heat recovery coil

exhaust air to outside

chilled water supply and return

Heat Recovery Unit Typical For All Fan Rooms

return fan

return air

exhaust air louver

heating coil

outside air louver

supply fan

vav box

cooling coil

vav box

air supply to upper level

air supply to lower level

CONTROL DIAGRAM—MULTIPLE ZONE AC SYSTEM, EXTERIOR

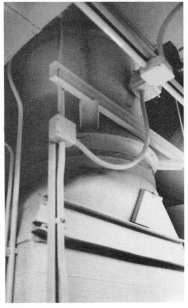

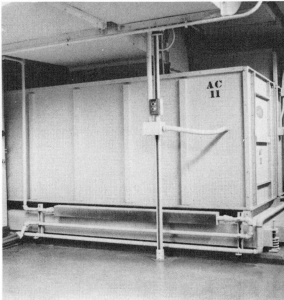

All air handlers are in linear penthouses that are a design feature of the AAL building. Basically two different types of air handlers (see diagrams) were used to serve three types of zones: 1) a single-zone air conditioner for interior zones, which, with a heating coil added to it, also is used for perimeter zones at the outside faces of the building; 2) a multizone air conditioner with hot and cold decks and damper-mixed air to handle large and varying heating and cooling loads for zones bordering the glass of the circular court, and for the glazed overpass. The chiller with a double-bundle condenser that acts as an internal source heat pump is at top. One of the packaged air handlers is above, right, and one of the variable-pitch-blade return-air fans is directly above.

Electrified panels of the access floor system bring power, telephone and communications to work stations. Now the building has 1200 such panels. A junction box occurs every 400 sq ft, with 6 to 8 flexible metal cables. The panels are fastened to the post supports, and also to each other for rigidity. They are covered with carpet squares kept in place by a magnetic coating on the backs.

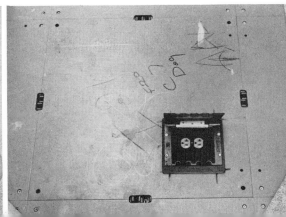

Air Products & Chemicals Headquarters, Allentown, Pennsylvania

For the corporate headquarters of Air Products & Chemicals, Inc., near Allentown, Pennsylvania, the design architect, Bernward Kurtz of The Eggers Group, wanted a sculptural feeling in the ceiling design without calling attention to the luminaires.

The solution, developed by Kurtz with his lighting consultant, James D. Kaloudis of Meyer, Strong & Jones, consulting engineers, is special pyramidal coffers supporting low-brightness, parabolic-type, twin-beam luminaires. And because partitions for some parts of the building could be as thick as 6 in. for fire protection purposes, Kurtz wanted ceiling runners 6-in. wide also, so that partitions would not interfere with the slope of the coffers. Since runners 6-in. wide were not available as stock items in pressed-steel sections, Kurtz found a fabricator to manufacture them, and he had the exposed 6-in.-wide strips finished in different colors to designate different floors. He also had the fabricator produce the metal framing and end panels for the coffer he designed—striking for its simplicity, and the ingenuity dis-

Don Fraser, Academy Studios Ltd.

played—to support the louvered parabolic luminaire and air diffuser saddle on top of the luminaire—scarcely a lightweight item.

The owner, represented by engineer Philip F. Newman, now manager of general services for Air Products & Chemicals, made

clear that the building should be not only flexible and efficient in the management of space, but also efficient in its use of energy. Flexibility for receptacle and communication wiring is provided by cellular flooring with in-floor fixtures, and H-cuts in the carpet to conceal the fixtures while allowing wiring egress.

The building consumes significantly less energy than similar existing buildings, according to John E. Plantinga, partner-in-charge for Meyer, Strong & Jones, even though it has some large areas with high heat loads and high fresh air requirements, such as the computer area, kitchen complex, cafeteria and print shop. Energy is saved by the lighting system (only 1.8 watts per sq ft), by the building envelope (precast panels are insulated, windows are double-glazed and take up only 25 per cent of the exterior), and by the hvac system (a variable-primary-air type that utilizes enthalpy control for optimizing free cooling via outdoor air). Electrical demand control also is provided as part of the building automation system.

Don Fraser, Academy Studios Ltd.

A 380,000-sq-ft corporate headquarters building, added to an existing campus of office, research and industrial buildings, for Air Products & Chemicals, Inc., in Trexlertown, Pennsylvania, has garnered several awards for its energy-conserving features. The headquarters is a series of four building units in a zigzag configuration. Exterior is insulated precast concrete panels and bronze-tinted, double-glazed windows. For most of the building, single-lamp luminaires were employed, using only 1.8 watts per sq ft, and providing about 75-80 footcandles in large open spaces. In several small partitioned interior spaces used by executives' secretaries, a single two-lamp luminaire was installed above the desks. In the drafting room, two-lamp troffers (one lamp above the other) alternate with single-lamp troffers to give more light. Ceiling runners suspend smoke detectors in the computer area.

Lawrence S. Williams

The coffer frame shown at the bottom of the page supports the luminaire and its associated air supply/return saddle. The frame for the luminaire is supported by the metal end panels together with the two stiffener pieces and angles shown. The metal panel is bent for rigidity and to provide a right angle section at the bottom to be received by the main runner, and also to provide a flange at the top to support lay-in acoustical panels. The 55-in. cross runners fit between the 10-ft main runners.

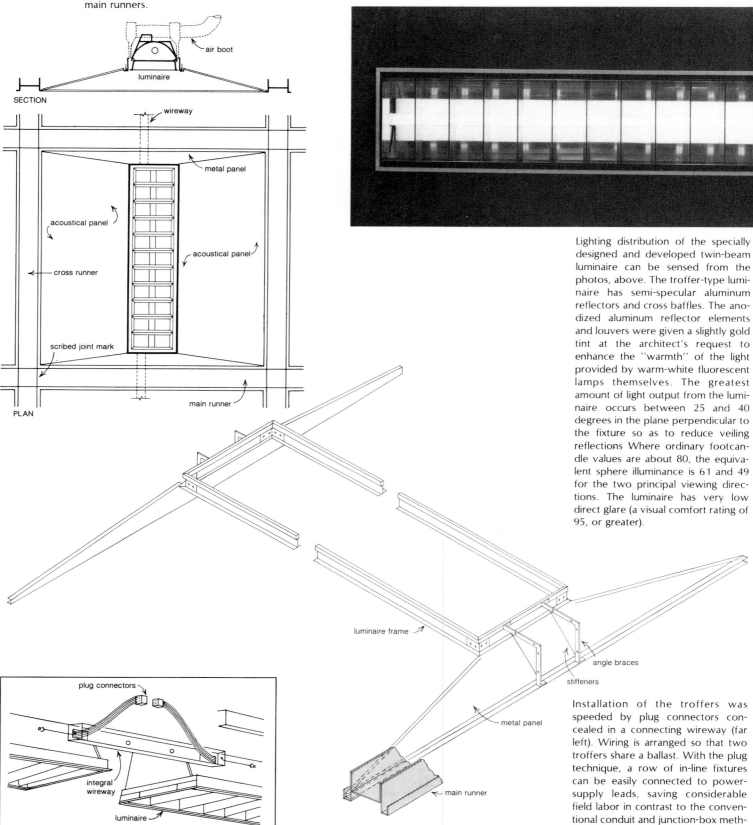

air boot

luminaire

SECTION

wireway

metal panel

acoustical panel

acoustical panel

cross runner

scribed joint mark

main runner

PLAN

plug connectors

integral wireway

luminaire

luminaire frame

angle braces

stiffeners

metal panel

main runner

Lighting distribution of the specially designed and developed twin-beam luminaire can be sensed from the photos, above. The troffer-type luminaire has semi-specular aluminum reflectors and cross baffles. The anodized aluminum reflector elements and louvers were given a slightly gold tint at the architect's request to enhance the "warmth" of the light provided by warm-white fluorescent lamps themselves. The greatest amount of light output from the luminaire occurs between 25 and 40 degrees in the plane perpendicular to the fixture so as to reduce veiling reflections Where ordinary footcandle values are about 80, the equivalent sphere illuminance is 61 and 49 for the two principal viewing directions. The luminaire has very low direct glare (a visual comfort rating of 95, or greater).

Installation of the troffers was speeded by plug connectors concealed in a connecting wireway (far left). Wiring is arranged so that two troffers share a ballast. With the plug technique, a row of in-line fixtures can be easily connected to power-supply leads, saving considerable field labor in contrast to the conventional conduit and junction-box method or to wire-splicing in channels.

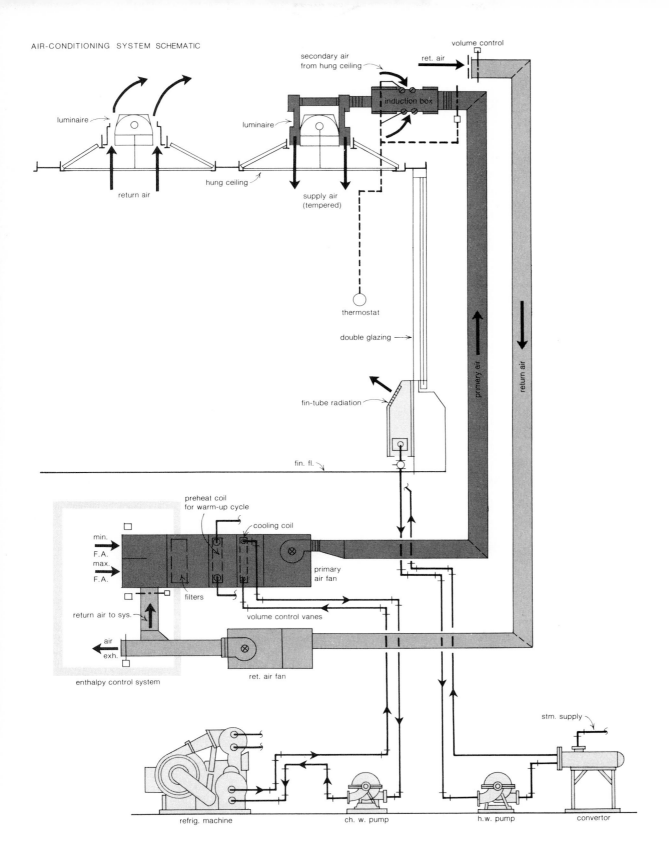

Spaces are conditioned by means of a variable-volume system. Supply air to spaces is constant, while the ratio of primary (cooled) air to return air is varied by the above-ceiling induction boxes in response to the room thermostats. The only source for tempering is the return air from the ceiling plenum. Primary air can be throttled to 40 per cent of maximum. Perimeter offices are heated by fin-tube radiation. Air is supplied to rooms and returned to the ceiling plenum through slots at the sides of the troffers. An enthalpy control system senses the temperature and humidity of outdoor air and "decides" when it can be used for "free" cooling. Because of the low energy taken by the lighting, the engineers were able to reduce the refrigeration capacity, air distribution and electrical distribution. A study on the cost implications of design features and on energy-system strategies, done for the client by consultant L. G. Spielvogel, concluded that the building generally meets the energy budget guidelines suggested by Federal agencies.

TASK/AMBIENT LIGHTING: AN IDEA WHOSE TIME HAS COME, BUT WHOSE IMPLICATIONS NEED TO BE BETTER UNDERSTOOD

Though precedents could be cited, the project at right—ARCO in Philadelphia—really launched task-ambient lighting as we know it. Literally thousands of architects, designers, engineers and owners have visited this installation, and now the idea is "red hot."

In 1975, only two manufacturers showed task/ambient lighting at NEOCON. One year later, at least ten had something to offer (though varying widely in technical sophistication), and others are about to announce their entry. Furniture manufacturers report that as much as 60 per cent of new office space is going open plan—and task/ambient lighting is a logical extension. So task/ambient lighting is, today, the thing. Is it a panacea? Definitely not. But now that it is so popular, some implications need to be examined more closely: What about reflected glare? What about work station and room brightnesses? What about wiring costs? How will people feel working in this new kind of lighting environment?

The pages that follow explore these questions. . . .

One big question is: how well do people like task lighting?

To help translate employee needs into the fabric of furniture and lighting for ARCO (Atlantic Richfield Company, Philadelphia), the interior design firm of Interspace, Incorporated involved environmental psychologist Ronald Goodrich early in their programming studies. In 1976, after two years' use, ARCO asked Goodrich to find out how well employees like it. Goodrich issued a questionnaire to 20 per cent of employees, top management to secretaries, and got an unusually high 70 per cent return. "The replies," Goodrich says, "showed that lighting

received the most positive response of any element of the design, save for the indoor plants." More of his analysis follows later.

As the programming studies developed, Interspace also brought in lighting consultant Sylvan R. Shemitz, who conceived the lighting approach and developed both the built-in lighting and the kiosks for uplighting and accent lighting. Guiding the project for the Atlantic Richfield Company was staff engineer Ben Cubler, who, as a committee-of-one, not only looked after client objectives and project scheduling, but also

was involved with lighting quality goals, and with such nitty-gritty as ease of setup and relocation of the furniture, detailed in metal and wood by JG Furniture.

In Goodrich's questionnaire, four questions dealt with how employees felt about the lighting . . . whether the characteristic mentioned mattered, "to some extent, to a moderate extent, or to a great extent." Question 1: Does this type of lighting create a more pleasant environment? Question 2: Is [a room with] this type of lighting easier to work in than one with

NO FIXTURES   FIXTURE AT DESK   UPLIGHT FROM WORK STATION   UPLIGHT FROM CABINET

standard ceiling lighting? Question 3: Does this lighting create less visual fatigue than standard ceiling lighting? Question 4: Does this lighting create a visually more attractive environment?

While Goodrich has not analyzed all the data, nor examined all the variables, his tentative conclusions from replies to the questionnaire are: Employees generally feel that the task lighting creates a more pleasant environment and makes it easier to work. Analysts and secretaries in interior spaces, some of whom are blocked off from windows,

gave lower ratings to the lighting as "creating less visual fatigue." Administrative employees on the perimeter were most positive on this question, while management personnel with private offices were less positive (75 per cent said it was true "to some extent;" 40 per cent said it was true "to a great extent"). Consideration of these replies, says Goodrich, suggests that: a) windows influence people's judgment about the standard of lighting, and b) different levels of employees have different conclusions about lighting—i.e., how much difference is perceived. In any event,

Goodrich says that more investigation of this question is necessary.

There were indications that younger people feel more positive about their environment in general, and about the lighting in particular. And people who liked their jobs, and described their jobs as non-routine, rated the visual environment higher.

Of all the design elements used in the offices, preference data showed that the task and ambient lighting was ranked either one or two as being the most important.

Task lighting can banish distracting brightness patterns

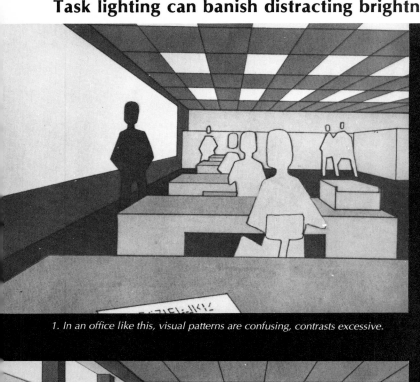

1. In an office like this, visual patterns are confusing, contrasts excessive.

2. A low partition cuts off "people distraction," but other problems remain.

5. A shelf added to the partition above the desk casts a shadow on the task area.

6. An under-shelf light brings back the illumination.

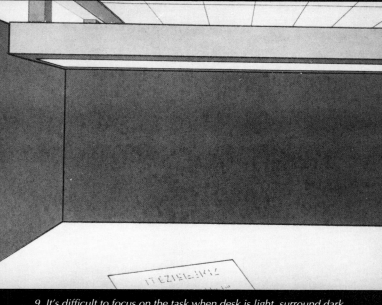

9. It's difficult to focus on the task when desk is light, surround dark.

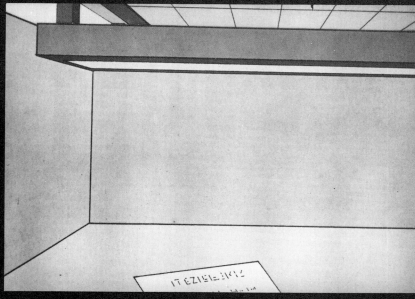

10. With brightness relationships in balance, the space is comfortable.

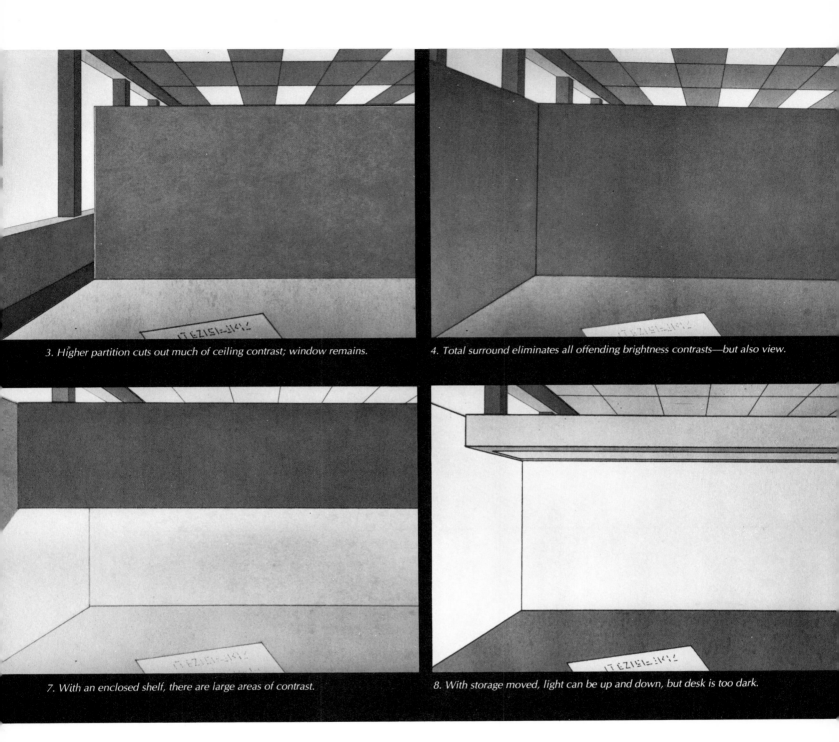

3. Higher partition cuts out much of ceiling contrast; window remains.

4. Total surround eliminates all offending brightness contrasts—but also view.

7. With an enclosed shelf, there are large areas of contrast.

8. With storage moved, light can be up and down, but desk is too dark.

Lighting consultant Sylvan R. Shemitz uses these black-and-white renderings to convey some of the visual-comfort problems common to many conventionally lighted offices, to indicate some the pitfalls on the way to getting rid of visual distractions and annoying ceiling brightness contrasts, and to emphasize the benefit to be gained from balanced brightness relationships via the task/ambient lighting approach.

In office design, it always has been good practice from the standpoints of lighting efficiency and visual comfort to use light colors for room finishes and for furniture, except where the tasks are not very critical. But, as Shemitz points out, this does not imply a

bland, lifeless interior environment. It does mean, however, careful attention to color schemes and textures, particularly with respect to the work stations and ceiling surfaces. While color of the carpet or the floor finish is not as critical from a contrast standpoint—though a marked difference could be distracting—it does have a significant effect upon the efficiency of the ambient lighting. The darker the floor, the less ambient light there will be overall. For example, in a task/ambient lighting installation for Texas Eastern Transmission in Houston, a light beige linen fabric was used for the vertical surface back of the uplight/downlight, and the work surface and the rest of the surround are light oak.

Once room distractions have been disposed of, the lighting design problem focuses on brightness relationships within work station furniture. The goal, says Shemitz, is to avoid striking brightness contrasts between work-station surfaces so that the eye does not need to make drastic adjustments when shifting away from the task and back to it. This involves control of illumination and reflectances.

When ambient lighting is provided by uplights within the furniture and from freestanding units, the lighting must be carefully designed to avoid "hot spots" of light on the ceiling which could be just as disconcerting as any checkerboard of bright ceiling luminaires and dark ceiling surround.

. . . A second generation of the task lighting approach

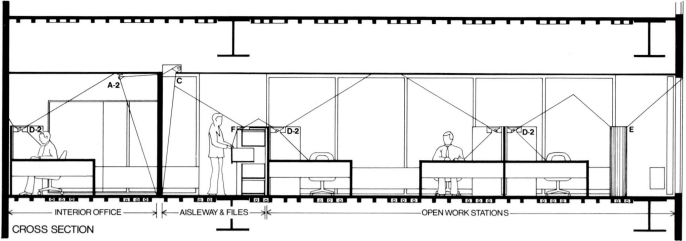

CROSS SECTION
INTERIOR OFFICE — AISLEWAY & FILES — OPEN WORK STATIONS

A-1: Recessed tungsten-halogen wall washer
- *precise coverage on walls without spillover*
- *essential ambient illumination*
- *accent lighting and display capability*

A-2: Surface tungsten-halogen wall washer
- *precise coverage*
- *supplementary ambient illumination*
- *accent lighting and display capability*

B: Concealed fluorescent ceiling washer (zone-controlled, with photocell override)
- *essential ambient illumination after dark*
- *precise and uniform coverage*

C: Recessed fluorescent wall washer (zone-controlled)
- *essential ambient illumination*
- *uniform coverage of core wall*

D-1: Fluorescent task light—private offices (zone-controlled, with individual circuit breaker; portable power pole)
- *illumination at work surfaces*
- *telephone and convenience outlets*

D-2: Fluorescent task light—open stations (zone controlled, with individual circuit breaker; portable power pole)
- *ambient illumination by up-component*
- *illumination at work surfaces*
- *telephone and convenience outlets*

E: Portable metal-halide kiosk (zone-controlled with photocell override)
- *ambient illumination in low-density areas*

F: Fluorescent file light
- *task illumination files in open areas*
- *added ambient illumination*

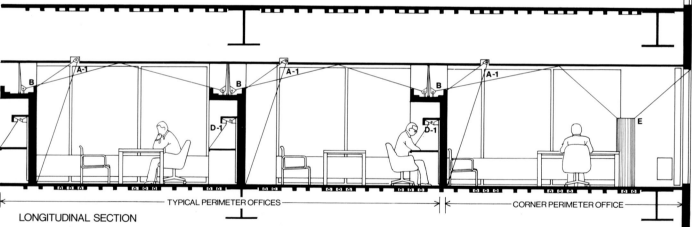

LONGITUDINAL SECTION
TYPICAL PERIMETER OFFICES — CORNER PERIMETER OFFICE

The design of 70,000 sq ft of office space for Crowley Maritime Corporation in San Francisco, by architects Robinson and Mills, goes far beyond using lighting "hardware" to provide task lighting, on the one hand, and uplighting, on the other. The architects and their lighting consultant, Sylvan R. Shemitz and Associates, jointly developed solutions through the use of both available and custom-designed fixtures, working closely with Knoll International in adapting lighting to the furniture. The result—evolving as a total architectural/lighting project—is an integrated concept of light to see by and light that is seen. As such, it might be viewed as the vanguard of a "second generation" of task/ambient lighting.

For task lighting, the installation uses fixtures built into portable furniture. But the ambient lighting—from a variety of ceiling washers, wall washers, and uplighting kiosks (see drawings)—produces not only general illumination for functional purposes, but also surface brightnesses (luminances) to create visual comfort and a sense of openness.

The plan has a variety of open and private spaces arranged around an expanded core for common uses, all joined by a generous circulation aisle lined with a distributed system of files.

The office areas, occupying four executive floors of One Market Plaza, in San Francisco, are divided into three general zones:

Zone I: Open-plan areas (lighting load: 1.01 watts/usable square foot). The white core wall is washed to provide ambient light and an interior source of soft brightness to balance the brightness of perimeter windows (fixture C on section). Work stations have one lighting fixture that provides both task lighting and uplighting. Low-density areas are supplemented by "filler" light from up-component kiosks. Some files in these areas are task lighted by a file light (fixture F) which also adds to the aisleway ambient level.

Zone II: Private perimeter offices (2.58 watts/USF). These offices gain ambient light through the windows on light days, and through built-in ceiling washers during dark

hours (fixture B). This ambient light is supplemented by recessed wall washers suitable for display of artwork (fixture A-1). Task fixtures are installed in custom work units (fixture D-1).

Zone III: Core and common use areas (3.00 watts/USF). Permanently-occupied interior core spaces have open-plan furniture with fixtures for task and ambient lighting, supplemented by wall washers (fixture A-2) for accent, display, and color variation.

The total installed capacity for lighting is 1.81 watts/USF. A central, visible master control panel has a switch for each zone, which is turned off when the zone is not being used. Ancillary lighting for use during non-daylight hours is controlled by a photocell override which limits its use to nighttime hours. All zones are programmed to turn off automatically after the last employee has left. Energy economics are enhanced by an arrangement with the owner by which unused energy credits are returned to the tenant (usage is monitored by a demand meter installed on each floor).

Engineers say some aspects of task lighting need more study

A number of new lighting concepts designed to cut energy usage have been explored since the energy crunch arrived. Task/ambient lighting has great potential in this respect. But . . . it may or may not use less energy than a well-designed ceiling lighting system. Without careful design, it can be troublesome from the standpoint of reflected glare. It can require more wiring at 120v. And the votes are still uncounted on some of the psychological aspects. For some expert opinion, engineer Steven Squillace; his associate, interior designer Leonard Else; lighting consultant James D. Kaloudis; and Dr. Ronald Helms were consulted:

Task lighting has great promise as a rational approach to putting light where it is needed. Also, it is giving lighting designers opportunity for dealing with the luminous environment in a new and creative way. But at the same time . . .

There are potential psychological and physiological problems that have not been dealt with before. One concern voiced by lighting designer James Kaloudis: How can task/ambient lighting systems be designed so the occupant is not "locked in" to one specific area for reading? What if he wants to turn away from the desk and lean back for reading? (Steve Squillace says if lighting solutions were more dynamic—with switching, dimming, etc.—this could be done. Kaloudis wonders about the cost.)

Task lighting also can present a unique physiological situation, as described by Kaloudis: With the light source located close to vertical surfaces of the work station, the luminance of the background may be very bright. If the background is brighter than the task, itself, then the eye may have trouble adapting. Think of it this way, says Kaloudis: The background luminance used to be the whole room, now it's a compressed envelope!

From a functional standpoint, "more science and less art" is needed, says Ron Helms. Inasmuch as quality of visual comfort and visibility are key factors, it is essential, he says, to develop proper light distributions (photometrics) . . . and this requires research money.

Two areas of lighting engi-

Steven Squillace and Leonard Else are with the Detroit firm of Smith, Hinchman & Grylls, architects and engineers. James D. Kaloudis is with the New York firm of Meyer, Strong & Jones, consulting mechanical and electrical engineers. Ronald Helms is an associate professor at the University of Colorado, Boulder, and has a lighting consulting practice.

neering that he feels need closer attention are: 1) the distribution of light from the indirect luminaires to avoid distracting patterns of brightness on the ceiling, and 2) the design of task lighting to avoid reflected glare (light from the source bouncing into one's eyes).

Helms is critical of indirect systems that produce "puddles" of brightness on the ceiling, creating visual clutter and drawing attention to the ceiling plane. This problem, he notes, is not confined to uplighting, but has been a common one with many direct systems, with bright ceiling fixtures and dark surround. Furthermore, some of these ceiling systems also are guilty of causing reflected glare because of the nature of their light distribution. Spotty ceilings can be avoided with care in the optical design of the luminaires. Such utilitarian lighting, he avers, should blend in with the interior environment, not conflict with it.

Helms says, further, that . . .

More awareness of reflected glare is needed. Putting the light source close to the task gets a lot of light on it, but this benefit may be negated if much of the illumination is reflected from the task at the occupant's viewing angle. Leonard Else and James Kaloudis, however, recently have noted that some manufacturers recognize the problem, and are showing a willingness to do something about it.

Both Squillace and Kaloudis agree that solving the reflected glare problem through design of the task light source takes careful thought. The trouble is that if the light comes from a narrow, linear source in front of the occupant, its mirror image can be reflected in the task, and, hence, cause glare.

If, because of work station design, the light source needs to be in front of the viewer, then a possible approach, says Squillace, is to block off the rays of light from the source in an area directly in front of the task. Because the task may not always be in the same location on the work surface, the solution, he feels, should have dynamic capability. Lighting designer Douglas Baker, reports Squillace, has been considering something along these lines. Kaloudis, equally conscious of the glare problem, thinks there is a solution to it even with a static luminaire design.

What about economics? As usual, some aspects are relative. Task lighting installations have been designed with installed capacities of from 1 to 2 plus watts per sq ft. On the other hand, some high-quality conventional ceiling lighting systems have been designed for less than 2 w per sq ft. Lower wattage lighting uses less power, but it may not use less wire. The reason is that most ceiling lighting systems are wired for 277-v distribution, but task lighting, so far, has been wired for 120 v. (A 277-v circuit can be loaded to 4300 watts, while a 120-v circuit can't carry more than 1800 w.) Why 120v for task lighting? Because the National Electrical Code states that branch circuits for supplying fixtures shall not exceed 150 v to ground unless they supply ballasts for lamps mounted in permanently installed fixtures; the fixtures do not have manual switch control as part of the fixture; and lampholders of the screw-shell type for electric-discharge lamps are not less than 8 ft above the floor.

But Steve Squillace believes there is logic from both engineering and safety standpoints for the code to be interpreted or changed to allow 277-v distribution to work stations. They could use an "umbilical cord" with a specially configured connector on the end for plugging into a floor cell. Even now, he points out, room switches for ceiling lights are connected to 277 v.

Manufacturers, in transition, are developing new designs

Eppinger is using a Lam, Inc. metal-halide uplight
that spreads out a wide pool of light from a point source.

Stow/Davis is working with ITT-Wakefield to refine a lighting cylinder
that is translucent on top and incorporates a diffusing strip lens on the bottom.

Knoll, one of the early entrants in the task-lighting field,
is using Shemitz lighting designs in several versions of furniture.

Steelcase has engaged Day-Brite Division of Emerson Electric
for development of new task-lighting fixtures.

Harvey Probber provides a swinging-arm work light for a workspace with
no place for a built-in task-lighting unit.

Westinghouse solves the problem of ambient and task lighting with a pedestal unit
that has uplight and a lens with narrow beam spread on the bottom.

Daylighting design aids emerge as interest grows in the technique

The rising cost of energy, along with the introduction of energy standards, has stimulated considerable interest in the potentialities of daylight, in combination with electric light, to produce energy savings. And this interest has given impetus to the development of procedures for economic evaluations, as well as for daylight designs. As one example, the daylighting section of the Illuminating Engineering Society's Recommended Practice for Daylighting is being completely rewritten. The Daylighting Committee has commissioned the College of Architecture and Urban Studies at the Virginia Polytechnic Institute and State University to undertake the revision under the supervision of professor Benjamin H. Evans, AIA. Objectives of the revision, which is expected to be available in about a year, are: 1) to help designers understand and appreciate the opportunities and constraints inherent in daylighting; 2) to provide sufficient computation processes to enable design decisions to be made with reasonable reliability at an early stage of the design process; and 3) to relate the use of solar energy for daylighting to the optimization of building design in all areas, including heating and cooling effects and life cycle cost-benefit analysis.

Yet even now, computer programs are available—or will be shortly—to assist the designer in getting some grasp of the economic potential of daylighting, or even in making precise predictions of ESI footcandle levels based upon assumed sky conditions.

Rohm and Haas Company has made a computer program known as SUN (Skylight Utilization Network) available to architects and engineers that analyzes the effects of skylights on the energy required for lighting, and on heating and cooling loads. The program is an outgrowth of work done at the Center for Industrial and Institutional Development at the University of New Hampshire, but has some refinements made by engineers at Rohm and Hass who added engineering data and computerized the procedure.

The Rohm and Haas program computes losses and gains caused by: 1) solar energy, 2) conductive and convective heat transfers through the curb and dome, 3) infiltration around the skylight, 4) illumination savings, based upon the kWhr saved when electric lights are not needed to maintain the design illumination level. Illumination calculated by the program is average footcandles on the working plane. Computer printout gives illuminance levels for each hour of the day for the 21st day of each month for clear days, overcast days, and for a weather-weighted average of the two. Illumination savings are counted only for the summer months because it is assumed that electric light contributes to the heating of the building in the winter—putting estimates on the conservative side. The program has the capability of computing savings for lighting in three modes: 1) savings only when the design lighting level is exceeded (it is assumed that electric lights are switched off at this point); 2) savings for any contribution of daylight up to and including the design level (it is assumed that lights have dimming capability); 3) savings computed up to and above the design level (while this is not a factor in savings, it does indicate the extent of the daylighting).

The lighting savings predicted by the computer program are then balanced against solar gain, conductive and convective heat transfer, and infiltration—which are additive or subtractive depending upon the season, and whether the building is being heated or cooled. Though solar gain, conduction, convection and infiltration add up to a deficiency in Btu's over the year, when the daylighting contribution is added, the computer runs show an over-all net energy savings achieved via the skylights.

In its present form, emphasis of the Rohm and Haas program is on the energy economics of skylights. The program does not determine the total energy balance within a space, as it does not include the losses through the building envelope, nor consider the type of hvac system used. What it does is to determine the energy tradeoffs between electric light and skylighting in providing average footcandles on a work plane. The skylight energy balance is in a form to allow energy credits for skylights as specified in energy conservation standards such as ASHRAE 90-75.

If the architect and engineer are looking for precision in the prediction of ESI (Equivalent Sphere Illumination) footcandles from daylight or a combination or electric light and daylight, this will be available in the Lumen III computer program of Smith, Hinchman and Grylls, Detroit architects and engineers, developed by Stephen Squillace, director of electrical engineering, and research assistant David DiLaura. As with Lumen II, which is for electric light, the new program will permit contour plots of equi-ESI values—a mapping of illuminance values in rooms. The "elegance" of the program is demonstrated by the fact that not only does it deal with the straight input of daylight into the room, but also takes into account the interreflectance of room surfaces. Even more impressive is the fact that the program is able to take into account the effect of overhangs or vanes, and even the effect of adjacent buildings (shadow effect, interreflectance between buildings, etc.).

To illustrate the potential energy savings through the use of skylights, Rohm and Haas took outputs from their skylight computer program to prepare maps and graphs such as those shown. It was assumed that when illumination from daylight reaches a specified level, the electric light will be regulated either manually or by automatic controls. The graph shows how energy savings vary with percentage of roof coverage by skylights. The percentages derive from the assumed use of 25, 36, 49 and 64 skylights for a 100-by 100-ft building.

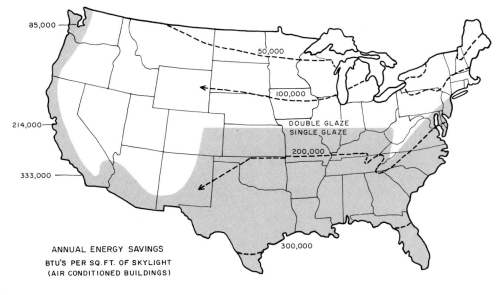

ANNUAL ENERGY SAVINGS
BTU'S PER SQ. FT. OF SKYLIGHT
(AIR CONDITIONED BUILDINGS)

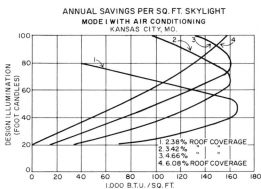

ANNUAL SAVINGS PER SQ. FT. SKYLIGHT
MODE I WITH AIR CONDITIONING
KANSAS CITY, MO.

1. 2.38% ROOF COVERAGE
2. 3.42% "
3. 4.66% "
4. 6.08% ROOF COVERAGE

EXAMPLES OF INNOVATION IN BUILDING OPERATION: EXPLODING SOME MYTHS ABOUT BUILDING ENERGY USE

By Lawrence G. Spielvogel, P.E.
Consulting engineer, Wyncote, Pennsylvania

The one factor that, more than any other, determines energy consumption of a building is how it is used. "How it is used" has more impact than the type of hvac system, or the boilers, or the chillers, or the energy source. More than how much glass, or insulation, or lighting a building has. It is the people who occupy a building that place the demands on systems and use energy. It is the *hours of operation* of systems and components that are the major determinant of energy consumption. What runs most of the time, and typically at full load? Prime examples are lighting, fans and pumps. In many buildings, the fans and pumps use more energy in a year than the chillers do.

While such statements may sound obvious, their reality is often ignored in many current studies and projections of building-energy use. Comparisons of buildings on the basis of installed capacities of hvac, lighting and other electrical equipment can be misleading because the quantity of energy used is not necessarily related either to design load or to installed equipment capacity.

The "occupant" factor is well demonstrated by studies on energy use by Princeton University[1] in "what would appear to be identical dwellings"— showing that during a given period of time, "a ratio of better than 2-to-1 exists between the highest and lowest users."

Furthermore, energy use can vary widely from year to year in dwellings, as is demonstrated by Figure 1, which shows metered energy for heating and cooling of a single-family dwelling in Indiana over a nine-year period. Heating- and cooling-energy consumptions vary by as much as 2 to 1.

Only a small fraction of annual energy use occurs during the extremes of weather

Most energy use in buildings occurs when the outdoor temperatures are moderate, which means that the hvac systems operate at part load most of the time. Only a small fraction of the energy use occurs during temperature extremes.

Figure 2 clearly makes these points. It is a curve showing annual energy use related to the outside temperature, for heating and cooling of a building in Ohio. In the 20F increment between 0F and 20F, less than 5 per cent of the annual energy is consumed, and in the 20F-increment between 80F and 100F, only 12 per cent of the total is used. But in the 30F-increment between 50F and 80F, 70 per cent of the total is used. Obviously, designers should be much more concerned about how efficiently the building and its systems operate during moderate temperatures than during extremes.

Space allocation directly affects efficiency of energy-using systems in buildings

Some of the most significant decisions affecting eventual energy use of a building are made in the very early programing stage. This is important enough that energy use should be included as one of the criteria in spatial organization of buildings. This means, for example, that particular attention must be paid to spaces that have only part-time occupancy such as conference rooms and auditoriums; and to spaces that are used round-the-clock, such as computer rooms.

A recent study[2] on the energy use of 50 office buildings in Philadelphia concluded that, "the single most important finding is that the variables most affecting energy consumption are the extent and type of building use, as determined . . . by presence or absence of computers, data-processing equipment and support facilities," in which case the energy use was 50 per cent higher than buildings without this equipment.

Virtually every one of these buildings was designed without thought being given to where computers would be located. While much of the 50 per cent premium in energy use can be attributed to the computers and their air conditioning, the fact that support facilities have to be provided for people working in these facilities is of major significance.

Most office-related systems are operated for 50 to 60 hours a week, while most computers are used for as much as 168 hours a week (24 hr a day). This means that it is necessary to provide lighting in the lobby, stairwells, corridors, lounges and toilet rooms, elevator service, vending machines, etc. for people working in these facilities. It may be necessary to provide almost as much energy for the services in the "spine" of the building as when it is fully occupied.

There have been cases where computer rooms occupying less than 10 per cent of the floor space of an office building consumed more than two-thirds of the annual electricity.

Big variations in energy budgets can result from changes in design and operation

Strikingly, studies of projected energy usage in buildings, using commonly accepted design

Actual energy use may turn out much different than presumed

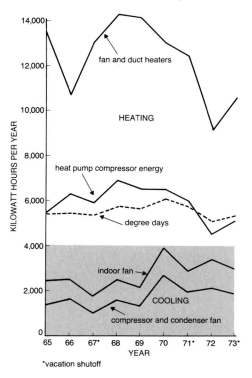

Figure 1: Annual variation in heating and cooling energy use for a single-family house with heat pump For this house in Indiana, maximum variation in heating and cooling loads was about 2 to 1. In 1968 when maximum heating load occurred, total energy use exceeded by 30 per cent, that of 1972, when minimum heating load occurred. Dip in heating energy consumption in 1966 presumably resulted from greater operation of the heat pump and less need for duct heaters.

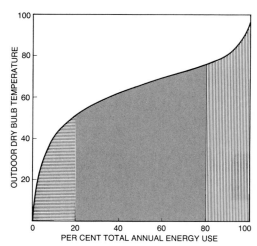

Figure 2: Hvac energy use as a function of temperature for a building in Ohio Up to a temperature of 50F, only 20 per cent of the total energy use occurred; above 80F only 12 per cent of the total energy use occurred.

practices, have shown variations as high as five or even 10 to one, depending upon systems selected and system operation.

While this is not usual, it is relatively easy to demonstrate variations on the order of two to one, as in Table 1[3] which lists energy budgets for a variety of system design and operations options for a proposed office building. Some of the items having significant impact include amount of ventilation air, hours of fan operation, control and capacity of perimeter radiation.

Even in buildings having reasonable energy consumption, it is possible to find further substantial reductions as demonstrated by Table 2. This 1-million sq ft building has a perimeter induction system and interior-zone reheat, and during one particular year had a *measured* energy consumption of about 70,000 Btu per sq ft per year. Through a combination of design, operational, and schedule changes, computer simulation indicated a possible reduction of 20 per cent.

Before going further, we should explain the commonly used meaning of the term "annual energy budget." It is defined as the amount of fuel, at its gross thermal value, used by a building, plus the kilowatt hours of electricity multiplied by 3,143 Btu/kWh, the total being divided by the square footage of the building.

A word of caution, though, about interpretations and inferences drawn from reported measured data (annual energy budgets). Good-quality energy consumption data and adequate information on buildings and their use is difficult and expensive to obtain. Scarcely any buildings are monitored by anything more than a kWh-meter, and bills for fuel oil, gas or steam. Seldom are individual pieces of equipment metered. For these reasons, when reported data is being used as a basis for comparison, the quality of the data must be carefully examined and carefully used—taking into account the presumed accuracy and sophistication of the people reporting the data, who is presenting the data and why, the validity of the sample, etc.

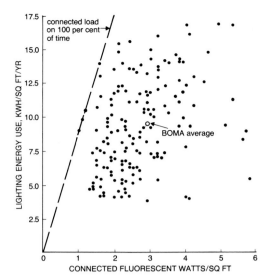

Figure 4: Plot of office building lighting energy consumption versus installed capacities
A survey of BOMA members across the country shows no correlation between yearly energy use for lighting and the watts per square foot of installed capacity.

Energy budgets vary from building type to building type and building to building

There seemingly is little consistency in annual energy consumption of buildings within given building types. And paradoxical as it might seem at first, statistics show that climate, itself, is not much of a factor. All of which tends to confirm the thesis that it is how a building is used and how much the systems are used that determine annual energy budgets.

Office buildings. Every year the Building Owners' and Manager's Association (BOMA) reports the air-conditioning operating costs of over 125 million square feet of office buildings on a city-by-city basis.

If air-conditioning operating cost, which in itself is fairly crude (how does one apportion the electrical energy usage among the various systems?) is plotted against cooling degree days, which also is fairly crude, on a city-by-

city basis, the plot is a scatter of points all over the place (Figure 3). In other words no consistent pattern develops. What a person might expect would be a series of points forming a diagonal line, starting low at the lowest degree days, and being high at the highest degree days. But this graph shows that cooling cost of office buildings has little relationship to climate. The reason is that most of the air-conditioning energy is used to offset heat gains from people, lights and equipment.

Another misconception is that the efficiency of equipment at full load is an index how efficiently a building will be operated, but this is not necessarily so. Again, it is how the building is used. Take an example: A centrifugal chiller for a high-rise office building might have an efficiency of 0.7 kW per ton, while some low-efficiency unitary units might take 2 kW per ton. But if one tenant wants to work late in an office building with a central system, it is necessary to turn on, say, one 500-ton chiller, a couple of 100 horsepower pumps, a 50-horsepower cooling tower fan, one 400-horsepower primary air fan, and a 100-horsepower return fan. Before you know it, almost 1000 kW are being used. Unitary air conditioners, on the other hand would take only about 2kW per person to keep late workers comfortable.

The case is not being made for unitary equipment, per se; not at all. Obviously a central system is more efficient where occupancy is uniform and consistent in a large building. The point is again made, however, that actual building use is a primary factor in energy use.

Earlier the statement was made that there is no direct relationship between installed capacity and energy consumption. This is borne out by data on lighting energy use in 307 office buildings across the country as collected by BOMA[4] (Figure 4). There is no pattern whatever between installed capacity and annual energy use.

Schools and colleges. This inconsistency we've been demonstrating is true of schools too. This is shown in Table 3, an energy-use study done on schools in Fairfax County, Vir-

Neither climate nor installed capacities of equipment are a guide to building energy use

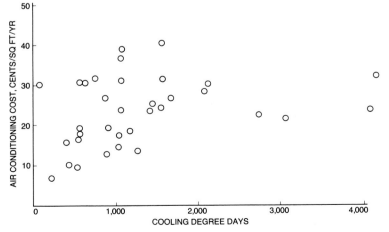

Figure 3: Plot of air-conditioning cost versus cooling degree days for 125 million square feet of office space
Statistics collected by the Building Owners' and Managers' Association show no correlation between climate and air-conditioning operating cost. The inference is that operating hours is a much more significant factor.

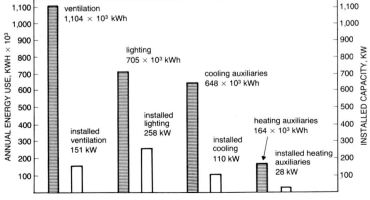

Figure 5: Relationships between installed capacities of equipment and energy consumption at an Ohio University
This bar graph indicates that there is no direct relationship between installed capacity and energy use.

ginia.[5] All the schools in this county operate under almost identical weather conditions; and, generally speaking, the architecture is similar. But look, for example, at how electrical consumption varies from school to school. Yearly costs range from 13.5 cents per sq ft down to 3.8 cents per sq ft—a ratio of four to one!

These schools are in an area where the utility company had an electric rate of a flat one cent per kWh with no demand, so the cost is directly related to the actual energy use. All the schools also pay the same price for fuel oil. so the cost figures are directly related to fuel consumption.

Figure 5 again confirms the concept that says, "I don't want to know so much how big the equipment is, I want to know how much it's used." This is a building at Ohio State University that has absorption cooling with a gas-fired boiler, which is also used for space heating.[6] Installed capacity of the ventilation equipment is only 151 kW, but look at the amount of energy it uses. In contrast, the lighting load is almost twice the installed capacity of the ventilation, but it uses only two-thirds as much energy.

University buildings of various types have been shown to vary by more than four to one in energy use[7] (Table 4). Obviously a chemistry building will use a lot more than a fine arts building. But the table shows that energy use of fine arts buildings at two different universities in Utah varied by 50 per cent.

Hospitals. Energy use in hospitals is intensive, as is shown in Table 5, from a study of three Veterans' Administration buildings in different parts of the country.[8] But climatic comparisons are also interesting. In Buffalo, where the winter design temperature is –10F, one would expect the fossil fuel requirements to be a lot higher than in Florida or California where the design temperatures are 30F to 40F. But not so. This table agains says when it comes to the amount of energy used, regardless of source, factors other than climate are the prime determinant.

Stores. There is an extreme range of energy budgets for stores, as is demonstrated in Table 6 which lists data from an enclosed mall-type shopping center about 50 miles north of Philadelphia. It is an all-electric building where each store has its own unitary all-electric heating and cooling system. Each store is metered and billed individually. The shopping mall operates a fixed number of hour per day, and days per week. Yet, there is a ratio of almost 10 to 1 in energy used, due primarily to the disparate functions of the stores.

The relevance of energy or power budgets is difficult to prove

There has been a movement toward establishing annual energy budgets for buildings as the basis for legislation or as guidelines for designers to meet. While this is favored by many knowledgeable people, there are many pros and cons.

In favor of the energy budget is that it establishes target energy consumptions without prescribing methods of compliance. The main

problem, however, is establishing the budget itself. Other problems include the means for determining compliance with the budget during design, and the means for enforcement after the building is built.

There has been a similar, but smaller, movement towards the power budget[9] which limits the installed capacity of the energy-using systems. But the power budget fails to account for the major factor in energy consumption: how the building is used.

Low life-cycle costs and low energy use do not necessarily go hand in hand
It may seem surprising, but there is no basic or implied relationship between low life-cycle cost and low energy consumption that holds true in all cases.

Table 1: Energy use variations with alternate designs for a three-story building

Alternatives	Estimated gas use, Mcf	Equivalent electricity MkWh	Approximate energy budget Btu/sq ft/yr
1* Base case 0.1 cfm/sq ft	10,127	2,415	73,400
2* Increased ventilation air	12,913	2,498	85,800
3 Single glass used	14,287	2,515	91,500
4* 68F-winter (20% relative humidity), 80F-summer	7,324	2,226	59,700
5* Heat recovery	9,165	2,856	75,700
6 Only 75% perimeter radiation installed	8,949	2,396	68,500
7 Modular radiation control	6,729	2,353	59,000
8 Perimeter radiation shutoff at night	6,749	2,356	59,200
9 Heat off over 50F	8,799	2,364	67,500
10* Reduced operation of air handlers	9,005	2,388	68,600
11* Increased operation of air handlers	17,851	2,869	110,600
12* Combines features	4,715	2,240	49,400

This table gives energy budgets for a three-story building with a central chilled-water system and a steam boiler, with a medium-velocity, variable-air-volume air-distribution system and perimeter radiation.

*1. The base case assumes the use of double glazing. 2. Ventilation air is increased to 0.25 cfm. 4. Base case (1) assumes 72F in winter and 75F in summer. 5. Heat recovery used, economy cycle (viz, outdoor air used for cooling) is turned off. 10. Startup is delayed until 8 a.m., and the system is shut off at 5 p.m., reducing operation by three hours. 11. The air-handling system is operated 24 hours a day, but outside air is shut off when the building is unoccupied. 12. Several of the energy-saving features are combined. They are not cumulative however, so energy saved is somewhat less than the sum total.

Tabie 2: Effects of design, operation and schedule changes on a million square foot building

	Annual energy use/sq ft					Percent savings		
	kWh	Btu	Steam (lb)	Btu	Total Btu	Heat	Cool	Elec
1 Building as is	7.9	26,963	42.3	42,300	69,263	0.0	0.0	0.0
2* Schedule changes								
a) 4 day week	7.7	26,280	40.3	40,300	66,580	8.5	3.7	3.4
b) daylight time	7.9	26,963	41.6	41,600	68,563	–1.6	4.3	0.3
3* Temperatures								
76-65 vs. 80-70	7.9	26,963	39.2	39,200	66,163	30.5	–4.2	0.4
4 Skin changes								
double glass	7.9	26,963	40.4	40,400	67,363	14.0	1.1	0.0
5* Air system changes								
a) reduced airflow	6.3	21,502	40.8	40,800	62,302	–4.3	11.8	20.6
b) vav + recirculate primary air	6.7	22,867	39.7	39,700	62,567	1.9	14.6	16.1
6* Central plant changes							Steam	
a) base load 500 ton chiller	7.6	25,939	38.2	38,200	64,139		9.7	4.5
b) electric 500 ton chiller	8.2	27,987	27.6	27,600	55,587		35.0	–3.2
c) electric 200 ton chiller	7.9	26,963	32.5	32,500	59,463		23.0	0.2
7 Combination of reduced airflow + recirculation + base load 500 ton chiller	6.0	20,478	35.6	35,600	56,078		16.0	25.0

The values in the table are the results of a computer analysis of an existing building with steam-turbine cooling.

*2a. Energy savings due primarily to reduction in number of startup and shutdown hours per week. 2b. Daylight-saving time reduced cooling energy but required more heating energy due to a one-hour earlier startup in mornings and the heating of ventilation air. The extra heating energy almost cancelled the cooling-energy saving. 3. Saving achieved by setting thermostat in winter at 65F instead of 76F, and 80F in summer instead of 70F. 5a. Savings due to reduction of air flow on both perimeter and interior systems to match actual load. 5b. Savings due to replacement of interior reheat coils with variable-air-volume boxes, and recirculating primary air for perimeter induction system in excess of that required for ventilation alone. 6. The central chilled-water plant consists of small, medium (500-ton), and large turbine-driven chillers. The medium-size chiller was used for the base load, Three of the alternatives included: 1) base loading the 500-ton turbine chiller; 2) substituting a 500-ton electric base-load chiller; and 3) installing a 200-ton electric base-load chiller.

For example, a recent study on a large high-rise office building recommended adoption of the system that had the highest annual energy requirement because it had the lowest annual operating cost. Reason for this apparent anomaly was that the district steam company had a 100 per cent demand ratchet charge for 12 months based upon maximum demand.

The system with the highest capacity, though more efficient than a lower-capacity (and lower cost) system, had the highest demand charge, and consequently, the highest operating cost. The cost for the actual energy used amounted to less than one-third of the annual energy bill; the remaining two-thirds was demand charge.

Energy consumption of buildings can vary by 2 to 1, or more

Table 3: Energy consumption cost of 17 elementary schools in the same county

Schools	Area (sq ft)	Cost of electricity per sq ft	Cost of fuel oil per sq ft
Greenbriar East	59,483	.135	.059
Fort Hunt	66,992	.131	.061
Brookfield	43,794	.127	.062
Kings Glen	64,023	.107	.073
Camelot	76,853	.100	.076
Forest Edge	80,843	.094	.050
Mt. Vernon Woods	40,051	.094	.066
Oak View	77,254	.092	.079
Wolftrap	49,082	.086	.056
Floris	19,637	.079	.089
Little Run	40,035	.074	.070
Quander Road	40,033	.062	.091
Cedar Lane	37,194	.061	.088
Beech Tree	40,333	.060	.070
Sleepy Hollow	39,045	.049	.101
Oak Grove	10,349	.039	.188
Crestwood	46,983	.038	.108

Table 4: Energy usage of university buildings in Utah

Building	Institution	Building area, sq ft	Heat	Energy budgets— MBtu/sq ft/year Electric	Total
Law	U of U	57,286	207	180	387
Pharmacy	U of U	57,790	129	51	180
Chemistry	U of U	95,160	429	158	587
Library	U of U	248,480	117	134	251
Fine Arts	USU	132,435	148	52	200
Eng. & Phys. Science	USU	142,580	119	30	149
Forestry & Bio Science	USU	118,827	128	54	182
Fine Arts	SUSC	18,849	95	39	134
Library	SUSC	45,168	70	70	140
Phys. Ed.	SUSC	50,349	227	24	251
Science	SUSC	45,609	147	24	171
Range			70 to 429 6.1:1	24 to 180 7.5:1	134 to 587 4.4:1

Table 5: Energy usage of three VA hospitals

	Btu/sq ft/year
Lake City, Fla	
Fuel	189,000
Electricity	73,000
Total	262,000
San Diego, Calif	
Fuel	285,000
Electricity	122,000
Total	407,000
Buffalo, NY	
Fuel	176,000
Electricity	41,000
Total	217,000

Table 6: Energy usage in a shopping mall

	Btu/sq ft/year
Auto center	74,000
Department store	114,000
Department store	102,000
Variety store	100,000
Restaurant	409,000
Bank	131,000
Drug store	129,000
Food market	205,000
Dry cleaner	688,000
Book store	104,000
Doughnut store	326,000

With computer simulation, how the building is used influences accuracy of results

From what has been said so far, one might be overwhelmed with the thought of predicting building energy use. There are, however, a number of computer programs available for this purpose. They have a wide range of capabilities and costs. No one computer program will be applicable in all situations. The key factor in selecting a program is its ability to handle the specifics of the building being evaluated in sufficient detail and flexibility to permit study of alternatives in adequate depth.

The cost of using these programs for new building design can range from less than $100 to several thousand dollars, plus about one to 10 professional man-days. Once a particular program has been selected, the main items of cost are the number of alternatives to be evaluated, and the complexity of the building and its systems.

How accurate are the results? Frequently, there are wide discrepancies between predicted and actual energy use because the use of the building turned out not to be what was presumed in the computer simulation. Then adjustments to the initial assumptions regarding hours of occupancy, night and weekend use, mechanical system operation, etc., are necessary to more closely match the predicted to the actual energy consumption.

Building owners must be able to control building energy consumption for efficiency

While the variations in building energy consumptions that have been demonstrated are probably best explained by use of buildings more than by their physical characteristics, this by no means implies that buildings and their systems should not be optimized for efficient use of energy in themselves. But the overriding factor still is the ability of the owner to efficiently control the energy consumption of the building, whether this be provision for switching lights off and on within reasonable building modules, allowance for part-load operation of systems, design for part-time occupancy of spaces or whatever.

References
1. Home Energy Use Gets Thorough Analysis *Electrical World,* July 1, 1974
2. Energy Consumption in Commercial Buildings in Philadelphia, Enviro-Management and Research, Inc., National Electrical Manufacturers Assn., 1975, N.Y., N.Y.
3. Computer Energy Analysis for Existing Buildings, Spielvogel, L.G., ASHRAE Journal, August 1975
4. Energy Conservation Applied to Office Lighting, Ross and Baruzzini, Inc., April 15, 1975, Federal Energy Administration, Washington, D.C.
5. Energy Study—Fairfax County Public Schools, Educational Facilities Laboratories, 1973, New York, N.Y.
6. Proceedings of the Conference on Energy Conservation in Commercial, Residential and Industrial Buildings, Ohio State University, May 1974, Columbus, Ohio
7. Campus Utility Costs, Furner, B.O., Heating, Piping and Air Conditioning, November 1973
8. Energy Conservation Study of V.A. Hospitals, Reynolds, Smith and Hills, Veterans Administration, 1974, Washington, D.C.
9. Ohio State Building Code, Chapter BB-48

BUILDING AUTOMATION: WHAT IT DOES, WHAT ITS BENEFITS ARE, HOW THE ECONOMICS FARE

by Donald E. Ross, partner
Jaros, Baum & Bolles, consulting engineers

Engineer Ross clears away some of the mystery surrounding building automation—explaining, simply, the terminology, and telling how electronic control is applied to building hvac, life-safety management and security.

Design professionals are finding it increasingly difficult to keep abreast of the new and sophisticated techniques continually being introduced in the field of mechanical systems for buildings. Nowhere has this dynamism been as extensive as with centralized control known as "building automation." Not only are many new techniques being used, derived from computer-based technologies, but many new and expanded functions have been added that rarely were included 20 years ago.

Building automation: how it is different from automatic temperature control

For years it has been possible to control room comfort conditions by adjusting a wall-mounted thermostat that regulates the amount of heating or cooling delivered to a space. Similarly, controls have been available that raise or lower the temperature of the stream of air or water being delivered throughout a large-size building to provide thermal comfort. Finally, traditional hvac design has included the ability to modify the operating mode of central equipment so that, for example: 1) controls at the supply-air system can set the system for either minimum outdoor air (summer cycle for a fan system), or variable outdoor air (winter cycle for a fan system), or 2) the flip of a switch can change the scheduled control temperature of a water system from cooling to heating, or 3) an operator, by adjusting a control-point adjuster, can raise or lower the temperature of the hot or cold water to modify performance for daytime or nighttime conditions. Also, the starting and stopping of fans and pumps could always be effected by depressing a start or stop button mounted somewhere near the unit. This type of regulation for a particular space or apparatus traditionally has been called automatic temperature control. Regardless of the function or means used to get a particular result, automatic temperature control involves the local adjustment of a device to achieve a desired effect.

But as soon as the control functions just described are centralized in a building so that a room thermostat, or the operating mode or supply temperature for building systems, can be adjusted from the building engineer's office, or a fan or a pump can be started from a remote centralized location, it can be said that the automatic temperature controls have been escalated to a building automation system.

Economics generally dictate sophistication of the air-conditioning system for a building

The consulting engineer has a limited number of alternatives to consider for the hvac system of a particular building. He is constrained by the architectural design, size of building, energy alternatives, and, finally, by the use of the building. Assuming comfort factors are relatively equal, the selection process is based largely upon economics: initial costs must be compared with operating and maintenance costs to permit an intelligent choice. The bottom-line rate of return on investment typically will control the decision process. Having selected the economically-correct system, the design engineer will provide for local automatic temperature control for the air and water systems, and local space temperature control as is required.

Whether the local temperature control should be advanced to central automation is governed by the same economic rules as for hvac system selection. Savings and/or convenience of alternatives must be compared. Savings in operating costs can result from reduction in energy use, as well as from a possible decrease in operating staff. The ability to tie alarm or malfunction points into an automation system can be not only a convenience and safety precaution, but also a money-saver through early notification of malfunction. This can reduce accompanying damage that might result from delay in removing the cause of alarm. Though justification of an automation system can be made, substantially, on economic grounds, subjective factors (prestige, for one) may also influence the decision.

Building automation, itself, has various degrees of sophistication—and costs

The ultimate automation system can provide, in one or more centralized control centers in a building, automatic monitoring and modification of the performance of a number of dif-

Before electronic technology was applied, building automation comprised panel-mounted indicators, alarms and controls that were hard-wired to individual sensors and devices at hvac equipment.

Now, with electronics, instructions can be transmitted faster; information presented faster and in more convenient form, and building operation optimized. Shown are a cathode-ray-tube display unit and operator's module (top); also the automation-system computer, a printer, and slide projectors (bottom).

Control and monitoring of subsystems for a large high-rise building is accomplished with equipment shown below: a central processor, operator's module, printers and slide projector. Electronic messages are coded and uncoded by a multiplexing unit (near right), and action is initiated by relays in an interlock panel (far right). Temperatures are measured by analog sensors, and on/off and alarm conditions are detected by digital sensors on equipment such as shown on the next page.

Control-center equipment in the engineer's office

One of many multiplexing cabinets (left). Interlock panel for life-safety system (right).

ferent building subsystems, including: 1) environmental control systems, 2) communication system, 3) life-safety and fire-management systems, 4) security system. It is this ultimate automation system that has been getting the most attention lately. There are, however, intermediate automation systems that, while not as exotic, are still applicable in smaller buildings.

Typical of these simpler systems is one that has dedicated hard wiring between each point or function within the system and a central control panel. This means that each control point has a pair of wires carried from it back to the central control panel. This hard-wired system usually permits remote starting and stopping of equipment, alarm indication, and perhaps some selected temperature indications. While this type of system may require the operator to start or stop a fan manually from the central control panel, it is possible to add sophistication by tying the individual fans into a time clock, or even a computer. Until about 15 years ago, the hard-wired system with a multiplicity of alarm lights and start-stop buttons on a panel in the building engineer's office was the only type of automation system being used. And it is still widely applicable for smaller, less complex buildings.

More recently it has become possible, through electronic technology, to transmit coded messages from a multiplicity of alternate types of points over a single trunk cable system to a central processor where they are deciphered. Over the same pair of wires it is possible to transmit requests for information, or to issue instructions that will cause a desired

change to occur at the addressed point. The signal transmission system that has had the widest application in the larger and more complex buildings comprises a two-wire or coaxial cable routed through the buildings. This type system is called a multiplexed system in that simultaneous multiple messages are transmitted and/or received over the same pair of wires. It is possible, however, to transmit the electronic signals over multi-conductor cable, with each point within the system having its own pair of wires, but this is being applied less frequently today than two-wire or coaxial cable systems.

How building automation works can be seen from a description of its basic components

The basic components are sensors and other remotely located devices that can transmit data to a central control facility. When interrogated by a central processing unit, these sensors cause an electronic signal to be generated that is transmitted to the central processing unit where it is deciphered. The deciphered message may be printed by a system-driven typewriter, appear on a cathode ray tube, initiate a visible or audible alarm, or even, automatically, cause some adjustment to be made in the system via a preprogrammed computer. The total system, when installed in this fashion, is a real-time system, or on-line system, in that the computer is analyzing data and acting on the data to effect an ongoing physical process from which the data is being received.

Though there are some proprietary differences in hardware and arrangements, it can

be separately typically into the following generic types and functions:

■ Analog Sensors are remotely located devices that measure temperature, pressure or flow. These sensors will measure quantities that vary as a function of time, such as temperature of an air- or water-supply system.

■ Digital Sensors are remotely located devices that indicate at the central control facility whether a particular piece of equipment is in an open or closed position, such as a fire-sprinkler flow alarm, heat detector, motor-starter contactor, or a door contactor used for security. These devices tell whether equipment is "on" or "off", "open" or "closed".

■ Resettable Devices are those such as a on-off motor control, door-security control, or opening or closing of a damper of an air-supply system. These devices initiate the action which is monitored by the digital sensors. Another resettable device is one that can change the set point of a thermostat or air-handling-system damper to whatever value is desired.

■ Multiplexing Cabinets are remote enclosures located throughout a building to which the sensors or controllers are connected by a pair of wires. They contain devices that convert the signals transmitted to and received from the central control facility into electronic pulses to which components of the system can respond.

■ The Transmission Trunk is a two-wire or coaxial cable, not essentially different from the antenna wire used for television sets, that is looped through a building and connects, in series, the various multiplexing cabinets. The

Analog sensors on duct can relay dew point and dry-bulb temperature of air.

Contact closure detects via pressure switch whether pump is running or not.

Analog sensors on chiller supply and return measure water temperatures.

Contact closures on expansion tank give alarm at high and low water levels.

cable terminates at the central processing unit.
▪ The Processing Unit is the central equipment that contains the logic for management of the total system. It can transmit and receive multiplexed information, and cause it to be presented. It has the ability to process all data in an orderly fashion, and controls the timing and flow of information to and from other elements of the over-all system. This processing unit may or may not include a computer. The significance of this is discussed later.

▪ Peripheral Devices are pieces of equipment attached to the processing unit in the central control facility to permit operating personnel to receive and transmit information to the system. They can include typewriters or other printers, a slide projector containing visual representations of the various building systems, a real-time clock (real time in this context means the actual clock time at which a physical process transpires), and a control module through which the operator can address the individual points in the over-all system, or request specifically programmed and retained information of what is happening in the building. Also typically contained within the control center is two-way voice communication to remote sections of the building through an audio channel that terminates, most often, at each multiplexing cabinet. This communication ability is handled by a separate wiring system in addition to the cable indicated above.

In review, then, the total system requires the installation of temperature, pressure and flow sensors, as well as, possibly, door-moni-

toring devices or alarm devices that are capable of transmitting data in the form of electronic signals to a central processing unit over the trunk cable that is looped through the building. The other function of the processing unit is to send instructions over the cable to change operational characteristics of systems by starting and stopping fans, adjusting temperature controllers, modifying damper positions, opening or closing locks on doors, etc. All of the transmission of data or instructions in either direction is digital and is handled in such a way as to be fully compatible with a computer.

In contrast to the hard-wired system, the multiplexed building automation system is easily expansible after installation. With the hardwired system, more panel sections and more wiring have to be added for the additional points. The digital system can be expanded in several ways, offering a whole range of potential uses.

Firstly, the system can be expanded by wiring additional sensors and devices into the existing multiplexing cabinets by making provisions for this in the original design.

Secondly, the system can be extended by adding multiplexing cabinets and trunk cable, if and when the project is expanded. This can be done without interrupting the functioning of the original system.

Thirdly, if there are extensive distances involved (for example, between a group of buildings miles apart), which makes it impractical to connect them by the trunk cable, communication to remote points can be accomplished

by using voice-grade telephone lines. A device called a modem changes the telephone signal into a digital signal, and vice versa. This means that the central control facility need be included in only one building, though peripheral devices such as printers, cathode ray tubes, etc., could be installed in the owner's satellite buildings.

Building automation is offered on a fee basis where costs preclude an in-house system
The capability of using telephone lines for transmission of data and instructions has been the impetus for several automation manufacturers and companies offering remote building monitoring and operation on a contractual basis. The companies, themselves, have a central control station on their premises, just like those installed in private buildings. Large numbers of buildings can be tied in, by means of leased telephone lines, to the company's central control station that is manned 24 hours a day by automation company personnel.

Such an arrangement permits scheduled start-up and shutdown of equipment in accordance with time, temperature or other variables, without the need for operating people performing these functions in remote buildings.

Furthermore, security points as well as fire-control functions in the remote buildings can be monitored at the automation company's central station.

The above-described approach permits many sophisticated techniques to be used in small buildings on a rental basis at reduced

Local control panel for a large air handler is shown in these photos. Electronic signals from the central processing unit are converted to pneumatic signals to activate reset devices within the panel. In turn, the reset devices actuate valves that control flow of hot and chilled water. On the panel cover are dials that indicate temperatures of water coils, temperature of supply air, zone temperature, zone relative humidity, and outside air temperature.

cost. These buildings, of course, must have had sensors and devices installed for the functions that are to be handled by the automation companies. The economics of this approach depends upon how many remote points are being handled. As the number increases, the cost of the service could reach the point where a separate system on the building premises is affordable. This is a great automation growth area, however, and will find wider and wider usage in the years ahead. Properly employed, it can save capital and operating labor for many buildings.

Once used mainly for environmental control, building automation now is more versatile

Centralized control is often used today to combine the building environmental, life-safety and security subsystems into a total integrated facility, though there still can be three separate control stations with different locations for each.

The environmental control station used by the operating engineers for controlling the environmental equipment typically is located in a room within or near a mechanical equipment room.

Location of the control station for life-safety and fire management, often called a fire-command station, is governed by requirements of the local fire department. While it can be part of the environmental control station, it is frequently located on or near the main floor of a building for ease of access by the fire department.

The security control station's location will depend upon the particular organization of the security staff.

All of the above stations are tied into a single, multiplexed, total-integrated building facility, with dedicated peripheral devices installed at each station. They usually will be interconnected by hard-wired telephones. The over-all integrated system should be so designed as to buffer the individual points monitored and controlled by each of the subsystem stations. It is not prudent, for example, to permit building operating engineers to access the security points in a building, and be able to permit secured spaces to be opened. Conversely, building security personnel should not be able to start or stop fans or pumps.

To enhance the reliability and flexibility of the over-all system, however, functions could be permitted to be switched back and forth between the various stations by means of a manual keying device or through electronic passwords. This allows continuous control, in the event of component failure at any one station. It also permits the manning of one station at night or on weekends by fewer people.

Degree of automation for the hvac system varies with building size, type, operation

In a relatively small building of less than 250,-000 sq ft, and with a single mechanical equipment room, the ability to start and stop fans in the engineer's office on the same floor probably could not be justified. On the other hand it could be reasonable to start and stop fans (as well as boilers and/or refrigeration equipment) from a remote-site automation system over

voice-grade telephone lines, as discussed earlier. Money could be saved by reducing the on-the-job hours of operating personnel.

In a large building, say in excess of 1-million sq ft, with multiple fan rooms and more complex operating schedules, automation systems usually will be included. For buildings between 250,000 and 1-million sq ft in size, the ability to support an automation system, and the extent of its complexity, can be resolved only through a careful engineering study of the building, its hvac and other systems, and its operating schedules.

With any building automation system, virtually all of the supply, return and exhaust fans and pumps will be started or stopped at the central control facility. Starting and stopping can be made automatic by providing a real-time clock at the central processing unit, avoiding possible human failure or delay.

Also, building automation systems will use their central processing units to scan analog temperatures throughout a building and compare them with stored temperature values (minimum and/or maximum) to determine whether there are excessive space temperature fluctuations. If such a condition exists, an alarm will be indicated by one of the peripheral printing devices.

Furthermore, the processing unit would continually scan the status of alarms on many building mechanical components and subsystems that indicate excessive or low water or air temperatures or pressures, high or low water levels on expansion tanks, etc.

And as mentioned earlier, both space temperature thermostats, and thermostats that control air- and water-supply temperatures, can be configured to be adjustable centrally.

With the automation of hvac systems, operators can check space temperatures and discharge temperatures of air-handling systems to analyze what changes need to be made (such as adjusting the discharge thermostat) to better control space conditions while also minimizing energy consumption.

The peripheral devices included with a building automation system permit the printing of hard copy of what is happening in the building for supervisory review. Among the types of logs that could be printed automatically on request are: 1) analog and digital alarm logs, as each occurs, 2) return to normal of these alarms, as each occurs, 3) alarm summary logs of all points currently in alarm, 4) individual point recording as a function of time, 5) groups of points indicating status, temperature, pressure, etc., on a programmed basis, 6) all-points logs indicating the status, temperature, pressure, etc. of all points connected to the system.

A total integrated building automation facility usually includes a two-way intercom. First of all it permits conversation between the central control facility and remote locations. But also it offers audible monitoring of the starting, stopping and running condition of remote motors, through control module commands. A separate hard-wired communication system should be provided for the life-safety and fire-management control system.

BUILDING AUTOMATION: ENERGY OPTIMIZATION BY COMPUTER

by Donald E. Ross, partner
Jaros, Baum & Bolles, consulting engineers

Right: control center for a large high-rise

A computer optimizes operation by checking what it is, and making it what it should be

The building automation system described so far is compatible with a programmable real-time computer. With the computer, all of the previously outlined functions can be performed in a more sophisticated and comprehensive fashion, but, in addition, it permits automatically-initiated optimization.

The concept of optimization involves the continuous monitoring and controlling of the building. The key word is "continuous," since operating personnel cannot perform operations as continuously as the computer. Possibly they may lag behind in sampling data and executing the required changes, with the result that building systems may drift from the optimal engineering path. To compensate for this lag, and to prevent temporary discomfort in the building, operators may take short cuts and operate the systems inefficiently.

The computer, on the other hand, is not time constrained, and will collect data, analyze it, make logical decisions, and perform or recommend proper changes in operation. These changes can bring about lowered operating costs without sacrifice of occupant comfort. This is the general meaning of "optimization." While the benefits of a control system with computer are similar to those of the basic control system previously outlined, they are at least one order of magnitude greater because of the ability of the computer to make logical calculations on the basis of operational parameters stored in its memory.

Some of the automation systems that perform monitoring and control operations use a central processor that is a non-programmable logic device (this is not a computer). This logic device is, however, computer compatible. It is possible to tie in a computer, as an additional system component, using an interface module placed between the central processor and the computer. With this configuration, the processor can be used even though the computer is not operating for any reason.

Without the computer, the programmed capabilities of the processing unit are limited to time functions (i.e., starting and stopping fans and pumps off the real-time clock) and reporting adjustable analog alarms by comparison of actual building conditions with discrete stored (and variable) values that are maintained in the limited memory of the processor.

In other systems that have been developed, the central processor is truly a computer, capable of performing optimization functions.

A third approach involves the use of microprocessors throughout the system, which act as slaves to organize and control the data being fed to a host computer.

Lower energy consumption and demand charges are possible with a computer

Reduced energy consumption derives from strategies, in the form of computer software, for manipulating the hvac and electrical systems. These strategies are complex, however, because of the interaction of many building systems, and because energy optimization schemes have an impact on many different functional aspects simultaneously.

Electrical power costs can be reduced by using software that reacts to the electrical demand approaching a new monthly peak value, and then sheds, or recommends shedding, of certain building electrical loads in accordance with a priority schedule.

Several automation companies offer purchase or lease of a computer that is dedicated primarily to demand or power management control. The computer is programmed to turn electrical equipment, such as fans, on and off for certain adjustable periods in every demand period.

The system's virtues are that it is simple, will have predictable savings, and can involve nominal initial investment. But starting and stopping fan or pump motors, especially large units of 50 hp or more, every demand period over an extended time, can shorten the life of motors as well as fan belts, bearings, etc. This is hard to predict, but should be considered, especially if it could lead to loss of a key fan.

A second liability of intermittent operation of fan equipment is possible acoustical problems because the human ear becomes accustomed to the noise level produced by moving air. When fans are off the silence is "deafening."

Another potential problem is that all building codes require a minimum input of outdoor air in occupied spaces. To avert any legal action, the owner should obtain a waiver of this requirement from the governing agency.

Finally, a disadvantage of these dedicated computers is the limited application of software programs: often only power management is available. In short, power management can be a useful, but often limited tool. It will probably find the widest application in buildings like department stores that have multiple fan systems with small motors. Other potential applications are schools, certain portions of hotels, and industrial plants.

Both tangible and intangible benefits result from centralized control by computer

- Improved efficiency of operating labor: This will be achieved by the control of thermostats, the starting and stopping of equipment, and the performing of other operator tasks, all automatically. A minimum number of operating people can concentrate their efforts in correct areas. Furthermore, the review of past and present performance and the projection of future needs will be a real guide for the operating staff.
- Data collection for analysis: The operating and optimizing functions outlined earlier provide a sound basis for economic operation of a building. As operating conditions, occupancy, or space utilization change, refinements and additions to control strategies may be required. Data collection would identify both system and external parameters to help ensure proper future operation.
- Preventive maintenance through anticipation: By intelligent review of equipment efficiency, performance, operating time, down-time and seasonal need, preventive maintenance can be better scheduled.

- Management reports: The analysis of accurate building and equipment operating costs should be of considerable value to building managements.
- Intangible benefits: The fact that wide variations in comfort and operating costs are encountered in many existing buildings suggests the virtue of computer-aided control.

The quality of computer optimization depends upon quality of the software

If we don't become bewildered by much of the jargon that has accompanied the development of building automation systems, we can concentrate on the one thing that matters—performance. The competence of a system including a computer becomes limited only by the imagination and engineering expertise of the software design team. Contrariwise, system performance will only be as good as the software.

To date, computer software has been limited largely to monitoring of system performance, miscellaneous alarms, data collection—though additional software routines have been promised by manufacturers. Because the state of the art is constantly changing, what it is at any given time can only be determined by proper specified definition at the time a system is developed, and by careful review of proposals when they are received.

One difficulty with the software developed so far is that is has been designed so it can be used in a variety of building types, which, inevitably, has meant some compromises. With software of this sort it has been possible for development costs to be shared by a broad customer base, thereby reducing the cost to any one customer. The difficulty is that constraints are built into programs in an effort to give them more universal application. This approach works in some instances, but in others, drawbacks result. One simply has to reflect on the differences between mechanical and electrical systems used in similar structures, such as an office building, to recognize the dilemma. Now think about making a computer-driven facility for an office building work for a hospital. It is a serious problem that results in compromises in computer software, and is simply another reason for careful specification and review.

Another drawback of some computer software is that it often is written in assembly language, rather than a higher-level language such as Fortran. While this results in the smallest consumption of computer memory core, it is virtually impossible to have the programs maintained or modified by people not familiar with both the assembly language for the particular computer and the development of the program itself.

The alternative exists of developing custom software for a particular building. This can be done by the automation company or other technical firms that have the in-house expertise on both computers and buildings. It should be understood, however, that custom software can get very expensive. Careful study of the needs of a building, and the areas requiring optimization, is a necessary precursor for development of proper software. An engineering firm that understands what is on the market

and what is needed can probably minimize costs by selecting standard software packages and having them modified for use in a particular project. This hybrid of standard and custom software can be successful (and save money) if the specifier understands the total process.

Automation costs include the control center, the sensors and the computer software

It is difficult to generalize, but if a minimum justifiable system for a building were to include 200 analog, digital and resettable points, the cost for the sensors or devices, the multiplexing cabinets and the coaxial cable connecting these points would be about $100,000 to $120,000. The cost of a central control console with central processing unit, teletype, operator's console, and intercom would add between $30,000 and $40,000 to that cost, for a base system cost of $130,000 to $160,000.

The addition of points beyond this base cost (including interconnection into multiplexing cabinets already installed) would add a per point cost (by function) as follows:

Temperature Indication	$200 to $300
Control-point Reset Ability	$400 to $550
Start/stop for Equipment	$400 to $500
Miscellaneous Digital Points	$200 to $300

This provides a basic system. To expand this into a simplified optimization facility with a minimum computer configuration and standard software could add about $50,000 to $70,000 more. If, however, a full-blown computer system is used employing bulk storage in the form of disc drive, a larger, more powerful computer, cathode ray tubes, a line printer, and other peripheral devices, the nominal addition of $50,000 to $70,000 could become $150,000 for hardware only. Software costs can vary anywhere from $40,000 to numbers substantially larger, depending upon the mix of standard and custom programs mandated.

These are all generalities, necessarily, but with an automation system in its ultimate form, first costs can be substantial. Another approach might be to take the cost of the automatic temperature control as 2 to 3 per cent of building cost. Automation could increase that percentage by 1 to 2 percentage points.

These foregoing figures should be recognized as order-of-magnitude costs—only proper study and analysis can determine the costs for an actual building. The economic justification should be maintenance costs—which can be 5 and 10 per cent of the first cost per year—and, of course, energy savings. Determining energy savings also is difficult, but conservative analysis of several projects has indicated that energy savings between 5 and 15 per cent, on an annual basis, can be obtained—with the lower figure almost a certainty. To this should be added labor savings and maintenance and equipment-failure cost deferrals, all readily obtainable. The larger the building, the better the return on investment.

A short summary of the hvac operations that a computer can help optimize

The list of hvac functions that can be subjected to a computer-directed control strategy is quite large, and will vary with the particular building

and the installed systems.
- Morning Startup Control: Subroutines for this function dynamically adjust the starting time for all building fans and pumps. The lead time for equipment starting is determined by the space temperature and the temperature of the outdoor air. Virtually all building equipment can be started automatically by computer at the latest possible time to develop comfort conditions at the desired time of day. The shortened time to get the building running both adds to equipment operating life and can save operating energy. Manpower needs are also reduced.
- Chilled Water Temperature Control: The least amount of energy required to refrigerate the chilled water in the summer can be achieved by the computer reviewing the building's needs and setting the chilled water temperature at its highest possible value.
- Outside Air Utilization: the computer monitors the relative heat of the outdoor air and the return air in the building, and then controls the optimum use of either to reduce the energy consumed by the air-supply systems.
- Interior System Control: The monitoring of selected points and control of interior systems will vary with the type of system installed. With a variable-air-volume system, the computer, in summer, should weigh the reduced fan horsepower possible against lower air temperature, increased refrigeration plant operating costs, and proper air distribution. In winter, the air-distribution criterion must be considered only against fan horsepower. For a reheat system, the computer must judge the highest possible system air-discharge temperature to minimize reheat, without sacrificing comfort.
- Exterior System Adjustment: One of the most intensive areas of energy consumption in a building is the exterior space, with its fluctuating needs due to varying solar and transmission loads. It is, therefore, space requiring intelligent control. It is also one of the most difficult to control because of the wide variation in systems applied. Accordingly, special software is usually needed to obtain proper results with these systems.
- Demand Control: Regular input from electric utility meters, and reduction by shedding electric loads when new monthly peaks are approached were discussed earlier in this article.
- Refrigeration Plant Monitoring: Refrigeration machines in summer are substantial energy-consuming devices. By monitoring performance and developing load profiles in easily understandable terms, such as kilowatts per ton or pounds of steam per ton, an operator can be advised as to which machines or combination of machines will most efficiently meet his needs as a function of the immediate requirements.
- Miscellaneous Functions: The effort to ensure total system performance and minimize over-all operating costs should ultimately involve virtually all equipment in a building. Control of heating systems, cooling towers, pumping systems, and special fan systems must all be reviewed and regulated to obtain the goals sought. These are areas where, as in the case of the exterior system, custom software is necessary since it is not available as a standard commercial package.

A FINAL WORD:
THIS IS JUST THE BEGINNING

As the introduction to this book suggests, the thinking expressed in this book is just a beginning.

Ten years ago almost no one was concerned with energy conservation. Today, everyone is *thinking* about it, *talking* about it, maybe even *worrying* about it—but too few are really *doing* anything about it.

We may soon no longer have a choice. It is my view that architects and engineers—especially those whose work or thinking is represented in this book—have made a stronger contribution to the cause of energy conservation than any other group in America. For instance: are you impressed with the efforts of the auto industry to conserve? Are you impressed with the public's attitude? But I think it is fair to be impressed by the work—and the very real savings—that have already been accomplished by design professionals and the building industry.

But, again, it is just a beginning. . . .

Walter F. Wagner, Jr.

INDEX